DATE DUE			

11/19

NO GOOD MEN
AMONG THE LIVING

NO GOOD MEN AMONG THE LIVING

AMERICA, THE TALIBAN,
AND THE WAR
THROUGH AFGHAN EYES

ANAND GOPAL

METROPOLITAN BOOKS
HENRY HOLT AND COMPANY NEW YORK

Metropolitan Books
Henry Holt and Company, LLC
Publishers since 1866
175 Fifth Avenue
New York, New York 10010
www.henryholt.com

Metropolitan Books® and m® are registered trademarks of
Henry Holt and Company, LLC.

Library of Congress Cataloging-in-Publication Data

Gopal, Anand, 1980–
    No good men among the living : America, the Taliban, and the war through
Afghan eyes / Anand Gopal.
        pages cm
    Includes index.
    ISBN 978-0-8050-9179-3 (hardback)—ISBN 978-1-4299-4502-8 (electronic book)
    1. Afghan War, 2001– 2. Afghan War, 2001—Personal narratives, Afghani.
3. Taliban. 4. Counterinsurgency—Afghanistan. 5. Peace-building—Afghanistan.
6. Internal security—Afghanistan. 7. United States—Military policy. I. Title.
    DS371.412.G66 2014
    958.104'7—dc23   2014001384

First Edition 2014

Designed by Kelly S. Too

Printed in the United States of America
3   5   7   9   10   8   6   4

CONTENTS

NO GOOD MEN
AMONG THE LIVING

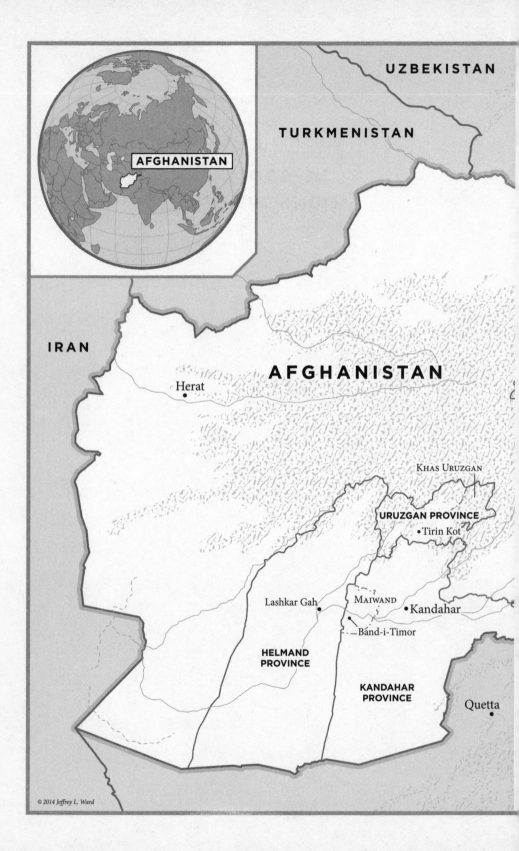

UZBEKISTAN

TURKMENISTAN

AFGHANISTAN

IRAN

Herat

KHAS URUZGAN

URUZGAN PROVINCE

• Tirin Kot

Lashkar Gah

MAIWAND

• Kandahar

Band-i-Timor

HELMAND
PROVINCE

KANDAHAR
PROVINCE

Quetta

© 2014 Jeffrey L. Ward

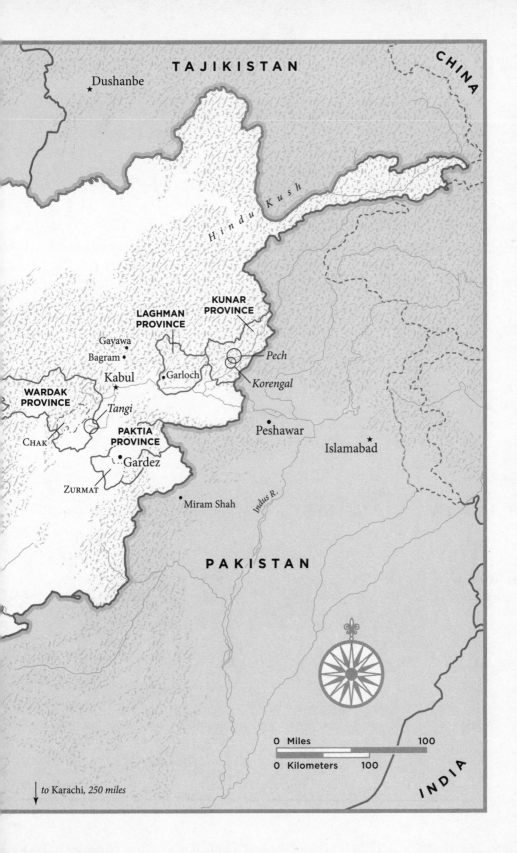

TAJIKISTAN

CHINA

Dushanbe

Hindu Kush

KUNAR
PROVINCE

LAGHMAN
PROVINCE

Gayawa

Bagram

KUNAR
PROVINCE

•Garloch

Pech

Kabul

Korengal

WARDAK
PROVINCE

Tangi

Peshawar

CHAK

Islamabad

PAKTIA
PROVINCE

•Gardez

Indus R.

ZURMAT

•Miram Shah

PAKISTAN

0 Miles   100

0 Kilometers   100

to Karachi, 250 miles

INDIA

Prologue

This is a book about categories that people create and then come to believe in—with a force of conviction so strong that sometimes it becomes literally a matter of life and death.

When the 9/11 attacks took place, I was living in lower Manhattan, and on that day it seemed that the categories of the world had revealed themselves with brutal, unmistakable clarity. On the one hand, there were those who had committed the atrocity, the terrorists, whose motives were so incomprehensible that we could only, as President George W. Bush put it, regard them as "evil." And on the other hand there were the rest of us, the good, we who wanted nothing more than a decent life of freedom and a better future.

That was the premise of the war on terror, and in particular of its opening salvo, the invasion of Afghanistan. You were either with us or against us, a principle that allowed the United States to sort friends from foes on a strange and distant battlefield. For a few years this approach appeared to work, and the country was at peace. Roads were paved, schools opened, and, for the first time in its history, the country voted in truly democratic elections.

It was not long, though, before things started to go wrong. By 2008, when I moved to Afghanistan as a correspondent, the situation had already slipped out of control. An anti-American insurgency was metastasizing, and large swaths of the country had succumbed to full-scale war. Errant air strikes, suicide attacks, and roadside bombs had killed thousands. Troops from forty-three nations had attempted to bring stability, working to build a national army, a police force, and a judiciary system. After years of effort, though, the army was weak, the police rapacious, and the judicial system still nearly nonexistent. A US surge of money and troops provided little relief. The hope pervading the early years was gone.

What had happened? Over the course of four years, I traveled through the Afghan countryside in search of answers. Much of the territory was off-limits to foreigners, so I was forced to adapt. I learned the language, grew a beard, and hit the road like a local, using shared taxis and motorcycles. In the process, I met many people and heard many stories that challenged my preconceived notions of the war and the categories we've used to fight it. When I mentioned this to one of the Afghans whom I had come to know well, he replied with a proverb, one he repeated often: "There are no good men among the living, and no bad ones among the dead."

Like so many Pashtun aphorisms, this phrase has many shades of meaning. At one level, it refers to the universal habit of ignoring or criticizing people while they are alive but remembering them fondly after they've departed. But for this man, an Afghan who had lived through decades of war, it also meant something more: that there were no heroes, no saviors, in his world. Neither side in the conflict offered much hope for a better future. The categories of the American war on terror—terrorists and non-terrorists, fundamentalists and democrats—mattered little, not when his abiding goal, like that of so many caught in the conflict, was simply to finish each day alive.

The more such stories I heard, the more I began to wonder whether the root of the conflict was Afghans' stubborn refusal to conform to the classifications that Washington had set forth, and America's insistence on clinging to those divisions. In these pages, I recount the stories of three people in particular who've lived this reality. One is an insurgent Taliban commander fighting against the Americans; another, a powerful member of the US-backed Afghan government; and the third, a village housewife—or, in the language of America's categories, our enemy, our ally, and a civilian.

PART ONE

- -

The Last Days of Vice and Virtue

Early in the morning on September 11, 2001, deep amid the jagged heights of the Hindu Kush, something terrible took place. When teenager Noor Ahmed arrived that day in Gayawa to buy firewood, he knew it immediately: there was no call to prayer. Almost every village in Afghanistan has a mosque, and normally you can hear the muezzin's tinny song just before dawn, signaling the start of a new day. But for the first time that he could remember, there was not a sound. The entire place seemed lifeless.

He walked down a narrow goat trail, toward low houses with enclosures of mud brick, and saw that the gates of many of them had been left open. The smell of burning rubber hung in the air. Near a creek, something brown lying in the yellow grass caught his eye, and he stopped to look at it. It was a disfigured body, caked in dried blood. Noor Ahmed took a few steps back and ran to the mosque, but it was empty. He knocked on the door of a neighboring home. It, too, was empty. He tried another one. Empty. Then he came upon an old mud schoolhouse, its front gate ajar, and stopped to listen. Stepping inside, he walked through a long yard strewn with disassembled auto parts and empty motor oil canisters. Finally, when he pushed his way through the front door, he saw them huddled in the corner: men and women, toddlers and teenagers, more than a dozen in total, clutching each other, crammed into a single room.

"Everyone else is dead," one said. "If you don't get out of here, they'll kill you, too."

In wartime Afghanistan, secrets are slippery things. The Taliban had planned a surprise attack on Gayawa, but the villagers had known for days that the raid was coming, and those who could had hired cars or donkeys and moved their families down into the valley. But this had been a hard, dry, unhappy summer. Times were not good and many villagers could not afford to leave, even though they knew what might await them. Of those who stayed, only the few hiding in the schoolhouse, where the Taliban soldiers never thought to look, escaped untouched. The rest met an unknown fate.

Back then, Gayawa was near the epicenter of a brutal, grinding war between the government of Afghanistan, controlled by the Taliban, and a band of rebel warlords known as the Northern Alliance. In their drive to crush the resistance, government troops waged a Shermanesque campaign, burning down houses and schools, destroying lush grape fields that had for generations yielded raisins renowned throughout South Asia, and setting whole communities in flight. In the region surrounding Gayawa, the Taliban enforced a blockade, allowing neither food nor supplies to enter. Those who attempted to breach the cordon were shot.

America's war had yet to begin, but on that September 11, Afghans had already been fighting for more than two decades. The troubles dated to 1979, when the Soviet Union invaded a largely peaceful country and ushered in a decadelong occupation that left it one of the most war-ravaged nations on Earth. The Russians withdrew in defeat in 1989, and in their wake scores of anti-Soviet resistance groups turned their guns on each other, unleashing a civil war that killed tens of thousands more and reduced to rubble what little infrastructure the country still had. Rival gangs robbed travelers at gunpoint and plucked women and boys off the streets with impunity.

In 1994, a fanatical band of religious students—the Taliban—emerged to sweep aside these warring factions and put an end to the civil war. On a fierce platform of law and order, they forcibly disarmed and disbanded many of the militias that had been terrorizing the populace and brought nearly 90 percent of the country under their control. For the first time in more than a decade, peace took root in much of the land. Criminality and warlordism vanished, and the streets became safe from rape and abduction.

In the process, however, the Taliban instituted a regime of draconian purity the likes of which the world had never witnessed. Moral and spiritual decay had dragged the country into civil war, the Taliban believed, and a puritanical version of Islamic law offered the only hope for salvation. All music, film, and photography—which the Taliban regarded as gateway drugs to pornography and licentiousness—were banned. They caged up women in their homes, executed adulterers, and whipped men of flagging faith. They prohibited, with only a few exceptions, all female education and employment. They outlawed the teaching of secular subjects in school. In many cities, roaming packs of religious police under the authority of the Ministry for the Prevention of Vice and Promotion of Virtue saw to it that no one missed the mandatory five-times-a-day prayer. All men were required to wear a fist-length beard and were beaten and jailed unless they complied.

A land of Old Testament rules, the Taliban's Afghanistan was brutal and vindictive. Relatives of murder victims were invited to gun down the accused; thieves had their hands lopped off; and obscurantist religious clerics, often semiliterate, decided matters of jurisprudence. If it were possible to distill the zeitgeist into a single devastating moment, it would be the Taliban's infamous demolition of two massive fifteen-hundred-year-old Buddha sculptures. Among South Asia's great archaeological treasures, the statues were brought tumbling down in an effort to rid the country of "false idols."

Yet Taliban rule did not go unchallenged. Remnants of some of the defeated militias fled to the mountains north of Kabul, Afghanistan's capital, where they regrouped in 1996 to form the Northern Alliance. For the next five years, Taliban troops fought a bloody campaign to subdue the north, meting out the greatest punishment to villages along the front line, like Gayawa.

Years later, I visited Gayawa to try to understand the Afghan world as it had appeared on the eve of 9/11. Some of the Taliban's old, rotting observation posts were still standing, and many houses remained abandoned. Memories of those war years lingered, and the rancor echoed in conversation after conversation. "The Taliban were evil. They were tormentors," Noor Ahmed told me. After finding those survivors in the schoolhouse on the morning of September 11, he had fled the area, returning only months later after a new government had assumed power. "They weren't humans. The laws you and I abide by, they didn't mean anything to them."

As I met more villagers in the area, I found that many of their stories centered on a particular roving Taliban unit, a feared team of disciplinarians who journeyed from village to village demanding taxes and household firearms. "Their leader was a tall man named Mullah Cable," said Nasir, a local. "We heard his name on the radio. He traveled a lot. He would search your house looking for weapons, and when you swore you didn't have anything, he'd bring out his whip, a cable. That's where his name comes from. He was a clever man—I don't know where he was from, but he was very smart. He was one of the first to use a whip on us like that. After a while, all the Talibs started carrying whips."

Mullah Cable. The very name spoke of the strange language that Afghans had acquired in decades of war. No one in Gayawa knew quite what had become of him. "When the Americans invaded," Nasir said, "all those Taliban vanished like ghosts."

I first saw Mullah Cable on an early winter evening in Kabul, the hour of dueling muezzins, dozens of them crooning from their minarets. It was 2009, and more than one hundred thousand foreign soldiers were on Afghan soil battling an increasingly powerful Taliban insurgency. When I approached him, he was pacing uncomfortably in a park, hands in his pockets, his eyes shifty, a black turban stuffed into his pocket. Tall and lanky, he stood with his shoulders hunched, as if he were carrying some dangerous secret. He wore glasses, unusual for an Afghan. Tattoos flowed down his arms and henna dye covered his fingernails. When he smiled, gold teeth glistened. Only his thick, spongy beard and a missing eye, a battlefield injury, placed him unmistakably among his Taliban comrades. Even without such telltale marks, though, as an Afghan you can never truly hide—a cousin, or an old war buddy, or a tribal chieftain somewhere would know how to find you. So I had tracked him down, and after months of effort I finally convinced him to speak to me.

"I don't come here often," he said. "Kabul is a strange place. I'm a village guy. I need the open spaces and fields to be able to think." As the typical Kabul evening smog settled in, commuters headed home, many with their faces wrapped in handkerchiefs. Toyota Corolla station wagons and minivan taxis, with arms and heads poking out, rattled by. A Ford Ranger police truck passed us, making Mullah Cable nervous. He had slipped in from the surrounding countryside and was worried about being noticed. We took shelter in a taxi, moving slowly through the darkening streets as we spoke in the back.

Almost a decade after battling the Northern Alliance, he was still fighting—now against the Americans. Though he didn't mention it, I later learned that the band of guerrillas under his command in the province of Wardak, a few dozen miles southwest of Kabul, had assassinated members of the US-backed Afghan government, kidnapped policemen, and deployed suicide bombers. On numerous occasions, they had attacked American soldiers. He fought, he told me, for "holy jihad," to rid his country of foreigners and to reinstate the Taliban regime.

This much I had expected, but he also surprised me. He admitted to not having received a single day's worth of religious instruction in his life. He could read only with great difficulty. Maps were a mystery to him, and despite his best efforts he could not locate the United States. In fact, growing up he had only the foggiest notion of America's existence. He cared little for, and understood little of, international politics. He had no opinions about events in the Middle East or the Arab-Israeli conflict. And even though he had been a Taliban commander in the 1990s, after the American-led invasion of Afghanistan in 2001 he had quit the movement and for a time actually supported the new US-backed government.

This is what fascinated me most: How did such a person end up declaring war on America? Nor was he alone. It turned out that thousands of Talibs like him had given up the fighter's life after 2001, but something had brought most of them back to the battlefield just a few years later. I wanted to learn his story. At first he was skeptical. "I don't understand why it matters," he said. "My story isn't very special. I think you won't find it interesting." I assured him that I would, and for a year we met regularly in the backs of taxis, in drowsy dark offices in Kabul, or out in the countryside. In his tale I found a history of America's war on terror itself, the first grand global experiment of the twenty-first century, and a glimpse of how he and thousands like him came to define themselves under this new paradigm—how they came to be our enemy.

As with so many Afghans, the beginning was hazy. He could not state where exactly he had been born, although he believed it was somewhere on the squalid outskirts of Kabul. Nor did he know when he was born, so he wasn't sure if he was three or five when the Russians invaded in 1979. That war had unfolded mostly in the countryside, and people in Kabul spoke of it the way they spoke of foreign countries, as something far off and vaguely interesting. But the Russian retreat, followed by the outbreak of civil war in 1992, brought the conflict home to the capital, and eventually he enlisted in a local militia. It was an "aimless life," as he put it, until the Taliban swept into power in 1996, inspiring thousands of young men to rally to their cause. He was one of them.

The Taliban provided a welcome home for unsettled youths like him who were repulsed by the chaos. In their regimented order he found a sense of purpose, a communion with something greater. "You have to understand," he explained, "we felt like we were the most powerful people in the world. Everyone was talking about the Taliban. The whole world knew about the Taliban. We brought good to this country. We brought security. Before we came, even a trip to buy groceries was a gamble. People stole, people raped, and no one could say anything.

"Under our government, you could sleep with the doors open. You could leave your keys in your car, return after a month, and no one would've touched it."

On the battlefield against the Northern Alliance rebels, he had risen quickly in the ranks, first leading a few dozen men, then heading a fifty-man unit, and finally establishing himself as one of the top commanders on the front line. By 2001, he was directing a force of a hundred or so fighters tasked with trekking through the mountains near Gayawa, hunting for rebel sympathizers. He was also chief of police for a district north of Kabul, occasional director of military transportation and logistics, and the sole authority responsible for disarming the population in any newly conquered territories. It was in this last duty that he acquired his nom de guerre, one that, in those days at least, he had carried proudly.

For five years, the fighting between his Taliban forces and the Northern Alliance ground on. For every insurgent hamlet put down, it felt as if another sprang up in its place. Then, on September 9, 2001, in the first suicide strike in Afghan history, a pair of young Arab men posing as journalists assassinated Ahmed Shah Massoud, the legendary leader of the Alliance. Rebel forces were thrown into disarray. For the first time, Mullah Cable could sense the prospect of total victory. On September 10, he and other Taliban commanders launched an offensive across the entire front line. By the morning of the eleventh, they had swept into the strategic village of Gayawa.

"We were on the verge of something great," he recalled, "but everything changed after the planes hit. That was the biggest mistake that ever happened to us."

Early on the morning of September 12, 2001, in the cracked, war-eaten office building housing Kabul's Foreign Ministry, a few turbaned Taliban officials sat watching the news on a flickering television—the only sanctioned set in town, as all moving images had been banned. As they stared at replays of the Twin Towers collapsing into an apocalyptic pile of burning ruins, President George W. Bush's warning flashed across the screen: "We will make no distinction between the terrorists who committed these acts and those who harbor them."

It was a moment some Taliban officials had long feared. To the most pragmatic among them, Osama bin Laden and his retinue of followers had been nothing but trouble since they had landed in 1996. The Arabs of al-Qaeda spoke a different language, practiced a distinct culture, and even followed a different form of Islam from their Afghan counterparts. Bin Laden was waging international jihad to overthrow US global hegemony, while the Taliban were concerned largely with politics within their country's borders. Bin Laden railed against the West, and his acolytes bombed US embassies in Kenya and Tanzania, while the Taliban were seeking Western diplomatic recognition. Quickly, America's bin

Laden problem had become the Taliban's as well. The two sides met throughout the late 1990s in an attempt to work out a solution, but cultural and political divides proved insurmountable. The Taliban agreed to place bin Laden on trial, but Washington, not trusting the impartiality of Afghan courts, demanded his extradition to US soil. The Taliban, for their part, doubted the objectivity of the American legal system. They agreed to hand him over only to a neutral Islamic country for trial, which Washington rejected.

The failed talks fueled Taliban hard-liners, who reminded their colleagues that bin Laden was helping bankroll the war against Alliance rebels. Both sides looked to Taliban leader Mullah Muhammad Omar for direction, but the enigmatic, one-eyed Commander of the Faithful, as he called himself, happened to be one of the most inscrutable and reticent heads of state in history. In his five years in power, he had never appeared on television; outside of a pair of grainy photographs, there is no visual record of his existence. During his reign, he traveled just twice to Kabul from his home in the southern city of Kandahar. He did not give speeches and avoided the radio. Indeed, to some Afghans he seemed a mythical figure conjured up by Taliban propagandists, an emblem of piety and virtue meant to serve as a focal point for Taliban rule.

The reality, however, was far more mundane. A lowly village preacher and minor figure in the anti-Soviet resistance, Omar had found himself, through an unlikely turn of events, thrust atop a fledgling state. As a mullah, a preacher qualified only to lead Friday sermons, he was at the bottom of the country's informal Islamic hierarchy, beneath a class of theologians who could interpret the scriptures and issue religious rulings called fatwas. Omar was a religious parvenu, a small-time priest giving orders to bishops. Projecting theological credibility to his more lettered colleagues, and by extension to the entire Muslim world, was everything, and the symbolism of surrendering bin Laden to non-Muslims would have been damaging to the very soul of the Taliban project. Their legitimacy as a state, such as it was, rested upon the notion that Islamic law had saved the country. In their view, they had ended the anarchy and bloodshed of the civil war by restoring society to its Islamic roots and submitting everyone—warlords and foot soldiers, landlords and peasants, men and women alike—to God's law. How then could

Omar justify extraditing bin Laden and subjecting him to the vagaries of secular Western justice? Bin Laden's presence was a problem that he saw no way to resolve. "Osama is like a chicken bone stuck in my throat," he once admitted. "I can neither spit him out nor swallow him."

Taliban pragmatists could see all too clearly the dangers that would befall them if the impasse continued. A week after the 9/11 attacks, they visited Omar in his modest Kandahar home. "We pleaded with him for hours" to expel bin Laden, one of them recalled, "but it was as if he covered his ears."

On September 20, President Bush increased the pressure, declaring: "The Taliban must act, and act immediately. They will hand over the terrorists, or they will share in their fate." When Taliban officials again went to see Omar, however, they found him in a defiant mood. "You just care about your posts and your money, your ministries," he said. "But I don't care about mine."

Behind the scenes, though, he was scrabbling for a face-saving solution. Twice he sent his top deputy to meet covertly in Pakistan with the Central Intelligence Agency's Islamabad station chief, Robert Grenier, in hopes of arranging bin Laden's transfer to a neutral third country—but Washington stood firm on its position of an unconditional handover. Meanwhile, Omar's intransigence was costing his government the few foreign supporters it had to its name, which became painfully clear when Pakistan, its key ally and patron, severed ties and sided openly with the United States.

Sinking into depression and paranoia, Omar was often on the verge of tears. He spent nights in a bunker underneath his home, a gas mask by his side due to rumors of an impending American chemical weapons attack. He restricted visits to his home to a few close aides and deployed troops to guard important armories and airstrips. Senior Talibs sent their families to Pakistan to wait out the inevitable.

Then, in late September, two developments gave Omar a glimmer of hope. First, Pakistani intelligence agents showed up at his home—without their government's knowledge. Contravening dictator Pervez Musharraf's stated policy, they pressed him to resist the invasion to the very end and assured him that he would have allies in Pakistan. It was the opening move in a perilous double game that the Pakistanis would play for the next decade. Second, senior Taliban figures, who until then were a threat to defect, decided to toss their lot in with the regime. "I was an original Talib," one said to me later. "I fought against the Russians with these people. We took Kandahar together. We almost died against the Northern Alliance. I realized that we couldn't abandon each other now, even if we disagreed."

In early October, President Bush warned the Taliban that "time is running out." A thousand troops from the US Tenth Mountain Division landed in Uzbekistan, near the Afghan border, while CIA agents and Special Operations Forces soldiers had already slipped into northern Afghanistan to work covertly with the Northern Alliance. Omar, meanwhile, kept himself and his family hidden in his bunker, passing messages to the outside world through a courier. On October 6, he received word from Pakistani agents that the American attack was imminent. That night, he gathered his senior lieutenants and delivered a last rousing address. "My family, my power, my privileges," he told them, "are all in danger, but still I am insisting on sacrificing myself, and you should do likewise."

The next evening, a few minutes before nine p.m., residents in Kandahar city saw the night sky flash a blinding white. In his bunker, Mullah Omar felt the house shake violently. The American war had begun. A missile had scored a direct hit on his compound, destroying a section and grievously wounding his ten-year-old son. Desperately clutching the child, he ran outside and, with the rest of his family, squeezed into an old Corolla. They sped to the hospital, where Omar begged the doctor to help his son. "He had very bad abdominal injuries," the doctor recalled, "and a badly fractured femur in his right leg, and we could not save him."

Distraught and furious, Omar jumped back into the vehicle and shouted to the driver, "Go! Go to Sangesar!" They raced through the narrow streets toward the village, where Omar had extended family, as dozens of townsfolk emerged from their homes to watch. On reaching the outskirts of Sangesar, everyone sprang out and hurried off on foot. Moments later, a missile slammed into the vehicle, blowing it to pieces. The Taliban leader and his relatives disappeared into the village. He would never be seen in public again.

--- --- ---

In Gayawa that night, Mullah Cable saw the darkened sky light up without warning in flickers of hot white and orange. He found it, in an odd kind of way, beautiful. He could tell that the bombs were off in the distance—in Kabul, probably, where the Taliban had many military installations. He glimpsed his men watching the sky, their silent faces briefly exposed with each strike. No one knew what they would do should the bombs reach their camp, except retreat to their bunkers and pray.

But not a single bomb fell anywhere near Gayawa that night, or the night following, or any other night that week. Mullah Cable began to consider the possibility that he had put too much stock in the Americans' technological prowess. In serious wars, there was no substitute for living and fighting in the mountains, for planning ambushes, coordinating artillery, and storming the enemy by sight and sound and gut alone. The Americans, on the other hand, hid behind the clouds, as if they knew all too well the fate of those who'd preceded them. By the fourth week of October, it was looking as if they would leave just as mysteriously as they came. "I thought the war would be over quickly, and then we could get on with things," he recalled.

Even when the strikes eventually hit the hills nearby during the first days of November, Mullah Cable remained unworried. His camp was too small, too insignificant to be picked out from above. Every night the planes would fly overhead without incident and disappear into the jagged country to the north, and the earth would tremble and the mountain peaks would light up, and his men would watch and talk about the pilots and wonder at their motives. It was only after one bomb struck close to their camp, in a neighboring valley, that they decided to go see for themselves what destruction the planes could bring. A group of the fighters assembled to investigate, but Mullah Cable opted to stay behind because his last pair of shoes had worn down to soggy rags. "Can you imagine?" he asked me later. "We were out there fighting for our country and God, and I didn't even have shoes." For days, his footwear problem had been all he could think about.

From his mountain perch, he watched his fighters drive their pickup trucks down the bluff away from the camp, then turn a corner and disappear. Over the radio, he heard them exchange greetings with another group of Taliban soldiers.

At that moment, a jet shrieked past, turned sharply, and dropped a series of bombs just where they had gone. The explosions were massive and deafening. "My teeth shook, my bones shook, everything inside me shook," he recalled. An enormous cloud of smoke rose above the mountains. All he could do was stand and watch.

The walkie-talkie had fallen silent. He waited for hours for some word. Finally, he decided that he had no choice but to go see for himself.

He drove into the basin and turned the corner and then stepped out of the vehicle. *Oh my God*, he thought. There were severed limbs everywhere. He inched closer. There were headless torsos and torso-less arms, cooked slivers of scalp and flayed skin. The stones were crimson, the sand ocher from all the blood. Coal-black lumps of melted steel and plastic marked the remains of his friends' vehicles.

Closing his eyes, he steadied himself. In five years of fighting he had seen his share of death, but never lives disposed of so easily, so completely, so mercilessly, in mere seconds.

"There's one still alive!"

He looked to see a villager coming toward him from a clutch of nearby houses. Inside one, he found his good friend Khoday Noor. Mullah Cable took his hand. "Khoday Noor! Khoday Noor! Can you hear me?" Noor stared back blankly. His right side was paralyzed and blood was draining from a wound in his back. They loaded him onto a vehicle, but he died en route to the nearest town. "He was just a young guy, a conscript," Mullah Cable recalled. "He had no reason to die."

Back at the camp, Mullah Cable washed his clothes and washed them again, but the smell would not go away. Those were men he'd known for five years down there in the valley—five years of mountain living, of meals and prayers shared. He sat there counting up the children they'd left behind.

The remaining men in the camp gathered for a dinner of naan and tea and offered theories about how the Americans spotted the convoy. Some said that they had advanced airplanes that could roam high above the clouds for days without refueling, picking out targets as they pleased; or that they could see every Talib in the country with a special type of flying camera, which beamed images back to commanders in the United States. Night washed over the mountains, the camp fell quiet, and Mullah

Cable retreated to his bunker to try to catch some sleep. As he lay there considering the day's events, he experienced something he'd never felt before about the Taliban: doubt.

Later that night, news came in over the radio: after a day's bombardment, 880 fighters were missing across the front lines. *Eight hundred and eighty*, he thought to himself—what kind of unimaginable power was this? Outside, his men stayed up, chatting anxiously until just before dawn, when villagers arrived with more grim news. They had found the body of the local Taliban governor—a powerful, feared man—cut clean in half.

In just two days, they had suffered more losses than he'd witnessed in the previous three years. He needed to calm down and think clearly. The trouble was, he hadn't slept since the bombing. That afternoon he retreated to his bunker for a short nap, but still sleep would not come. Instead, he stared at the ceiling for hours. A few of his fighters entered with rumors that whole Taliban units had defected up north. He said nothing.

In the evening, a message from supreme leader Mullah Omar, still in hiding, came by radio: "The people are suffering, but this is a test we shall pass, God willing." The test was from God himself, Omar said, and the goal, he explained, was "martyrdom."

Mullah Cable simply couldn't believe it. To defend his country he would take deadly risks, suffer cold mountain nights, go for months without his family—he would do it all, gladly, but martyrdom? Talk of martyrdom from a man in hiding? For reasons he did not fully grasp, the Americans were trying to kill him and everyone around him. The Northern Alliance was still trying to kill him. And now, he realized, his own leaders were encouraging his death.

Then and there, he decided not to die in the service of hopeless causes. A thousand armies at Mullah Omar's command could not stop a power like the Americans, not with the sort of jet he had watched eviscerate his comrades. If his leaders were planning to abandon him to such machines, then he would abandon them first.

He went over to see his men, who were busy checking provisions and talking among themselves. He knew that the scent of cowardice in his decision was unmistakable. He wasn't the type to run or shirk responsibility. But it would be criminal to ask his fighters to sacrifice themselves for Mullah Omar, a man they'd never even seen. He gathered them together. Jets were shrieking overhead and the mountains echoed with booms like some otherworldly storm, and a few of his men were already in tears. "Go home," he said. "Get yourselves away from here. Don't contact each other." Not a soul protested.

By morning, messages from other commanders were flooding in over his walkie-talkie, proclaiming battle plans and announcing this or that new mission. In communiqués broadcast on the national radio, the same words were on every fighter's lips: martyrdom, jihad, infidels. They formed the quintessential elements of their argot, forged from years fighting the Russians and the Northern Alliance warlords. Yet it was only talk, aired for their superiors and perhaps for each other. Mullah Cable figured that in reality, Talibs everywhere were probably defecting. After all, hundreds of commanders up and down the front lines don't just spontaneously announce missions at the same time, not without prior coordination. He was sure that only the Arabs of al-Qaeda and their foreign allies would fight to the death because they had nowhere else to go. Retreating to their home countries was simply not an option. As Afghan natives, however, the Taliban could hold out hope that they'd be allowed to return to their home villages in peace and, when the chaos ended, start afresh. This was how things had gone for decades. His countrymen had learned to switch sides when necessary or give up the fighter's life entirely—anything to survive.

As Mullah Cable stood shoeless atop his mountain base, he considered his fate. If he somehow could make it out alive, he promised himself that he would abandon politics forever. He'd get a job with his in-laws, who owned a shop in Kabul, where his wife and children lived. But getting there would not be easy. Chaos reigned: rumors were pouring in of fighters across the front lines throwing their weapons in ditches and fleeing. They were bribing locals for shelter, or heading off to their home villages—and often dying in the effort. The Taliban's crumbling forces were up against a thousand or so highly motivated Northern Alliance rebels, a seemingly endless stream of American warplanes, and CIA agents and Special Operations soldiers directing the whole effort. The enemy was barreling toward Kabul—at this pace, Mullah Cable figured they might reach it any day—and he knew that he had to get there first to have any hope of making it into the city.

The fifty-mile journey along serpentine dirt roads through the mountains was hazardous and unpredictable. Capture by the Northern Alliance would mean detention and possibly death, a logic he understood all too well given how the Taliban had treated their own captives. And if his own superiors caught him fleeing, he would fare no better. Worst of all, with fighters switching sides in droves, he could trust no one. It was every man for himself, a world with no comrades, only enemies.

He walked over to the few fighters still in the camp. He hugged each in turn, boarded a Toyota HiLux pickup truck, and drove off alone.

It was November 6, 2001, and the war was about a month old. The first winter winds were gusting through the valleys and avalanches were tumbling majestically down the distant peaks of the Hindu Kush. But driving through small mud villages, past fields of wheat and corn, Mullah Cable kept his eyes fixed on the road. The trip proved humiliating. Whenever locals glimpsed his HiLux, a signature Taliban vehicle, gunshots soon followed. In one village, he saw even housewives firing out from their windows. From then on he opted for the spine-jarring back roads, and eventually he made it to Parwan, the next province.

He crossed a bridge and noticed that there was not a car or pedestrian or goat in sight. He glanced up, but the sky was empty. Groves of fruit trees stood in rows, Soviet war ruins lying here and there between them. He drove on, the road sloping down into a broad plain. He passed clusters of abandoned mud houses and neglected fields and then, up ahead, he saw vehicles approaching. They soon pulled up before him, blocking his path. Men in white turbans jumped out and pointed their Kalashnikovs and shouted. There was little he could say or do. Before he knew it, he was assailed by fists and rifle butts and shoved unceremoniously into the back of a vehicle. Someone shouted that he was a coward for forsaking his country. In the front seat, a Taliban commander turned to him and said, "We kill people like you."

From their turbans and their accents, he knew that this was no ordinary

Taliban force. This was the Palace Guard—"crazy Kandaharis," as he used to call them: elite special forces from the Taliban heartland provinces of Helmand and Kandahar. They were taking him back to the front lines.

Later that afternoon he was pressed back into service. For three days, he and other captives were ordered to fire on various Northern Alliance outposts and to guard weapons caches. At nightfall, he was shackled and tossed into an improvised prison.

By the third day, their food supplies were dwindling. Men were melting snow to drink. A fellow captive begged Mullah Cable to shoot him and end his misery. He began to wonder if he should have held out longer in the mountains and kept his unit together. It had been foolish to assume that the Taliban would simply fall over, not with these brutish Palace Guards keeping everyone in the fight. Maybe the Taliban were stronger than he'd suspected. Maybe this war would take months or even years.

But how did any of that matter? It was no life, sleeping in the mountains, hiding from killer machines that he could barely see, watching friends erased in a flash. Even if the Taliban stood for a hundred years, he decided, he would never go back. But he couldn't stay here, either.

He had certainly gotten out of worse before. Two years earlier, during a routine inspection near his mountain camp, he had come across a shepherd boy guarding his animals with particular zeal. Something didn't seem right. Mullah Cable had questioned the boy, and, when he clammed up, he ordered his men to inspect the flock. Pulling back the wool on one sheep, a Talib found a gun firmly tied to its belly. They searched the others. Every single one bore a weapon. Mullah Cable headed back to the camp and found his weapons cache nearly empty. It was only then that the boy spilled the truth: Northern Alliance rebels had been bribing villagers to steal from the Taliban's weapons stock, in the process bulking up their own supplies. Mullah Cable's unit was now nearly defenseless.

It would take much too long for backup to arrive. That evening, as the sky dimmed, panic had spread among the unarmed fighters. As the Talibs prepared to flee, the first fusillade of gunfire rang out not far away.

From the sound of it, the rebels would be reaching the camp's front entrance in minutes. Mullah Cable scanned the darkness for an escape route. In one direction was a road heading straight downhill, right into the enemy's clutches. In the other, a small knoll. According to his spotters, rebels were circling around and about to close in on that, too. Then he looked at his truck, idling nearby, and inspiration struck. Calling over a Talib, he ordered him to drive up the knoll with headlights off, then turn around and drive back down, headlights on—and repeat, again and again. From the rebels' vantage point, it would appear as if vehicle after vehicle of reinforcements was flooding into the camp. He then got on the radio—which he knew the rebels monitored—and let slip that thousands in backup were on their way. Soon enough, the firing died down. His sentries breathlessly called in with news that the rebels had broken ranks in retreat. The unit was saved.

That had been back before the whole business with the Americans, when he was the confident commander of hundreds. Now a prisoner of his own side, he stood there silently as the Kandaharis hurled obscenities at him. Without food, however, he and the other detainees could hardly lift their Kalashnikovs, let alone march through the mountains. It was only then, the end of his third day in captivity, that the Palace Guards finally agreed to head to the nearest town to collect supplies. The captives assembled in a row for inspection, and when the guard saw Mullah Cable and another man in a shoeless state, he selected them both to take along.

They were brought to a small bazaar where men and boys were crowding around a few stalls and vendors were calling out their prices. The Kandaharis fanned out in every direction, and Mullah Cable and his fellow captive were dispatched to collect bread. When he neared a pyramid of tomatoes, he glanced back at the Kandaharis, who were busy looking over vegetables and talking among themselves. Slipping behind the tomatoes, he whispered to the other captive, "Follow me!" They broke into a sprint and just kept running.

It was long dark when they arrived at a level plain stretching south to the horizon, an open country of old mud huts and mud streams known as Bagram. Mullah Cable stopped in a field to examine his feet, now bruised a dark purple. All around him were the remains of a major Soviet military base, the fields littered with the detritus of that now-ancient occupation: rusting tanks, orphaned turrets, decaying mountains of wheelless jeeps, and, a short walk away, a gigantic, corroding warehouse made of corrugated iron—the perfect place to spend the night.

As he worked to pry open the door, a pair of headlights appeared in the distance. He moved faster as they careened toward him. Before he knew it, a jeep drove right up and armed men jumped out. Another Palace Guard patrol. He and the other captive were kneed and slapped and ridiculed and thrown into the back of a jeep. During the ride, Mullah Cable cried out from the pain of men sitting atop him and the broken road beneath him. When he tried to speak he was hit with something hard.

The Taliban camp, when they pulled in, was already a frenzy of activity. News over the radio told that Alliance rebels were pulling close, and a guard handed him a Kalashnikov with the words, "Don't be a coward." Not long after, the night erupted in gunfire. Men were shouting orders in the darkness. It was being said that the rebels had reached the front gate, but he could not see anything in that direction save the hills, dark against the sky. He fired wildly and then thought better of it, tossed his weapon aside, and broke for the rear exit. He was nearly out of the gate when something stopped him in his tracks: a pair of makeshift sandals that had been carved out of old army boots. Fortune was finally on his side. Strapping them on, he headed down the main road into the black night.

Some hours later he came upon another fleeing captive who reported that the camp had fallen and the surrounding fields were teeming with Palace Guards trying to find their way home. They, too, were not eager for martyrdom.

A twelve-hour walk to Kabul lay ahead. The road was lifeless, no sound anywhere but for his sandals on the gravel. He neared some darkened mud houses and slowed to see if anyone might be home but then changed his mind and kept walking. Some hours passed and fatigue set in. He came upon another row of houses that stood in perfect silence. Suddenly a flashlight blinked on and a voice yelled, "Stop!" Men in turbans were gathered ahead, and his heart sank.

A Taliban officer stepped forward. "Where are you going? he asked, sounding nervous. "Who are you?"

Mullah Cable had to think quickly. "I was up in Bagram visiting family. I'm on my way back to Kabul."

The officer studied him. "What kind of shoes are those? You don't look like an ordinary person." Mullah Cable responded with more lies, whatever came to mind, none of which made much sense. It turned out he had stumbled into Qale Nasro, a garrison town still in Taliban hands. The soldiers conferred, not knowing quite what to do. In the end, they decided to keep him at their guard post for the night.

When he awoke at dawn, the soldiers were already deep in discussion. They looked tense, clutching their walkie-talkies and listening to reports on the advance of Alliance rebels. It would be thirty minutes, or an hour at most, before the rebels reached Qale Nasro. The soldiers no longer seemed to have the slightest interest in him. Without hesitating, Mullah Cable slipped away and returned to the main road heading to Kabul.

He walked for hours as the sun climbed steadily overhead. When a minivan taxi appeared, he ran to catch it and it rolled to a stop, but the driver took one look at him, with his Taliban-style black turban and strange sandals, and refused to unlock the door. The two men negotiated through the open window. Mullah Cable pressed his case, repeating that he was a civilian visiting family up north, and the driver continued to look him up and down and kept the door locked. Finally, Mullah Cable unclasped his gold Swiss watch. A gift from his beloved brother, eight years deceased, it was the most valued thing he owned, the only item of luxury he'd allowed himself in the mountains. The driver took it and let him in.

They drove south. Mullah Cable wondered if the shame of what he had just done would ever leave him. What would his brother have said? It was all happening too fast. Just weeks before, he would have been driven anywhere he wished, by taxi or passing civilian alike, for free.

The van continued on. Had Mullah Cable looked at the country passing him by, he would have seen rows of ruined grape trees standing bare against the sky. He would have seen flame-blackened one-room shops, and mud houses with missing doors and windows and outer walls. It had all been done by his people, by the movement he had sworn his life to, but he saw none of it. Instead, he stared blankly ahead, wondering about the days to come, the friends he'd lost, and the end of life as he knew it.

— — —

Late on November 12, 2001, Mullah Cable entered Kabul. He found a hollow city. The roads were cratered, just as they had been when he'd left for the mountains all those years before. Shops and restaurants stood shuttered, and there was almost no one about. Crossing the Kabul River, he stared at the stinking mixture of mud and trash and goat droppings. He walked through neighborhoods he hadn't seen in years, where refuse sluiced down hillside drains into street gutters. The stench of sulfur and human waste was smothering. Up in the mountains, he'd forgotten how little governing the Taliban had done outside their drive for security and order. Everywhere he looked, there was nothing but spectacular neglect.

Near the city center, he arrived at a small house and for the first time in months saw his wife and daughter and the panoply of cousins and uncles who shared his roof. As they hugged, his relief was profound. He wanted nothing more than to stay in their company and live quietly and honorably. Peacefully. He hoisted up his sore feet and told them everything, and they listened with great concern and admiration. They said they didn't know what they would have done had he not returned to them. It was not long before they left to prepare dinner and he drifted off to sleep.

That evening, he awoke to visitors. Two cousins from the outskirts of town had heard that Northern Alliance rebels would be entering Kabul in the next day or two. As he ate his meal, Mullah Cable considered the news. He understood what everyone in town had long known: the civil war had compartmentalized Afghanistan's nearly forty ethnic groups into political blocs. The Taliban drew their recruits almost entirely from ethnic Pashtuns, who made up about 40 percent of the country, while the Northern Alliance typically gathered support from ethnic Tajik, Hazara, and Uzbek minority communities. Now most Pashtuns, even those who disliked the Taliban, felt anxious about the prospect of Northern Alliance rule.

When Kabul fell, he knew, not a single Talib would be left alive. It would be madness to stay. But where could he go? No province seemed safe, and the possibilities of retribution—at the hands of Alliance rebels, the Americans, or even civilians—bloomed in his imagination.

Only one option remained, and he could not deny it. The next morning Mullah Cable sold everything he owned to the neighbors, raising about $1,000. He, his wife, his daughter, and two other relatives squeezed into a minivan taxi. They passed the southern gates of Kabul, then the hills circling the city's edge, and finally Bala Hisar, a set of mud-walled castle ruins that the Taliban used for storage. Mullah Cable watched as men climbed out of the castle windows, weapons in hand. Looters. Government vehicles were being stolen. He knew then that Kabul was falling, and that it would be lost forever.

The taxi emerged onto a broad, vacant escarpment, and the road curved southeast. It was empty in both directions. Dark brown mountains lay in the far distance; beyond them, Pakistan. On the radio, the BBC was reporting scenes of jubilation in the city they had left behind. He sat deep in thought. The ignominy of his flight fit no narrative he knew. You worked hard, were clever and careful, and through patronage or charisma you became someone who mattered. You were brave in battle and loyal in life, and it paid off—but not for him. He was escaping like a common thief, turning his back on the movement that had made him who he was. "That was the beginning, I can tell you that," he recalled years later. "That was the start of my depression. I was thinking, *What will happen to me?* I pressed my face against the glass. I was crying, but I didn't want anyone to see. It felt like the sky was falling."

Two mornings later, Mullah Cable and his family arrived at a small way station at the foot of the dark brown mountains. They waited through the day until a smuggler appeared, and Mullah Cable spoke with him briefly. Just ahead was a stand of pine trees, and the group left their taxi behind and headed toward it on foot. Soon they found themselves making their way through a thick forest. A few miles ahead lay the tribal badlands of Waziristan, a region of Pakistan home to "murderers, backbiters, and thieves," as he explained to his wife. It was terra incognita for him, but he had heard enough tales of travelers being robbed and knifed there, or kidnapped and never seen again. Worse yet, Pakistan's official policy was to arrest any Talib they found.

With the smuggler as their guide, they headed off the path, hacking their way through the bracken, clearing their way as they went. Every so often, they were directed by the smuggler to lie motionless on the ground. Mullah Cable looked at his wife, suffering these hardships in silence, picking her way through the trees in her burqa. Guilt welled up in him, guilt for her ordeal and for having ever gotten mixed up in politics. He told himself that she shouldn't have to pay for his sins. The smuggler had given him a hunting rifle, and Mullah Cable decided that if someone came for his family he would fight to the death. "If I tell you to run," he told her, "just do it. Don't ask me, and don't wait for me."

After many hours they emerged into a clearing. A smooth, paved highway, a sight he'd never seen anywhere in Afghanistan, stretched out before them. Some time later, a truck rolled to a stop and picked them up, as arranged. Once they were on their way, he noticed the driver staring at him. "I've been doing this for a long time," the driver said. "But I've never seen anyone as anxious as you."

They drove on as the highway curved through forests of pine and holly. Every so often a Pakistani military vehicle trundled by and Mullah Cable ducked his head out of view. He knew that if he were caught he'd be turned over to the Americans or banished to a Pakistani prison, and the thought filled him with anger. What had it all been for? A mad village preacher throwing away the country for nothing?

The forest thinned into a broad clearing. Up ahead, straddling the highway, stood a military checkpoint. They drove up and the driver waved and the Pakistani soldier nodded and they continued on. They drove through a second and third checkpoint, and Mullah Cable was not even questioned. He could not make sense of it.

They crossed a dried riverbed and came upon street after street of low mud-brick houses. The driver announced that they had reached the town of Miram Shah. For the first time in three days, Mullah Cable and his family sat down to eat. The next morning they set out again, heading for the anonymous streets of the port metropolis of Karachi.

Back in Afghanistan the bombing continued, but the Taliban's end was near. Thousands of their soldiers were fleeing, and while some made it back to their home villages, the less fortunate among them ended up in Northern Alliance hands. Many of these were executed, including hundreds who were locked inside giant containers and suffocated to death. Though he didn't realize it, Mullah Cable had only narrowly escaped a similar fate. Shortly after he left the Taliban garrison town of Qale Nasro, rebels overran the outpost and seized whomever they could find. A *New York Times* reporter traveling with them learned that a Taliban soldier hiding in an irrigation ditch had been dragged out, stripped of his belongings, and shot. For good measure, a rocket-propelled grenade launcher was then driven into the corpse's head.

When his family reached Karachi, relief washed over Mullah Cable. If he could keep out of sight of Pakistani authorities, he could begin to piece together a Taliban-free future. He had a new world to look forward to, a new set of possibilities. A life at peace.

— 2 —

The Battle for Tirin Kot

On the day Jan Muhammad was scheduled to die, he awoke around dawn. He sat in the corner amid the darkness, until the familiar sounds of the morning began: the creaking of the hall gate, the deep thudding footsteps on the dirt floor, a series of bangs growing louder, and then the heavy rapping on his door. His Taliban jailers had adopted this tradition because you couldn't hear the muezzin in here. He stood to pray.

For the next two hours it was quiet. Then the sounds came again. Muhammad quickly groped around until he found the ornamental box where he had hidden the money. The door swung open and the hallway's dull light filled the room. Grabbing his jerry can, he followed the guards through the windowless corridor. He entered a large room of yellowing tiles and buzzing flies, where prisoners were hunched over and whispering softly. They were brought here daily to empty their cans, which they used to relieve themselves. With no drains, the effluent sat in puddles, sometimes for days, until one of the men was ordered to scrub the floor clean. Jan Muhammad retrieved the money he had concealed in his pants and quickly stuffed it into the fist of another prisoner. It was everything he had, $2,000, collected patiently from family visits and the sale of contraband over the last year.

"It's yours now," he whispered. "Take it." But he had been spotted. The guards surrounded him, and before he knew it he was thrown against the wall, kicked on the shins, and slapped across the face.

He was used to such impromptu beatings by now. When he was first brought to this Taliban prison, he had been thrown into a tiny room and shackled to the wall. Then the guards, mere teenagers, had entered with glass-studded belts. They came every day. By the time they left, he could barely stand. Now and then they even forbade him from praying. It was the one thing he couldn't live without. After fifteen days he was broken, sobbing and begging God to let him die.

That had been a year ago. Now, on December 5, 2001, his desperate plea was about to be answered. The American invasion was almost two months old, but here in Kandahar the Taliban were still in charge and eager to clear their prison of potential troublemakers.

Back in his cell, Jan Muhammad paced and prayed and thumbed his worry beads. Then he sat down against the wall, staring at the door. At that moment, his children were probably out working the farm. So, too, were his cousins and friends, except for a few who had most likely fled the country or were hiding in the mountains. He'd had no news from any of them for months. In fact, he'd had no news at all from the outside world. He continued to pray. Hours passed, and then he again heard the crescendo of approaching steps. The door swung open. Jan Muhammad looked at the guards and then stood up and followed them.

He wanted to be brave, stoic even, so that everyone would know what kind of man he was. So that his family would speak proudly of him for generations. But it was hard. As he was led past the cells of men he'd gotten to know from their time scrubbing jerry cans, he lost control. He found himself shouting, "Don't leave anything for these dogs!" In response, inmates banged on their doors. A few hollered, "God is great!"

He stepped outside into an open courtyard, under the blazing Kandahar sun. The fresh air felt pure and clean. From another section of the prison guards brought out Muhammad Nabi, a former enemy. It had been a year since Jan Muhammad had seen him.

Soon, the warden came out, an old man with flaking skin and a cold stare, surrounded by gun-toting Talibs. He had overseen much torture and humiliation, taking, it seemed, an almost sadistic pleasure in it all. But now he seemed nervous.

Ten minutes passed. More guards stepped into the sunlight to watch.

Jan Muhammad kept his gaze fixed on his feet. Everyone was quiet. The armed guards assembled, and he was pushed, with effort, to the wall.

Once, things had been different. You could have found Jan Muhammad sitting on plush velvet cushions, his arms folded across his massive lap, surrounded by friends, nephews, and hangers-on who listened with admiration to his every word. For many years, he stood at the center of all things political in Uruzgan Province, a mountainous little corner of southern Afghanistan. His had been a rags-to-guns-to-riches tale that could only have happened in this country. A school janitor when the Soviets invaded, Muhammad had joined the mujahedeen, the "holy warriors"—CIA-backed Islamist rebels fighting against the Russians—and quickly rose to commander. In those days, such a climb was possible if you had charisma and political skill, qualities that, it was said, he wielded with particular success. By the early 1990s, with the Soviets gone, he was governing Uruzgan and commanding the loyalty of thousands of men.

Yet Uruzgan, like much of the country, plunged into civil war after the Soviet withdrawal, and various mujahedeen groups vied to depose him. When the Taliban movement erupted in 1994 and swept through the province, Muhammad was stripped of his post and his weapons. He joined an underground anti-Taliban network that, unlike the Northern Alliance, was cut from the same cloth as the Taliban: ethnic Pashtuns from the deep south.

This "southern alliance" was headquartered in the Pakistani city of Quetta, where, in a stately home surrounded by bougainvilleas and orchids, there lived a former humanitarian worker named Hamid Karzai. The scion of an elite Kandahar family, Karzai was weaving together a network of tribal elders and former anti-Soviet commanders who shared his driving desire to overthrow the Taliban. "Hamid hated them," his brother Ahmed Wali told me. "He so badly wanted Afghanistan to join the international community. He didn't want his country to be a pariah state."

The alliance attracted dozens of important figures, but none were more crucial to Karzai than Jan Muhammad, the key node in a prodigious web of contacts throughout the south. The two formed an unlikely pair: a rakish, worldly college graduate and an illiterate, rough-hewn guerrilla. Yet they stood united in their belief in the power of tradition to deliver their country from what they saw as the Taliban's alien impositions. Hailing from the same Pashtun tribe, the Popalzais, the two carried themselves, in the words of Ahmed Wali, "like brothers."

Their bond had been forged on the front lines of the anti-Soviet war. Back then, Karzai, who worked for a Pakistan-based NGO, would slip into Uruzgan to deliver humanitarian assistance under Muhammad's protection. Once, as they were crossing a mountain defile, a rival mujahedeen group, presumably after the aid themselves, opened fire. While his men fought off the ambush, Muhammad spirited Karzai away to safety. Afterward, Karzai tearfully hugged his friend and swore that he would never forget what he had done.

Under the Taliban, Muhammad would secretly trek from Uruzgan to Pakistan to meet Karzai and plot the government's overthrow, slipping past authorities using every bit of ingenuity he could muster. Once, he bribed officials to plant false news of his whereabouts on the radio; another time, he passed off his old Soviet-era war wounds as new injuries, claiming to be heading to Pakistan for treatment. By 1999, however, the Taliban was tightening the clamps on all opposition activity. That year, assassins gunned down Abdul Ahad Karzai, Hamid's well-known father, for his antigovernment stance. Not long after, Jan Muhammad was arrested in his Uruzgan home and thrown into prison in Kandahar. News of the 9/11 attacks and the American invasion never reached his cell, and in October 2001 he was informed of his scheduled execution.

From the moment his friend had been arrested, Karzai vowed to do whatever it took to save him—and his country—from the Taliban. His plan hinged on a belief in tribal power: the Taliban were uncultured clerics who had upended the social order, but tribal elders, the guardians of tradition, could stir a counterrevolution. So Karzai spent months fostering a network of contacts in the heart of Taliban country, meeting them regularly in Pakistan to earn their trust and win their backing, waiting for the right time to foment an uprising. Now, with the American invasion imminent, he finally saw a chance to put this long-cultivated vision into effect.

With his urbane, professorial ways, however, Karzai was not a likely man of action. For a generation, the country's major figures had been fighters—war heroes (or villains, depending on where you stood)—but Karzai's close call in Uruzgan was one of his few tastes of actual combat. Instead, he had worked in a minor political capacity for the mujahedeen, mainly in Pakistan, which left his name absent from most histories of the Soviet war. Nor did he possess the aristocratic stature of his father, leader of the politically influential Popalzais. Friends knew him to be mercurial, edgy, and, in a pinch, given to tearful outbursts like a "spoiled child," according to a former aide.

Still, he could show flashes of brio when it mattered most. After his father's assassination, for example, he had defied Taliban threats and led a funeral procession into Kandahar. The daring march was something of a political coup, raising his stock in the opposition and prompting his coronation as head of the tribe. In politics as on the battlefield, timing was key. With the American campaign about to kick off, he knew that everything depended on his ability to convince the United States that an uprising was possible. Yet even though Washington was actively seeking a Pashtun counterweight to the Northern Alliance, American officials were skeptical. Karzai had few contacts outside of the CIA, which made him a relative unknown in Washington. It would not be easy, especially with Jan Muhammad behind bars. But given his hard-won network of tribal allies on the ground, Karzai was sure the people would be ready. They just needed a leader.

As the American bombing commenced, Karzai decided to make his move. He would infiltrate Taliban country himself to spark a tribal insurrection—with or without help. Only then did the CIA sign off on his plot, equipping him with satellite phones and bags of cash. "I thought he was mad," his brother Ahmed Wali recalled. "It was a suicide mission and we begged him not to go. But when Hamid gets an idea in his head, he listens to no one."

On a morning in mid-October, Karzai and a few aides, with shaggy beards and large turbans, mounted old motorcycles and slipped across the border into Kandahar Province. Capture meant certain execution. They rode along the cracked highway, past scrubland dotted with ramshackle homes. By lunchtime they had made it to Kandahar city and spent the day there in hiding. The next afternoon, they headed out by car toward the clay-colored cliffs of northern Kandahar. Just beyond lay Uruzgan, home of many Taliban leaders and key to Karzai's plan. If he could launch a rebellion there, in the Taliban heartland, the regime would never recover.

Night was drawing near when they saw flashing lights ahead—a Taliban roadblock. Karzai covered his face and sat quietly in the back. A Taliban guard pointed to the large sack on the seat beside him, containing the CIA-supplied satellite phones, and said, "Open that up."

They panicked. "There are women's cosmetics in there," said Muhammad Shah, Karzai's security guard, playing on cultural prohibitions against unrelated men handling women's intimate possessions. The guards looked unconvinced. "I started begging them, negotiating with them, trying everything," Shah recalled. "I was sweating. It seemed like the end. I was crying and telling them that my family members had been killed in the American bombings."

The guard seemed puzzled, and suddenly it dawned on Shah that the soldiers at this isolated outpost had not the slightest idea what was happening on the front lines, where their movement was rapidly crumbling under the power of American bombs. Shah quickly explained that air strikes were flattening military targets in province after province, and that Mullah Omar was nowhere to be found. The guards looked shaken. When Shah began insisting that an air strike could come at any minute, the soldiers waved them on.

Later that evening the men arrived in Uruzgan, driving with headlights off through the back roads and country lanes. They were guests in the houses of friendly elders and mullahs, sleeping in a different bed every night for security. At each stop, Karzai laid out his plan. The elders listened politely, but it soon became apparent that here, Karzai's grand vision of a Taliban-free future meant little. Everyone knew what happened if you stood against the Taliban—you swung from a tree. Karzai's tiny band of insurgents seemed impotent, even pathetic, in the face of such repression. The elders understood what Karzai did not yet seem to grasp: political victories in southern Afghanistan came not to those with the most inspiring ideas or far-reaching programs, but to those with the deepest pockets and biggest guns. And that was something that only the Americans could deliver. "You have a phone," one of the elders reportedly told Karzai. "Have the Americans bomb the Taliban command here." Karzai answered that he could not do that. "Then you will never win," the elder replied.

Soon word came that the Taliban had learned of their presence, and Karzai's team fled into the mountains. By the next day the Taliban had surrounded the area and were closing in fast. "It was bleak," an aide said later. "We were on the verge of a complete disaster."

Finally, Karzai switched on his satellite phone and dialed the CIA in Pakistan. Helicopters were rushed in for a nighttime weapons drop, and the freshly armed insurgents managed to fend off the Taliban and escape farther upland. Over the next week they were spirited from one remote safe house to the next, always a village ahead of their pursuers. At each stop, not a single local stepped forward to join them.

Weary and dejected, the team settled into a remote mountain fastness to regroup. Once more the Taliban caught wind of their location. "We had maybe an hour to live," Shah recalled. "I was thinking of my family." Again Karzai dialed the CIA. This time, in the nighttime blackness, he was plucked from the wilderness by a team of Navy SEALs and covertly choppered to a secret US base in Jacobabad, Pakistan.

The conclusion was unavoidable: Karzai's plan, two years in the making, had failed. The Taliban maintained their vise-like grip on the south, there was no "southern alliance" to speak of, and Jan Muhammad remained in prison, awaiting his execution.

Years later, in an ill-lit hotel bar in Washington, DC, I met Lieutenant Colonel Jason Amerine, the man who would help turn Karzai's fortunes around. A Green Beret with the Fifth Special Forces Group, Amerine had an action figure's contours and boot-camp posture, forged by years of training as a specialist in risky parachute insertions behind enemy lines. His unit had deployed to Jacobabad shortly after the 9/11 attacks, and he first met Karzai on the night of his rescue. "No one really believed in

Hamid on our side," Amerine recalled. "When I was sent down, they said, 'Have your team see who this guy is, but don't do anything crazy.'"

Amerine, however, sensed something exceptional in the guerrilla leader. He wasn't your typical Afghan warlord, not with his bookish cultivation and soft-spoken mien. "In a word," said Amerine, "he was a statesman." And Karzai's unswerving belief in a tribal uprising, despite his setbacks, was undeniably impressive, even though Amerine knew that the odds weren't in his favor. Karzai was insisting that the uprising had foundered only because he had failed to demonstrate that American power stood behind him. So he floated an even more daring idea: he would return to Uruzgan, this time with American soldiers by his side. Capturing the province, he promised, would "rip the heart out of the Taliban" and usher in the fall of Kandahar.

Even with Uruzgan elders clamoring for American support, however, Karzai had an obvious image problem on his hands. Every Afghan leader since the 1970s had lived and died with foreign backing, and many of them had plotted their coups and revolutions from Pakistan. How was he any different? His plan needed a nationalist gloss, a way to maintain the fiction of a homegrown uprising, if it was to have an air of legitimacy in the eyes of the country and the world. Ever the politician, Karzai got on his satellite phone with CNN and the BBC, proclaiming that he was on the run in the Afghan mountains when in fact he was safely ensconced at a CIA airbase in Pakistan.

Meanwhile, it was becoming clear to Washington that without a Pashtun proxy, the war could take a dangerous turn. With Kabul's fall imminent, the Northern Alliance was openly hinting that after taking the capital they planned to press south until the whole country was "liberated"—an advance certain to spark a civil war with the Pashtun-dominated south. Karzai's plot received the green light.

In the predawn stillness of November 14, five Black Hawk helicopters alighted on a mountaintop in central Uruzgan. Jason Amerine and nine other Green Berets trekked down the slope, bringing with them CIA agents, Delta Force commanders, and Hamid Karzai. They found their way to a small cove, were billeted in the residence of a friendly elder, and waited. They were miles from the nearest town, deep in Taliban country, not far from Mullah Omar's childhood home. Locals would join them, Karzai promised, so Amerine planned to spend weeks, if not months, training an insurgent force. Through it all, they would have to somehow avoid Taliban detection.

For two days, farmers came, took weapons, and disappeared into their villages. Most of them never returned. Then Karzai learned that the Taliban mayor of Tirin Kot, Uruzgan's capital, had either been deposed or had fled, leaving the town in the hands of its residents. It was not what Amerine wanted to hear. He still lacked a fighting force and, without adequate intelligence, heading into Tirin Kot could be a suicide mission. But he was certain that the Taliban would send reinforcements, and without help the town would be crushed. He'd have to move fast.

That evening, the Green Berets led Karzai and his smattering of guerrilla fighters in a caravan of pickup trucks, vans, donkeys, and horses on a four-hour journey across Uruzgan's parched moonscape. Upon arriving at the provincial capital, they found an adobe city, a warren of sienna-hued compounds surrounded by mud walls, each indistinguishable from the next. "Hamid had warned us there would be celebratory fire," Amerine recalled, "but when we got to town, there was nobody on the streets. It was a ghost town. That's when I knew it was a precarious situation."

The team took over a local residence and set up a command center. Then Amerine left his men and followed the insurgents through the darkened streets, past shuttered one-room shops, until they arrived at a squat concrete building. It was the governor's mansion. Karzai was already inside, seated with graybeards and stately-looking men in turbans and waistcoats. Some had taken part in whatever machinations had resulted in the mayor's departure; others had only emerged after the changeover. Some had once been Karzai's enemies because of his friendship with Jan Muhammad, their rival from the civil war days—but for now, in the shadow of American power, old grudges were overlooked.

The Afghans were just settling down to end their Ramadan fast when Karzai broke the news: a large Taliban convoy was en route from Kandahar to recapture the town, and they would likely arrive sometime in the morning.

It was exactly as Amerine had feared. He was invited to stay and eat, but he was in no mood for dinner. It was already close to midnight and, judging by the map, the enemy could arrive as soon as daybreak. A large convoy—that meant hundreds or even thousands of enemy troops against twelve Special Forces soldiers and maybe thirty ragtag Afghan militiamen, if Karzai could muster even that.

Back at the command center, Amerine relayed the news to a roomful of silent Green Berets. Men pored over maps, assessing possible Taliban infiltration routes. Incoming intelligence was now suggesting a convoy of nearly one hundred trucks. Amerine looked at the dozen men in the room. There was only one equalizer in a situation like this.

Shortly after one thirty a.m., Sergeant Alex Yoshimoto, an Air Force combat controller, received word that a patrolling F-18 fighter jet had spotted eight trucks speeding toward Uruzgan. It might be the lead element of the convoy. Yoshimoto looked at Amerine. "Are we clear to engage?"

Amerine was a man of solidity, a fighter who thought deeply about the conduct and meaning of war. With a bachelor's degree in Arabic, he had a facility with foreign cultures rare for a soldier. He quoted Tennyson and the Stoics and spoke of duty and honor. Now, for the first time in this mission, he faced the grim calculus of wartime, where a mistake could wipe out whole families or, conversely, throw your own men into danger.

In the end, for him, as for ground commanders everywhere, the choice was never really in doubt.

He told Yoshimoto, "Smoke 'em."

What could possibly compel anyone to face the might of American airpower? It was something I often wondered as I followed the invasion in the news. Back then, every day seemed to bring reports of dozens or hundreds of Taliban mowed down, only to have more of them sprout anew days later. They had the faceless quality of old Hollywood henchmen, always willing to sacrifice themselves in a mindless drive to satisfy some devious master. That certainly didn't sound like anyone I'd ever met, and it was one of the things I found most interesting about the Taliban.

Years later, I asked Jason Amerine for his thoughts on the enemy. "For ten years I had a lot of questions and what-ifs," he said. "You wonder who they were really and what they were after. What they were really about." Amerine had come to Afghanistan because, on some level, he felt he was responding to his country's needs after 9/11. It seemed to me that his counterpart, the Taliban commander rushing in to retake Tirin Kot, might, in a way difficult for us to grasp, feel similarly—that he, too, might regard himself as responding to his country's needs, or whatever warped perceptions of these needs he held.

When I mentioned this to Amerine in the hotel bar, he set his whiskey down and stared hard at the table. Then he said, "You know, I wish I could meet him. Sit down and talk to him. Or at least find out somehow what he was thinking."

In 2011, I visited the guesthouse of a tribal elder living in Kandahar city. Men sat in the shade of the porch out front sipping their tea and fanning themselves, looking on wordlessly as I approached. They were wrapped in pattus, the woolen shawls customary in those parts, and their beards glistened with sweat. It was past noon. The street outside was still and desolate and the people inside were readying themselves to sleep the sleep of a Kandahar summer's day.

Mullah Manan rose nervously to greet me, his pattu concealing everything but his eyes and forehead. He spoke quietly and with great precision, as if under examination. When he removed his shawl, it revealed a gaunt frame, high cheekbones, and shy eyes. Back in 2001, he said, he had helped lead the Taliban's push to retake Tirin Kot. He was, in other words, Jason Amerine's counterpart.

"I knew Karzai was up there with some fighters," he said. Refusing a chair—sitting in them wasn't his habit—he instead curled up on the floor in the corner, his eyes on his lap as he spoke. "We had all the intelligence. So my job was to capture the town and get rid of him."

As Jason Amerine and Karzai pulled into Tirin Kot, Mullah Manan's soldiers, nearly a thousand of them, had climbed onto dozens upon dozens of flatbed trucks and armored personnel carriers and HiLux pickups, some fitted with antiaircraft guns, and headed north from their Kandahar base. They drove along dirt roads, kicking up plumes of dust that could be seen for miles. By early evening, they had reached the red foothills of Uruzgan's southern border.

The mountain shadows were running long over the land and Manan found his thoughts turning to mealtime after the day's Ramadan fast. They stopped at a tiny roadside village with a lone restaurant, and the crowd of soldiers soon overwhelmed its supplies and began dipping into their own provisions for the coming days. Manan knew that they'd probably have to spend a few nights in Tirin Kot, so he radioed back to his base in Kandahar to request additional meal rations. An eight-truck convoy carrying food and blankets was promptly dispatched.

After breaking their fast, the soldiers stretched out on the gravel road, leaning against their truck tires, drowsy with food. On the horizon, the dark forms of Uruzgan's mountains stood waiting. As a native son, Manan understood the province well. He'd grown up an illiterate farmer, and joined the Taliban after witnessing the criminality of the mujahedeen warlords. Now he found himself in charge of hundreds of lives, but that wasn't troubling in the least, for the Tirin Kot he knew was an unimpressive little town with unimpressive defenses: an old, rusted antitank weapon from the Soviet days and a few rocket-propelled grenade launchers. His side had everything you could have asked for: mines, mortars, and, most important of all, many loyal men.

Manan and his three fellow commanders decided to rest the troops here and hit the road again at first light. Settling in next to a tire, he listened as his men chatted away under the stars. A few were already asleep, stretched out on the backs of their trucks. Somewhere in Tirin Kot, he thought, Hamid Karzai and his insurgents were probably finishing their own meal, getting ready to turn in for the night. *They'll be fast asleep*, Manan realized. If his men moved now, they could strike before Karzai even knew what hit him. He mentioned the idea to the other commanders, but they were united in opposition. Karzai's group could just as easily be handled at daybreak, they said, especially since intelligence reports indicated an enemy numbering no more than twenty poorly equipped fighters. To Manan, it seemed that the element of surprise should never be squandered, but he kept these thoughts to himself. He had never been one to invite confrontation. Instead, he'd always tried to be all things to all people, the consummate diplomat. It was how God had made him, and it had gotten him this far without a problem. He curled up next to his tire, and the night fell silent.

The sky paled and the muezzin sang and Manan awoke to say his prayers. The others clambered onto their trucks and started the engines. He checked his walkie-talkie and his rifle, a trusty semiautomatic in use since the Russian days, and rolled out to near the middle of the convoy. As they picked up speed, Manan noted that the eight-truck convoy bringing supplies had never shown up. There must have been confusion at headquarters, an occurrence far too frequent for his taste.

The trucks carried the men through the empty reddish desert. Up ahead lay the Tirin Kot pass, a narrow defile cut into the coppery mountains that formed Uruzgan's natural southern wall. The town lay twelve miles from the pass, the mountains extending in a semicircle around it like half of a giant earthen bowl.

As the first touches of orange streaked the eastern sky, Manan's radio came to life. "I can see the governor's house," said his friend Rahim from the lead vehicle. Rahim had made it through the pass and was inside the bowl, a good mile ahead of him. They would reach the town in no time.

As the pass appeared, Manan prepared to steer through. It was then that he noticed the sound of planes, not too far away.

It was near four a.m. when Hamid Karzai showed up at Amerine's command center with the small band of guerrillas he had managed to cobble together, many of them friends and relatives of Jan Muhammad. Amerine loaded the recruits and his own team onto pickups and headed for the Tirin Kot pass.

The vehicles drove across the rolling earth through a web of hills that stretched for miles. The desert eventually gave way to a two-hundred-foot-high ridgeline, and the trucks pulled to a stop. It was a perfect vantage point overlooking the pass, two miles off. From here, the Afghan guerrillas could fire rocket-propelled grenades and Amerine's men could call in air strikes.

The Afghans were placed in fighting positions, and the Green Berets set to work establishing communications with air support. Not long after, the team spotted dust clouds near the pass. Amerine glassed the area with his binoculars and saw something coming straight toward them. It was moving fast, and it was not a car or a truck—it looked like an armored personnel carrier. He issued an order and Sergeant Yoshimoto radioed to the F-18s waiting above. Moments later the air pulsed with a massive boom, but the vehicle appeared untouched. A second strike sent a shock wave across the basin. When the smoke cleared, all he could see was a burning lump of metal.

Amerine turned to his guerrillas—but they were scrambling back to their vehicles. After the first bomb missed, they decided that they'd seen enough. "Hey, what the fuck is going on?" a soldier shouted. "Where are they going?" The first trucks pulled away. Amerine and his team would be stranded, left to the Taliban. For a moment, he contemplated shooting the drivers. But what would Karzai think? Or the townsfolk? He'd have to go with them, even if that meant abandoning the position. He and the other Green Berets jumped onto the last vehicles as they were about to speed off.

The developing situation had now caught the attention of command centers in Pakistan and back home. A dozen or so Green Berets were facing the largest Taliban assault of the entire war, and every available air asset across the theater was directed to Uruzgan.

Meanwhile, a few miles away, Mullah Manan eased his vehicle through the pass. When he emerged, he gasped—Rahim's armored personnel carrier was a heap of burning metal and billowing smoke. He looked skyward for planes. Nothing. For a moment he considered stopping to look for bodies, but the basin was too exposed. He pressed ahead, toward a shallow ridgeline.

Back in Tirin Kot, the Americans unloaded the guerrillas and drove two jeeps back themselves to a small hillock just outside of town. Amerine surveyed the area. If the Taliban made it past here, he knew he wouldn't be able to bring himself to authorize air strikes—not with all those people, all those houses. If Taliban trucks breached this point, the town would be theirs.

Mullah Manan forced himself to concentrate on the road. He told himself that Rahim was resourceful, that he would have made it out somehow. He'd go back for him after securing Tirin Kot. His vehicle was now moving so fast that every bump sent a jolt of pain up his spine. This blitzkrieg-style attack, which he'd learned against the Northern Alliance, almost always caught the enemy off guard. He estimated he was about six miles from town.

On the hill, Amerine received word from pilots that the Taliban trucks had split into three columns. "Put it all on the center column for now," he said.

Manan was focused on keeping a tight distance from the truck in front of him when a massive blast slammed the column to his right, spewing dust everywhere. It felt like an earthquake. *The Americans are here*, he thought, searching the sky.

On the hill, the Green Berets were busy coordinating strikes. When Amerine looked up, he saw Tirin Kot residents—men, women, and children—emerging from their homes, coming up to the hill to watch them work. News of the awe-inspiring strikes was spreading, and cheers erupted with every blast. Many of the onlookers were Jan Muhammad's tribespeople.

By now, vehicles were exploding into flames all around Manan. Yet scanning the ridgelines, he couldn't see a soul anywhere. Where were the Americans? What kind of impossibly advanced machines were they using? This wasn't a battle, not when you couldn't even see your enemies. No, it was some sort of wizardry, majestic and cowardly all at once. He pressed his sandaled foot to the pedal and barreled ahead. He was now four miles from town.

Amerine had a problem—there were just too many trucks. The sky was stacked with at least thirty aircraft, but there was no end to the Taliban vehicles pouring out of the pass. Short on payload, pilots began strafing runs, which he knew would expose them to antiaircraft fire. But with the convoy largely intact, there seemed to be no choice.

That was the first time Mullah Manan actually spotted one of the planes. It swooped in, firing rapidly at the column to the east, and he saw windshields fracture and heard a tire somewhere pop. Already the column was breaking up. Trucks struggled to turn around or lay jackknifed across the road. But Manan was not panicking. It looked like there were just one or two planes in the fight, and they were targeting the other columns. His drove on untouched. *They must not be able to see us*, he thought. He was now only three miles from town.

"Work on the western column, and then the eastern one," Amerine ordered. Within moments, a jet dove toward Manan. He heard machine-gun fire and looked up to see the plane's belly flash past. The first vehicle hit was a food truck, which crashed into a second truck, scattering loaves of flatbread everywhere. Manan swerved, only to see another jet speeding toward him. He veered off the road just as it flew past, machine-gunning a truck behind him. Grabbing his walkie-talkie, he screamed: "Turn around!"

Amerine received news of the arrival of a fresh wave of jets carrying 500-pound bombs, which they were dropping up and down the column.

Manan looked up. The sky filled with an almost deafening roar. He started praying, promising God that if he made it out of this he'd quit fighting forever. Driving back toward the pass, he ran into a stream of oncoming trucks. Vehicles were stacking up in both directions, a traffic jam right there amid the hills. Without hesitating, Manan slammed on the brakes, tossed aside his weapon, leapt out, and ran, heading east toward the sunrise. He didn't look back.

On the hill, Amerine caught sight of a truck that had somehow made it all the way to Tirin Kot. Suddenly, machine-gun fire erupted somewhere nearby. For a dark moment he thought the Taliban had penetrated the town. But then he saw that it was the townsfolk firing at the truck, sending the driver scrambling away.

Everywhere, explosions echoed through the basin. Manan's fighters were abandoning their vehicles and fleeing on foot. The townsfolk jumped into trucks to give chase. Those they caught, they executed. The battle was over, and soon the Taliban would be as well.

News of the victory at Tirin Kot spread fast, spurring Taliban officials throughout the south to defect. But it could easily have been otherwise. When I described Mullah Manan's account of the battle to Jason Amerine, he leaned back thoughtfully. Had Manan convinced his comrades to drive on through the night, Amerine said, his team would not have been in position in time. "We would have lost. We wouldn't have held Tirin Kot because there was no way I could have bombed the town."

For two days the Green Berets waited for a counterattack, but nothing came. Still, Amerine knew the war wouldn't be over until Kandahar city

was theirs, and he prepared to march south with Karzai's growing guerrilla army. Before leaving, however, he wanted to fully explore the area.
There was one valley in particular, about ten miles due east, yet to be
visited. When he raised the possibility with Karzai, though, it was dis-
missed. The guerrillas shouldn't venture there, Karzai said, because
"they don't like us and we don't like them."

In that very valley, Mullah Manan was sitting in a stranger's home,
shell-shocked and nursing his wounded ambitions. He had hiked for
hours through a maze of hills in order to seek refuge among his clan, members of the Ghilzai tribal confederation. They had long been marginalized
in an Uruzgan dominated by the Popalzais and related tribes. The Taliban
had upset this hierarchy—the sole reason a poor Ghilzai farmer like
Manan could ever have risen to command hundreds. In steering Amerine
away, Karzai understood what his American friends did not yet grasp: not
only individuals but entire tribal communities were winners and losers in
the invasion. Time would reveal this in a most painful way.

More than anything, Manan wanted to hear from his comrades in
the convoy, or from the Kandahar leadership, or from anyone at all with
news. But for three days he heard nothing. He needed direction, a sense
of how the others were coping, an idea of what would come next. He
would have to risk a trip to his home valley.

Walking up the dusty bazaar road of his hometown, he headed
toward the office of the town mayor, a friend of his. Just then, a shopkeeper stepped out and shouted, "Where's your weapon now?" Someone
else jeered, "You call yourself a man? Go home to your wife!" Five years
of Taliban authority were crumbling before his eyes. A week earlier, these
shopkeepers would have hugged him and prayed for his safety. It was
hard to believe.

At government headquarters he learned that the mayor had fled,
along with his assistants, the gardener, the tea boy, and the night watchman. Manan headed home. Embracing his sisters and parents, he
recounted his harrowing escape. Then he went to the backyard and
hoisted himself onto the mud wall overlooking their tiny wheat field.
There was his brother, hunched over in sweat, as always. He'd turned
down the fighter's life for a chance to run the farm. At that moment, as

his brother turned the soil with his bare hands, Manan saw the honor of simple work, the type that belongs to you alone.

That month, thousands of Taliban confronted the same reality. Their movement had failed a great test of endurance and legitimacy. Now the mandate of authority was passing to the Americans and their Afghan allies.

On November 30, almost two weeks after the battle of Tirin Kot, Jason Amerine's Green Berets escorted Hamid Karzai and his CIA handlers to Kandahar with a caravan of Afghan militiamen and tribal elders. Along the way they passed through the battle-scarred hills of the failed Taliban assault, the roadside dotted here and there with circles of rocks, hasty graves erected wherever fighters had fallen. On reaching Uruzgan's southernmost mountains, the edge of the bowl, they stopped at the same ramshackle village that had hosted Manan's forces a few weeks earlier.

Thousands of miles away, in Bonn, Germany, various Afghan political factions were meeting to decide on a post-Taliban government. The Northern Alliance held the majority of delegate seats, followed by an assortment of groups associated with the former king Zahir Shah, in exile since 1973. After much wrangling, Abdul Sattar Sirat, an ethnic Uzbek close to the king, was chosen as the country's interim president. Hamid Karzai, whose stock had been soaring since the Tirin Kot battle, was awarded the vice presidency.

The following day, Amerine's team stopped about fifteen miles north of Kandahar city, at an eerily silent and apparently deserted town. Everything was still, except for the Taliban's signature white flags flapping atop the buildings. As the team pressed closer, Kalashnikov fire erupted nearby. It was a leftover Taliban contingent, putting up last-ditch resistance. Over fifteen hours, the Green Berets and Afghan insurgents slowly advanced through the wadis and fields, getting into close-range firefights and calling in air strikes. At times, the fighting grew intense—one Green Beret survived a bullet through the neck—but the Americans eventually captured a strategic hill overlooking the main tributary flowing into Kandahar.

By the next morning the outpost had been transformed into a hub of operations for the insurgency, with local elders streaming in for audiences with Karzai. Around eight thirty a.m., Karzai headed to a command post to meet some newly arrived tribal leaders who had come bearing an important message. Suddenly everything exploded: windows burst, slabs of the ceiling came crashing down, and Karzai was thrown to the ground. When he looked up, he saw smoke and blood and groaning, soot-covered men.

The Americans had called in an air strike—on themselves. Although threat of a Taliban counterattack had been minimal, American bombing had continued (largely on orders of Amerine's superior, who had flown in to join the mission). In the process, an errant 2,000-pound satellite-guided bomb struck their own encampment. Miraculously, Karzai escaped with only bruises, but some of his most trusted commanders were killed. In all, five Afghans lost their lives in the blast, along with three American soldiers, and many more were wounded, Amerine among them. He was evacuated from the country.

Minutes after the blast, Karzai's satellite phone rang with a call from the BBC's Lyse Doucet. "What's your reaction to being named as prime minister?" she asked. It was news to Karzai. Behind the scenes, US officials had been busy reversing the decision that Afghan groups had reached in Germany. The Americans had apparently wanted their own man, a Pashtun, in the presidential palace.

Moments later, Karzai got another dose of surprising news: the Taliban were sending a delegation to meet him.

After two months in hiding, Mullah Omar was losing his grip. Initially, he had exhorted his senior lieutenants to fight on, assuring them that he was "ready to leave everything, and to believe only in Islam and my Afghan bravery." But his mettle deserted him after the war's fateful first night. Since then, he had been hiding in the houses of close friends, emerging only at nightfall. He was suffering from apocalyptic dreams and anguish over his decision not to surrender bin Laden. His moods veered wildly between intense defiance, including pledges to fight to the death, and bouts of boundless terror that brought him close to tears. Even worse, the rest of the Taliban leadership, who had come to see their cause as hopeless, were pressing him to capitulate.

Two weeks before the battle of Tirin Kot, Omar had ordered an assistant to reach out to Karzai through tribal intermediaries to explore the possibility of surrender. Karzai had received the call on his satellite phone at the airbase in Pakistan, as Jason Amerine sat within earshot, and passed the message to the CIA, who reportedly relayed it all the way up to Secretary of Defense Donald Rumsfeld. The Taliban leader hinted that he was seeking a face-saving abdication of power, which meant an "honorable immunity," in the words of an associate. Rumsfeld's response was clear and direct: Washington would accept nothing short of unconditional surrender.

After the defeat in Tirin Kot, the Taliban leadership gathered secretly at a house in Kandahar city. Throughout the afternoon, an increasingly sullen Omar pleaded with the others to head for the mountains and launch a guerrilla war. But "this wasn't happening," a top military commander told me later. "We all knew time was up. Fate laughs at even the best schemes."

His back to the wall, Mullah Omar drew up a letter to Hamid Karzai, acknowledging his selection as interim president. The letter also granted Omar's ministers, deputies, and aides the right to surrender and formalized the handover of his vehicles, books, and other possessions to tribal elders.

On December 5, a Taliban delegation arrived at the US special forces camp north of Kandahar city to officially relinquish power. According to a participant, Karzai was asked that he allow Mullah Omar to "live in dignity" in exchange for his quiescence. The delegation members, which included Defense Minister Mullah Obaidullah, Omar's trusted aide Tayeb Agha, and other key leaders, pledged to retire from politics and return to their home villages. Crucially, they also agreed that their movement would surrender arms, effectively ensuring that the Taliban could no longer function as a military entity. There would be no jihad, no resistance from the Taliban to the new order—even as leaders of al-Qaeda were escaping to Pakistan to continue their holy war. The differences between the two groups may have never been so apparent, but as Washington declared victory, they passed largely unnoticed.

It was December 7, less than two months since the first American
bomb had fallen. Across Afghanistan, men and women looked with won-
drous anticipation toward the end of twenty-one years of war. In Kandahar, a convoy of Afghan militiamen, Green Berets, and Karzai with his
CIA escorts snaked through acres of farmland and approached the dusty
outskirts of the city. As they entered the mud-walled maze of narrow
streets, they passed a large irrigation tunnel. Inside, Mullah Omar and
other senior Taliban leaders were huddled together, fearing that, despite
Karzai's promises, they would be handed over to the Americans.

Later that evening, as Karzai and the Americans occupied Mullah
Omar's home and announced the official end of the Taliban regime, as
crowds celebrated in Kabul and other cities across Afghanistan, as the
world heralded the end of one of the most oppressive governments in
memory, Mullah Omar stepped out of the tunnel. With the open country before him, he bid farewell to his friends and said that they should
attempt to contact him no more. They were now and forever on their own.
Then he climbed aboard an old Honda motorcycle, drove out along the
highway, and disappeared into the desert.

The day that Karzai survived a US bomb and learned that he had been
selected president, a prisoner was walked out of his cell and into the
courtyard of a Kandahar prison. The sun weighed down heavily; the
guards gathered in the shade. No words were spoken, as dozens of eyes
fixed on the condemned.

Then a door to the courtyard banged open and a man strode in, followed by a group of bodyguards. Jan Muhammad recognized him as a
high-ranking Taliban official. He watched as the man whispered something to the warden.

The pair walked toward Jan Muhammad. The warden reached behind
him and slipped a key into his wrist shackles.

He stared at them. "Is this a joke?" It was all that he could think to say.

"I hope you'll forgive us for what we did to you," the official said. He
then undid the cuffs of the other prisoner, Muhammad Nabi. "You are
free. A car is waiting outside."

Karzai had not forgotten his promise. Upon meeting the Taliban delegation, he'd stated that he would accept their surrender on one condition: the immediate release of his dear friend Jan Muhammad.

Muhammad was driven to the American camp, and when Karzai first caught sight of him he burst into tears. After they embraced, he took a step back and gasped: his once corpulent friend had shriveled up, skin hanging from his bones.

Only in Karzai's camp did Muhammad finally learn about the events of the previous two months, of 9/11, the US invasion, and the Taliban's impending demise. He drove home to Uruzgan to see his family and returned the next day with scores of jubilant tribesmen. The following day, the whole group would march with the Americans into Kandahar city, Afghanistan's political crucible, as men of power.

When I met him years later, Jan Muhammad's ample frame had filled out, and he was living once again in a world of supplicants and hangers-on. I had sought out Mullah Cable to understand the US invasion from the perspective of the losers, and now I was meeting Muhammad to explore just what it had meant for the winners—and few had won as much as he. It was a quintessentially Kabul meeting: the cluttered living room with its gaudy leather couches still in their plastic covers, the glass coffee table, the portrait of Karzai hung proudly on the wall, the children peeking in shyly from behind a kitchen door. Jan Muhammad showed me how his body had become a battlefield over the years, bearing the remnants of Soviet slugs and Taliban torture. A coarse gray beard hung wildly from his jowls, and a turban sat so haphazardly atop his head that you had to fight the urge to reach over and straighten it. One eye was damaged and useless; the other squinted at you with a touch of suspicion.

I asked him what his initial thoughts had been upon his release, and he replied that from his first free step, he was consumed by a single idea. It churned inside him, invaded his dreams, and gripped his imagination. It commandeered his public life, even though he knew it was wrong, and it had destroyed many of his personal relationships. He looked at me, with an unflinching stare, and said: "I wanted revenge."

3

The War from Year Zero

The old man sat legs folded on the asphalt, facing a bullet-ridden building. Spread out before him were Colgate toothbrushes and colored plastic combs and glossy cigarette packs promising "American flavor." The building was like a crumbling cave, with its collapsed roof, buckling support beams, and a yawning hole for a front door. He pointed to the structure. "There," he said, "was once something glorious."

He had lived in this sweltering city of Lashkar Gah, the capital of Helmand Province, selling trinkets and toiletries for as long as he could remember—"before the Americans, before the Taliban, before the Russians," he explained. In the 1970s, the building had served as the Helmand Cinema House, the only movie theater in all of southern Afghanistan. On a Friday afternoon, you could catch double features imported from around the world. One of the most popular was *Laila Majnu*, a Bollywood take on a classic Arab story of unrealized love. Qays, a farmer, falls hard for a girl named Laila, but her father forbids the marriage and she is given to another man. Despondent, Qays roams the desert for years, earning the sobriquet *majnun*, madman. Eventually, his body is found next to the grave of his beloved, his final ode to her written in the sand nearby.

The old man had gone back repeatedly, even though he didn't understand most of the Hindi spoken, until he had the film memorized. He had grown up in a world segregated by gender, where marriages were arranged, and this was his first love story. "It gave us all hope," he told me, "that we would find something special in our lives."

But one afternoon in 1992, the mujahedeen arrived in town and shut down the theater forever. Later, they rocketed it for good measure. When the Taliban seized power, the building was converted into a state-run radio station. After 2001, under the American-backed regime, the place became an opium den. A whole generation grew up never having seen a film. But the old man still remembered, and he told anyone who would listen about the time when, for two hours a week, a madman and his lover were all that mattered.

The first years after 2001 were like a dream. Society had effectively been on hold for two decades, and now, with the war over, it was as if the very notion of public life had been unearthed from a time capsule. It was a new beginning, a Year Zero. Barbers were among the first to reemerge, unrolling their mats onto busy sidewalks; for a few pennies and a cup of tea you could shave your Taliban-mandated beard, shearing away the weight of the past. Music once again rang out through the streets, and Hollywood and Bollywood DVDs, once traded like samizdat, were selling openly in Kabul.

Millions of refugees returned after years away. Investment dollars poured in, as television stations and cell phone towers sprouted seemingly overnight. An influx of aid organizations formed part of the broadest international humanitarian initiative in history, and abandoned homes were repurposed into offices for gender experts and development specialists. One result of all the outside attention was the 2004 constitution, drafted with heavy Western input and hailed as one of the world's most progressive. In addition to protecting basic civil liberties and minority rights, the document guaranteed women 25 percent of parliamentary seats (surpassing the proportion in the US Congress).

Yet I wondered if all this was enough to erase the memories of the Taliban past. What did it feel like to emerge from those brutal years? One afternoon in 2010 I met a woman, Heela, who would help me understand what the post-Taliban world really meant for civilians. At first, however, she hesitated to talk. "I don't know anything about these wars," she told me. "I'm just an ordinary woman." So ordinary, in fact, that she seemed the very embodiment of Afghanistan—troubled, tried, resilient, and ultimately beholden to a foreign power. She appeared to typify exactly the sort of person the US invasion had saved, and I wondered if perhaps, in her newfound freedom, she would offer a glimpse of the best of American influence.

Heela, then thirty-seven, was the doyenne of a tiny clan of boys. Walid, the youngest, was a torrent of mischief; Omaid, the oldest, was a pensive teenager with lugubrious eyes. Between them were Nawid and Jamshed, both of whom had a penchant for skipping school and wandering far and wide, but who always came home in time for dinner. Heela lived a life of jangled nerves and frequent distractions; when speaking, she raced ahead breathlessly, hopscotching in her story from one place to another, zigzagging across time and space like some postmodern conversationalist. She stood taller than average, with a youthful smile and large, winter-gray eyes.

As with Mullah Cable and Jan Muhammad, I was interested in Heela's experience in the new American-backed order. But to start her story with the US invasion would be like "watching a movie from the middle," as she put it. In truth, Afghanistan's real Year Zero was 1979, the year of the Soviet invasion, and nothing—not the Taliban, or the American invasion, or the trajectory of Heela's life—makes much sense without first coming to terms with the Russian occupation and its aftermath.

In the veritable Afghan prehistory of peace and anonymity, the era before the Soviets, there lies a world lost and yet to be recovered. In 1972, the year that Heela was born to a family of journalists and professionals, Kabul was a quaint, relaxed mountain town. An important stop on the "hippie trail"—a well-trodden route for Western stoners and flower children often heading to India—the town had reinvented itself in a few short generations. A wave of progressive reforms had rippled through Afghanistan in the 1950s, resulting in a government decree that veiling was optional for women. In 1964, they were granted the franchise. Photographs from the era show besuited men accompanied by women in short skirts and beehive hairdos; there are movie theaters, broad paved roads, and tree-lined sidewalks.

Out in the heavily tribal Pashtun countryside, however, conservatism still reigned and women lived cloistered in their homes. The state was largely absent, and civil society nonexistent; politics worked through kinship and patronage, leaving clan leaders and landlords to run their own fiefdoms. If you managed to make it out to Kabul and attend university, you came away with a tantalizing taste of what your country could become, and a stark, unremitting sense of the inadequacies of the world you'd left behind. As with so many other developing nations of that era, this disjuncture spawned a crisis of modernity, and the disillusioned urban intelligentsia struggled to articulate a response. Two rival currents emerged: one embracing Communism, which looked to the Soviet Union and third-world liberation movements, and the other, Islamism, which took inspiration from the Muslim Brotherhood and related trends in the Arab world.

For many years these were merely undercurrents, but they rushed to the surface in the late 1970s. Heela was in the third grade when, one afternoon, she happened upon a large demonstration. Throngs of students wearing black headbands were carrying a body and chanting slogans. They had symbolically tied cloths around their own jaws, the way Afghans did with a corpse to prevent its mouth from swinging open. Some were shouting and firing rifles in the air, or waving flags bearing the likenesses of Che Guevara and Karl Marx. It was April 1978, and the Communists were rallying against the government for killing Mir Akbar Khyber, one of their leaders. "This was the first time the Afghan people raised their voices. It was like an earthquake," she told me. "None of us in my family understood it yet, though. We weren't political people."

The Communists used the killing of their leader as a pretext to launch a coup against dictator Daud Khan. Within days, army units had seized the palace and executed Khan and his family. But the Communists themselves were riven into two feuding factions, which immediately took to conspiring against each other. For the next year, chaos gripped the country, as the Communist leadership pushed through land reform, killed thousands of tribal elders, landlords, and religious figures, and plotted to knock one another off. The government seemed on the verge of devouring itself. On Christmas Eve 1979, the neighboring Soviet Union invaded, ostensibly to end the internecine fighting and put in place a more stable leadership. But their occupation only intensified the bloodshed: in the decadelong war that followed, it is believed that a million Afghans were killed and five million became refugees. Soviet bombers wiped whole villages off the map, while Soviet troops imprisoned and tortured thousands. The decade marked a cataclysmic rupture; nothing for Afghans, or indeed the entire Muslim world, would ever be the same.

While the Communists waged devastation on the countryside, within the big cities they managed to win a semblance of support through the provision of services. They built modern housing complexes and subsidized health care and basic foodstuffs. Record numbers of women went to college. "I don't know about their political views," Heela said of the Communists, "but they helped build Kabul. We liked them for that." She also approved of their liberal take on women's rights. "There was complete freedom in those days," she said. "No one could tell a woman where to go or what to do." Even the headscarf, that shibboleth of societal conservatism, had become a matter of familial discretion. Heela was supposed to wear one, but upon leaving the house she would stuff it into her purse.

Education was Heela's abiding ambition. At seventeen, she won admission to Kabul University, the nation's premier institution of higher learning. She majored in economics, hoping to go on for a master's degree.

One day during her junior year, her family brought home a young man for tea. It had become a regular occurrence, for at nineteen she was well into her marriageable years. Heela was to stay quietly in the adjacent room until called; usually, she would be brought out to meet the visiting family, some words would be exchanged with the adults, and then modesty would call for her to retreat again. This time, though, as she was introduced, she saw that there were no relatives accompanying this visitor, no throng of curious aunts. There was only a tall, pale young man standing shyly in the corner. He had a sharp nose, prominent cheekbones, and—impossible to ignore—a disarming smile.

Heela knew that it would be improper to inquire about him openly, but over the next few days she gleaned snippets here and there. His name was Musqinyar, and he'd come alone because his family was down south. He had been living by himself in Kabul, something she'd never heard of before, working for the government. She also learned that he was a Communist and a fervent defender of women's rights. Over the following weeks, Heela registered her approval the way a good Afghan girl did—by saying nothing at all.

During her daily walks to the university she found her thoughts wandering to him. It was killing her not to know what the two sides were discussing, or if they were talking at all. One afternoon, she had almost reached the campus when suddenly Musqinyar appeared in her path. *Oh my god*, she thought. They stood staring at each other. She could see the scandal, the tears and screams at home, the accusations about a couple skirting their families and taking matters into their own hands.

Before she could say anything, he broke into a wide grin and announced that he would like her hand in marriage. Not knowing what to do, she turned and hurried the other way. She fought the urge to look back.

Some days later he appeared again. This time, before she could flee, he blurted out that he wanted to get to know the woman that he might spend the rest of his life with. He meant no harm, he insisted, and no one would know that they had spoken. It was just for his peace of mind.

She agreed to walk with him. He quickly slid into lengthy monologues about politics and religion and the war. He was distinctly modern, progressive, in a way she'd never seen before in a man. He assured her that only the Communists could save the country, that the stories filtering in from the countryside were exaggerated. By the end of the walk, she finally plucked up the courage to ask if he would allow her to work. He shot her a wounded look, seeming insulted that she'd even asked. It was a woman's natural right, he said.

Soon he became a fixture on her daily walk. They spoke of Pashto poetry and overbearing relatives, of traveling the country after the war and some day visiting central Europe, where Kabul's electric trolleybuses were built. They would go to Germany, he promised, after peace arrived. They'd ride the trains, even the ones that ran underground.

In 1991, they were wed. Shortly after, they moved into a small Soviet-built apartment near downtown Kabul. Musqinyar was making good money working for the Ministry of Health, and Heela, upon receiving her diploma, found a job as a teacher. In her spare time she took courses in nursing and midwifery, which led to a moonlighting gig with the World Health Organization. It wasn't long before she gave birth to a baby boy.

Life was good. Infused with tiny, daily acts of hope, their imagination told of a future that belonged entirely to them. But beyond city limits, in the rust-hued mountains girding Kabul, that future was being unwritten.

Even before the first Soviet tanks crossed into Afghanistan in 1979, a movement of Islamists had sprung up nationwide in opposition to the Communist state. They were, at first, city-bound intellectuals, university students and professors with limited countryside appeal. But under unrelenting Soviet brutality they began to forge alliances with rural tribal leaders and clerics. The resulting Islamist insurgents—the mujahedeen—became proxies in a Cold War battle, with the Soviet Union on one side and the United States, Pakistan, and Saudi Arabia on the other. As the Soviets propped up the Afghan government, the CIA and other intelligence agencies funneled millions of dollars in aid to the mujahedeen, along with crate after crate of weaponry. In the process, traditional hierarchies came radically undone. When the Communists killed hundreds of tribal leaders and landlords, young men of more humble backgrounds used CIA money and arms to form a new warrior elite in their place—which was how, for instance, school janitor Jan Muhammad reinvented himself. In the West, we would call such men "warlords." In Afghanistan they are usually labeled "commanders." Whatever the term, they represented a phenomenon previously unknown in Afghan history. Now, each valley and district had its own mujahedeen commanders, all fighting to free the country from Soviet rule but ultimately subservient to the CIA's guns and money.

The war revolutionized the very core of rural culture. With Afghan schools destroyed, millions of boys were instead educated across the border in Pakistani madrassas, or religious seminaries, where they were fed an extreme, violence-laden version of Islam. Looking to keep the war fueled, Washington—where the prevailing ethos was to bleed the Russians until the last Afghan—financed textbooks for schoolchildren in refugee camps that were festooned with illustrations of Kalashnikovs, swords, and overturned tanks. One such edition declared: "Jihad is a kind of war that Muslims fight in the name of God to free Muslims. . . . If infidels invade, jihad is the obligation of every Muslim." An American text designed to teach children the Farsi alphabet began:

Aleph [is for] Allah; Allah is one
Bey [is for] Baba (father); Father goes to the mosque
Tey [is for] Tofang (rifle); Javed obtains rifles for the mujahedeen
Jeem [is for] Jihad; Jihad is an obligation. My mom went to the jihad.

The cult of martyrdom, the veneration of jihad, the casting of music and cinema as sinful—once heard only from the pulpits of a few zealots—now became the common vocabulary of resistance nationwide. The US-backed mujahedeen branded those supporting the Communist government, or even simply refusing to pick sides, as "infidels," and justified the killing of civilians by labeling them apostates. They waged assassination campaigns against professors and civil servants, bombed movie theaters, and kidnapped humanitarian workers. They sabotaged basic infrastructure and even razed schools and clinics. (This litany of terror pales in comparison to Soviet brutality but is relevant for what came next.)

With foreign backing, the Afghan resistance eventually proved too much for the Russians. The last Soviet troops withdrew in 1989, leaving a battered nation, a tottering government that was Communist in name only, and a countryside in the sway of the commanders. For three long years following the withdrawal, the CIA kept the weapons and money flowing to the mujahedeen, while working to block any peace deal between them and the Soviet-funded government. The CIA and the ISI (Inter-Services Intelligence), Pakistan's spy agency, pushed the rebels to shell Afghan cities still under government control, including a major assault on the eastern city of Jalalabad that flattened whole neighborhoods. As long as Soviet patronage continued, though, the government withstood the onslaught.

With the collapse of the Soviet Union in late 1991, however, Moscow and Washington agreed to cease all aid to their respective proxies. Within months, the Afghan government crumbled. The question of who would fill the vacuum, who would build a new state, has not been fully resolved to this day.

- - -

It was an unseasonably warm evening in April 1992 when one of Heela's neighbors appeared at the front door. "Sister!" she pleaded. "Do you have a headscarf? The mujahedeen are coming!" Heela rarely wore Islamic head coverings anymore, inside or out. But she knew that she would have to find something, for the mujahedeen's reputation preceded them. In the closet, she discovered two large pieces of torn cloth. Her neighbor took one, wrapping it around her head. Heela kept the other and waited.

Although there had been occasional assassinations and terrorist attacks over the years, during the occupation the mujahedeen had never openly set foot in Kabul, lending them such an aura of mystery that they were dubbed *dukhi*, ghosts, by the Russians. Now, with the government collapsing, Kabul residents began to burn their state-issued ID cards to avoid any visible link with the previous authorities.

Musqinyar and Heela stepped outside. The streets were empty and the shops shuttered, but the wind carried in shouts from the distance. They moved toward the commotion, stopping at the neighborhood's main thoroughfare.

The voices grew louder. On terraces and balconies, people stood watching. Heela looked down the road and saw a crowd of men walking her way. They had on *pakols*—woolen flat-topped hats resembling berets, worn in the mountains—and green jackets. Everyone was carrying arms, and a few were pulling along artillery pieces. As they approached, the shouting coalesced into a distinct call, resounding down the street: "God is great!"

They swarmed around a pair of government asphalting vehicles and set them ablaze. As smoke filled the air, Heela heard, again and again, the cry of "God is great!" The rebels surged past them toward a government rations center, torching it as well. Heela and her husband looked at each other. A new order had arrived.

For the next few mornings, whenever she looked outside she saw an ashen daylight, fed by columns of smoke rising on the horizon. The mujahedeen ransacked the library at Kabul University, burning the books in a pyre. They confiscated thousands of bottles of alcohol, piling them up and crushing them with a captured tank. They banned female television announcers from the airwaves.

Outside the capital, mujahedeen rule veered into the tyrannical. A commander in the northwestern province of Faryab decreed it permissible to rape any unmarried girl over the age of twelve. In the western city of Herat, authorities curtailed musical performances, outlawing love songs and "dancing music." It was the mujahedeen—not the Taliban, who did not yet exist as a formal group—who first brought these strictures into politics. Many of these same commanders would be returned to power by the United States to run the country after 2001.

Soon enough, the Supreme Court demanded that the government oust female employees from their jobs and girls from their schools, because "schools are whorehouses and centers of adultery." It decreed:

> Women are not to leave their homes at all, unless absolutely necessary, in which case they are to cover themselves completely; are not to wear attractive clothing and decorative accessories; are not to wear perfume or jewelry that makes any noise; are not to walk gracefully or with pride in the middle of the sidewalk; are not to talk to strangers; are not to speak loudly or laugh in public; and they must always ask their husbands' permission to leave the home.

Noisy jewelry would soon be the least of anyone's problems. A few days after the takeover, Heela ventured to the school where she taught, now closed because of the troubles. Along the way she noticed something terrible-smelling in the drainage ditch, wrapped in dark plastic. A premonition told her not to look, but she couldn't resist and pulled back the plastic—and recoiled. It was a dead body. She glanced around. The street was ghostly still, not a car in sight, the buildings locked and the shops closed. Somewhere in the distance, she could hear the patter of gunfire. She turned and ran home as fast as she could.

The Afghan civil war had begun. At home, Musqinyar explained that the newly victorious mujahedeen factions, cut off from their American and Pakistani patrons, had turned their guns on each other in a scramble for power. The first mujahedeen group to make it into the city had been Jamiat-e-Islami (the Islamic Society), headed by a wizened, kind-faced professor named Burhanuddin Rabbani and counting among its ranks the war's most famous commander, Ahmad Shah Massoud. A system of rotating presidents was established to share authority among the various factions, but Rabbani refused to relinquish power when his term ended. In response, a rival group, Hizb-i-Islami (the Islamic Party), rained rockets down on the city from an encampment in the suburbs. Their leader was the notorious Gulbuddin Hekmatyar, an erstwhile CIA favorite known, above all, for his ruthlessness. A number of other factions also jostled for power, forming alliances and switching sides with the seasons.

The civil war stretched from 1992 to 1996, and no one escaped unscathed. Some, like Jan Muhammad, were eager participants, waging endless battles over tiny scraps of territory, but most had participation thrust upon them. One day, in a dusky cluttered office on the outskirts of Kabul, I asked Mullah Cable about his memories of the time. He glanced at me, then looked down at his hands. "Well," he finally said, "I guess that war is why I ended up like this."

He had grown up in Shah Shahid, a rough neighborhood in the south end of the capital, where his family lived on a narrow dirt lane crisscrossed by electrical wires and clotheslines. It was a life of pranks and street fights, of barefoot poverty and cousins too many to count. He was known then by his given name, Akbar Gul, and he had a bit of a reputation. "People would call me *badmash*," a sort of raffish hooligan, he said with pride.

For as long as he could remember, jobs had been scarce. His father had never held steady employment, and he had always expected to get married, settle down, and grow old in a refugee camp somewhere. In the meantime he earned some notoriety on the streets as a quick-witted hustler, a lanky teenager with a penchant for mischief and an entrepreneurial eye, which he took to Kabul's scrap yards to scavenge spare parts for sale. Eventually he fell into drug running, one of the only sure forms of employment around, and wound up in and out of jail. Still, he harbored a secret desire to get out of the drug business and follow the path of his two older brothers, the pride of the family, who worked as policemen under the Communist government.

With the outbreak of the civil war, government functions ground to a halt and his brothers stopped receiving paychecks. The family spent whole

days indoors, listening to the radio and waiting for word of the resump-
tion of services. In the evenings, Akbar Gul and his cousin Manaf would
climb onto the roof of their house, stretch out under a warm summer
sky, and talk themselves to sleep, dreaming idle dreams of escape. For
weeks, he wondered whether he could make his way to Iran. Friends
who'd gone there had found jobs—and girls, too. The problem, as always,
was money. The Iranians didn't hand out visas to just anyone, so you had
to hire a trafficker to smuggle you across the border. The Hindu Kush
presented another possibility. He'd heard that in the peaks of the Panj-
shir Valley you could hunt for gemstones, that some mine floors were
literally covered with them. You wouldn't even be able to carry back all
that you found in a single trip. But that was mujahedeen territory, which
both he and Manaf wished to avoid.

In time, however, the mujahedeen came to him. Early one morning,
militiamen showed up in his neighborhood, going house to house, bang-
ing on doors, ordering people out for "inspections," and taking whatever
they liked—jewelry, embroidered cushions, sometimes girls. They plun-
dered so meticulously that locals christened them Gelam Jam, the Rug
Collectors, for it was said that when they looted your home nothing would
be left, not even the rugs. After Gelam Jam took over a nearby street corner, Akbar Gul stopped sleeping on the roof.

One afternoon, he was in a crowd of pedestrians on his way to buy
motorcycle parts when a man stepped out of an alley and blocked their
path. He was clutching a Kalashnikov and his eyes shone crimson. The
stench of alcohol was unmistakable. "Where are you going?" he shouted.
It was a Gelam Jam militiaman. Other gunmen stood farther back in the
alley, watching. "We're just walking, brother," an elder said. "We aren't
part of this war." The gunman stood glaring, and then his gaze fell upon
a group of burqa-clad women. "Get on the ground," he yelled. They did
as they were told, no one uttering a sound. Keeping his weapon trained on
the crowd, he walked over to the prone women and seized one of them.
She screamed and struggled and almost broke free. "I'll kill you now if
you don't shut up," the militiaman snapped, dragging her into a giant
shipping container by the roadside.

Akbar Gul kept his face to the asphalt, and for a few moments everything was still. Then he heard a long, shrill scream and looked up to see the woman burst through the container door. Her burqa was torn, exposing a breast. An elder ran to help. A fighter leaned out of the shipping container and shouted, "We told you to stay down, you dog!" and fired two rounds into him. Another fighter chased down the woman and hoisted her over his shoulders. After returning her to the container, he slammed the door shut.

From then on, even life's simplest acts took on a new meaning. Akbar Gul learned to plan walks to the grocery store meticulously, and to go only when absolutely necessary. For families with children, school was out of the question. Women stopped going outside. Yet the looting and killing and rapes continued. At the time, historian and Kabul resident Muhammad Hassan Kakar wrote that "adults wish not to have new babies," and if they have them, "they pray to God to give them ugly ones. Women hate themselves for being attractive."

At home, Akbar Gul's family was finding it increasingly difficult to make ends meet. The city faced acute food shortages. Meals had become nothing more than stone-hard, days-old bread soaked in water and parceled out, the smallest children and the elderly getting priority. Finally, Akbar Gul's oldest brother, Muhammad, decided to brave the streets and head for the police precinct office to see if he might collect the salary he was owed.

He did not return that afternoon. The family waited into the evening, but he still did not come back. Akbar Gul spent the night in front of the house, but he saw no sign of his brother.

The next afternoon, as Akbar Gul was floating in and out of sleep, he heard a knock on the door. It was a neighbor, looking nervous and uncomfortable. He said to come quickly but wouldn't explain why. A sick feeling overcame Akbar Gul. Whatever it was, he wanted to hear it first with his own ears. Finally, he forced out the words: "Did they kill him?"

"Pray for his soul," the neighbor answered.

The rest of the day was a haze of wailing women and visiting relatives. Even amid his tears, Akbar Gul simmered inside. Muhammad had been the trailblazer in the family, the first one to land a job, the first one to marry. He had done everything the right way, while Akbar Gul had taken the easy path. Fate, it seemed, had picked out the wrong man. Gelam Jam were killing the good ones, the honest ones, and it filled him with disgust.

In search of a fresh start, his parents decided to abandon Kabul for Pakistan, and in short order his sisters and cousins, too, fled the country. Only Akbar Gul, his cousin Manaf, and his remaining brother stayed behind, planning to sell the house and the family's possessions before joining the rest. Yet they could not find any takers, for everyone in the neighborhood appeared to be doing the same. Moving to Pakistan did not come cheap—for a start, you'd need to bribe dozens of commanders who had set up checkpoints along the way. Akbar Gul's brother had an old friend in the neighborhood who owed him money, and he felt that he had no choice but to venture out and track him down. This time, Manaf tagged along for protection.

Later that evening, Akbar Gul learned that his brother and cousin had been stopped on a street corner and, along with other military-age males, ordered to the wall. In full sight of the passersby, they were executed.

For weeks, Akbar Gul could hardly eat. He spent his days in bed, blaming himself for letting the two of them go. The bitterness he felt was deep and growing. In every militiaman who passed his window he saw the men who had ruined his family. It felt as if God Himself were taunting him, sparing the wicked and condemning the just, rewarding criminals like Gelam Jam and idlers like himself. He had visions of living in a refugee camp in Pakistan while Gelam Jam fighters occupied his home, trekking through in their shoes, spitting and hacking where they pleased, bringing in people from the streets to do what they pleased.

It was time for a change. He would honor his brothers, live by their example, live an honest life. He'd stay behind, guard the family home, and help ensure that no one else suffered what his parents had. But how? All around him, families were crumbling. There seemed to be no rhyme or reason to it—it didn't matter what you thought, whether you supported the mujahedeen or the Communists. The only households surviving unscathed, he knew, were the neighborhood's few Uzbek families, members of the same ethnic group as Gelam Jam.

He wasn't interested in this war, but the war seemed interested in him. There were no more innocents, no more neutrals, only sides already chosen for him. The choice was clear: pick a side, or end up like his brothers. It would have been unthinkable before the war, but now he felt he could trust only his fellow Pashtuns. They had borne the brunt of Gelam Jam in his neighborhood, it seemed. At first, they had hidden their ethnicity, speaking only Farsi in public, but soon they were getting plucked from their vehicles to have their pronunciation checked—and if their speech sounded Pashtun, they were often killed on the spot. This was a war against people who spoke like him, who looked like him, and if that's what the enemy had decided, then he'd play by their rules.

So one morning he went to a camp of Hizb-i-Islami, a Pashtun-heavy militia, and sought out an acquaintance. "I want to do jihad," he announced.

The man broke into a broad smile. "Welcome," he said.

Thousands of young men, many of them now orphans and widowers, flocked to the various factions feuding for power in the civil war. There were no heroes; each group proved as responsible for the bloodshed as the next. Broadly, the factions were organized along ethnic lines—not so much due to ethnic nationalism but because in the face of perpetual instability, with a weak or absent state, you allied with those you knew and trusted. In fact, it was often unclear what ideological differences, if any, divided the men fighting each other on Kabul's streets. Still, the struggle for power and survival was imbued with meaning: more than simply a battle of wills, for many the war was "jihad."

The West responded to the civil war by simply ignoring it, and after the 2001 invasion the years from 1992 to 1996 were all but stricken from the standard narrative. It was dangerous history, the truths buried within it too uncomfortable and messy. If the mujahedeen had been no better than the Taliban or al-Qaeda, any attempt to bring the principal actors of that period to account could only lead to the highest echelons of Hamid Karzai's government, and, by extension, to American policy over the previous thirty years.

Yet it isn't difficult to uncover this history, for every Kabuli has a story to tell. Deadly roadblocks, disappeared neighbors, and decaying bodies were woven into the fabric of daily life, like going shopping or saying your prayers. Every day brought fresh destruction; any date picked out of the calendar is the anniversary of some grisly toll.

On May 5, 1992, for example, Sher Muhammad climbed to the roof of his house in southern Kabul to wash his face under the spring sun. He had just returned to Afghanistan after ten years as a refugee, hoping to relaunch his singing career. As he stood there, a Hekmatyar rocket crashed into the nearby Brezhnev Bazaar, a sprawling market of corrugated tin roofs that had once sold stolen Soviet supplies. Seven people were killed, including an orphaned boy. Then another rocket overshot its target and slammed into Muhammad's house, killing him and three others.

Or take February 2, 1993, when Muhammad Haroun was arrested by an ethnic Hazara militia as he walked past a school. Fifteen days later, after surrendering a fortune in bribes, his mother was led to his body. It lay in a dry well, burnt from head to toe, the eyes gouged out.

That same year, Hazara militiamen stormed the house of Rafiullah, a Pashtun vegetable peddler. His hands and feet were bound and he was thrown into a corner of the room. As he watched, the militiamen forced themselves upon his screaming daughter. After finishing, they seized his wife and did the same. Unable to face their community after the attack, the family fled, leaving most of their possessions behind. Later, it was said, his daughter committed suicide by throwing herself down a well.

November 25, 1995: Gelam Jam fighters broke into apartment number 38 of the Microrayon housing complex. They killed a pregnant woman and her three children, then stripped the apartment clean. A month later another group came to the housing complex, this time to apartment number 4, killing a woman and kidnapping her daughter. She was never seen again.

May 24, 1996: A rocket struck the house of Abdul Karim, injuring him and killing his three-year-old son. When his wife went to visit him at the hospital, she was abducted and gang-raped.

And so it went.

By 1993, Ahmad Shah Massoud had allied his forces with those of Abdul Rasul Sayyaf, an Islamist professor and mujahedeen leader. A staunch fundamentalist, Sayyaf would one day invite Osama bin Laden to take refuge in Afghanistan. (Nevertheless, he would be counted as a US ally during the 2001 invasion, eventually landing in parliament.) On February 7, 1993, Massoud and Sayyaf's forces attacked Afshar, a Hazara enclave in western Kabul. They began by lobbing mortars blindly into the densely populated neighborhood, killing scores. Then soldiers went door to door, seizing able-bodied men, lining them up against the walls, and executing them in full view of their wives and children. As news of the massacre spread, residents began to flee. Massoud's forces, on a mountain overlooking the neighborhood, fired down at the crowds, killing many more. Meanwhile, the house-by-house manhunts continued. Militiamen stormed the home of a woman named Mina and carried her husband away. Later that afternoon, a second group of fighters forced their way into the home; finding no adult males left to kill, they seized her eleven-year-old son. "They held him and asked where his father was," Mina said later. "They aimed their guns at him and I threw myself over him. I was shot in the hand and leg, but he was shot five times. He died." As she lay bleeding next to her son's corpse, three soldiers held her down while a fourth raped her. Then they took the rest of the women in the house, including two teenagers, to the basement for their turn.

Like victors in a medieval battle, the mujahedeen attacking Afshar hauled captives and booty away. Some Hazaras, like resident Abdul Qader, were forced into slavery. First, he was pressed into service carrying loot from his neighborhood; then was taken to a militia base outside the city, where he was jammed into a giant shipping container with other prisoners. Eventually he was moved to another base, forced to work for his captors by day and kept manacled at night. He would remain enslaved for three years.

After two days of bloodshed, most of the population of Afshar was dead or missing. Nearly five thousand homes had been destroyed. An unknown number of people—probably at least one thousand—had been killed. Photographs of the aftermath show a stricken neighborhood: Swiss cheese holes in concrete walls, hollowed-out buildings, and bones—many bones. Sometimes, it seemed that killing alone was not enough. An old man named Fazil Ahmed was decapitated and his limbs sawed off; his body was found with his penis stuffed into his mouth. It was as if the violence sprang from some far deeper, more complex drive than simply planting flags in a civil war. Could it have been a collective post-traumatic stress disorder response to years of Russian brutality? It's hard to say, especially since there has been no national reckoning with the civil war, no truth and reconciliation process.

What is certain, however, is that the Afshar violence had clear enough political motives: to eliminate a Hazara militia stronghold. Human rights investigators subsequently found that senior mujahedeen commanders were aware of the massacre and, in many cases, helped carry it out. At the top of the chain of responsibility sat the operation's architects, Massoud and Sayyaf. (Despite this, Massoud is still considered a hero in some circles.) A number of their sub-commanders bear direct culpability, yet every one of them has emerged politically unscathed. Marshal Muhammad Fahim, who oversaw the operation and commanded an important outpost during the siege, became a key American ally during the 2001 invasion, earning himself millions in CIA dollars. Eventually, he became vice president of Afghanistan. Baba Jan, who also helped plan and execute the siege, became a key Northern Alliance commander. After 2001, he grew extravagantly wealthy as a logistics contractor for the US military. Mullah Izzat, who commanded a group that led house searches, also struck gold after the invasion—counting, among his considerable holdings, Kabul's only golf course. Zulmay Tofan, complicit in the house searches and forced labor, reaped his post-2001 windfall by supplying fuel to US troops.

The twin dislocations of the Soviet invasion and CIA patronage of the mujahedeen irrevocably reconfigured Afghan society, leading directly to the horrors of the civil war, then to the Taliban, and ultimately to the shape of Afghan politics after 2001. Still, when Zbigniew Brzezinski, who as national security adviser to President Carter helped to initiate Washington's anti-Soviet mujahedeen policies, was asked in the late 1990s whether he had any regrets, he replied: "What is more important in the history of the world? The Taliban or the collapse of the Soviet empire? Some stirred-up Muslims or the liberation of Central Europe and the end of the Cold War?"

--- ---

It was in those years that the future Mullah Cable began to regard his brother's gold watch as a talisman, one of his few remaining links to a world now dissolved. In his new reality as a member of the Hizb-i-Islami militia, Akbar Gul's days of streetwise insouciance, his idle afternoons with brothers and cousins, were now behind him. His life now structured by a militia's responsibilities, he grew up quickly. Duties included patrolling, checking weapons stocks, and staffing roadblocks. He learned how to use firearms and operate communication systems, how to target mortar fire and conduct reconnaissance—skills passed on from those who once trained in American-funded Pakistani camps.

One day, his unit was patrolling near an abandoned palace on the city's edge when they stumbled upon a weapons depot. "As we came nearer," he told me, "we could hear people's voices, just barely. I held my ear to the door and then I knew that there were people locked up in there. They were shouting, so we shot the door open.

"There were a lot of women and some men in there. Some of them had already died, and the smell made me sick. A few of the women were completely naked. They were crying and screaming and told us they had been in there for days. They were all Pashtuns—the Hazara groups had done this to them. When we saw this, we couldn't control ourselves, and we decided to do the same thing to their people. We went down to Dasht-e-Barchi"—a Hazara neighborhood—"and made retribution."

I asked if he was personally involved in the retribution. He stared into his lap for a long moment. Then he said, "I managed to save three Hazara girls from having a very big problem during the incident. We should not get revenge on children."

Initially, families with money had ways of avoiding the war. Musqinyar, Heela, and their infant son, Omaid, moved to Microrayon, an upscale neighborhood with Soviet-built apartment complexes where the fighting was not intense. Schools were still closed, so she spent days with Omaid in the park, listening to the rat-a-tat of faraway gunfire. Sometimes she ran into her neighbor Orzala, who had a small daughter of her own, and the two would sit and watch the children play.

They were resting in the shade one afternoon when Heela heard a pop and saw Orzala's daughter drop to the ground. Neighbors tried to rush her to the hospital, but Massoud's fighters were blocking the roads and refused to let them pass. They brought her back home, where she slipped into a coma and died.

It was difficult for Heela to process. A stray bullet right there in her neighborhood, in that tucked-away little park. She could no longer bring herself to leave the house. It was just as well, for the sound of gunfire echoed louder by the day. Rashid Dostum and his Gelam Jam militia had abruptly switched sides and joined Hizb-i-Islami, who were battling Massoud's forces. Some evenings, the fighting swelled to such intensity on the street below that she was forced to sit in the darkness—a neighbor had once left her lights on and received a bullet through the window. "I went to sleep expecting to die," she recalled, "and woke up thankful for another day. We focused very hard on our prayers, because that's all we had."

Through it all, Musqinyar went about his days calm and resolute. He had stopped going to work at the Ministry of Health after it was taken over by mujahedeen, but still made informal house calls delivering medical supplies to neighbors in need. He was convinced that the war's end was near, that the various factions would snap to their senses. It was his habit to see the good in all people, a stance that Heela regarded with a mixture of admiration and despair. While the days of dinner parties and casual visits were long gone, friends still showed up from time to time. A positive outlook was a precious find, worth braving a trip across neighborhoods.

The winter came and went, the fighting unconquered by the snow, and spring arrived late. Occasionally Musqinyar would risk visiting friends in other parts of town, returning with news of the neighborhoods and streets of their youth reduced to rubble. Heela did her best to wish it all away. In the evenings she would curl up with Omaid and ask Musqinyar to read to them. It didn't matter what it was; she simply loved the rise and fall of his soft voice. It soothed her like nothing else.

Early in 1994 she became pregnant with her second child. In those days, this was no simple matter. She heard that militiamen had once stopped a vehicle carrying a woman in labor to the hospital. The fighters, almost all teenagers, had never seen a live birth. They stripped the woman naked and forced her to deliver right there at the roadside as they watched.

So Heela planned to give birth at home, but as she neared term that summer the fighting pressed so close that Musqinyar couldn't even leave for extra medical supplies. Soon enough, a battle erupted over control of their apartment block. It was late evening, and artillery shell explosions pounded the air. They crouched in the corner. Then the room shook violently, blanketing them in dust. A rocket had hit somewhere close by, maybe even next door. Heela clung to Musqinyar and Omaid. A second explosion rattled the room, loosening slabs of concrete in the ceiling. One fell, hitting Heela squarely in the face. She lost consciousness.

When Heela awoke, the first thing she saw was Musqinyar's bright, relieved smile. They were somewhere she didn't recognize. She immediately asked about her baby, but he wouldn't answer. She started crying, pleading with him, and he looked at her silently. Then he reached over and gently caressed her head.

In the following days, Heela noticed a change in Musqinyar's demeanor. He stopped talking about the old neighborhoods or the possibility of a coming peace. In fact, since the miscarriage he hardly talked at all. Instead, she watched him spend hours staring out the window into the ruined street below, a scarred no-man's-land of bullet holes and collapsed buildings.

"God rarely gives second chances," he announced one day. He had been saying this sort of thing for days now, seemingly having abandoned his secularism, but Heela now noticed a flicker of purpose in his eyes. If they squandered this opportunity, he said, they'd have no one to blame but themselves. There wasn't a safe neighborhood left in the city, and the truth was becoming painfully clear: it was time to flee. But where? Pakistan was out of the question; they knew what life could be like in the squalid refugee camps and had no desire to run from violence to abject poverty. Iran was a possibility, but Musqinyar had heard that only refugees who practiced the Shia version of Islam were welcome. There was just one obvious destination: his ancestral home, the southern backwater province of Uruzgan. He'd heard that things were calmer there. He knew that the deep countryside was no place for a city-bred woman like Heela, but what was the alternative?

That evening brought another round of fighting. Once again the sky rumbled and flashed while the family huddled together in a corner. Early the next morning, during the lull in the shooting that came with the first call to prayer, they decided to make their escape. Heela took whatever she found within arm's reach: a teapot, two mugs, a few stacks of stale bread. "We left in such a hurry that we left our apartment wide open," she recalled, "and everything was there for the mujahedeen to take, money, jewelry—everything. I had to leave my wedding ring and wedding shoes behind. I'll never forgive myself."

At the taxi stand dozens of families were crowding around a pair of TownAce vans. The drivers, struggling to fend them off, were demanding huge sums. The road south out of Kabul, crisscrossed with roadblocks, passed through no fewer than a dozen warlord fiefs, a ride that drivers risked at their peril. Musqinyar squeezed his way through and waved cash—about $100, everything he had managed to take with him—and they were allowed aboard.

Not long after they hit the road, the van rolled to a stop in a small town just beyond the outskirts of Kabul. Posters of Hekmatyar, the leader of Hizb-i-Islami, were pasted everywhere. Fighters had billeted in the shops, and artillery pieces sat here and there.

A teenage fighter strolled up to Heela's van. Peering through the window, he inquired after their destination. By now this was a well-practiced ritual; everyone surrendered whatever money and jewelry was on hand. Then the fighter caught sight of Heela and slowly smiled. A woman on the road was a prize, a rare jewel. He rapped on the window, gazing at her intently.

Then another van pulled up behind them—carrying more women. The gunman, having found a new object of interest, waved Heela's vehicle on.

Hours later, they turned off the main highway and rattled down a rock-studded road. Staring out the window, Heela saw that they were in desert country now, with massive rufous boulders and miles upon miles of blood-red sand. This was a land of cattle raiders and feuding clans, a place untouched by the state or any other formal authority for almost two decades. In her twenty-two years, Heela had never ventured far from Kabul, certainly not this deep into the countryside—not into the vastness, the emptiness, that was now swallowing her. She found herself drifting back to Kabul, to the crowds at the Friday bazaar, to her school and her pupils—to opportunities lost, a motif for a whole generation. The war years were not only about survival; they also meant the wedding you never attended, the trip you never took, the movie you never saw.

When Uruzgan's snowcapped peaks came into view, the van stopped at a small market. Musqinyar stepped out to speak with the locals and returned with tea and a small plastic bag. Heela asked about the situation in Uruzgan and learned that people were complaining of a cruel and vindictive warlord. His name was Jan Muhammad.

Musqinyar handed Heela the bag and she opened it and stared. She could not believe it had come to this. Folded inside was something she'd never handled in her life: a soft, sky-blue burqa. Immediately she protested, but Musqinyar was insistent. In mujahedeen-controlled Uruzgan, it was simply unthinkable for a woman to travel open-faced. Grieving, weary, and fearful, Heela decided not to resist. "At that point," she recalled, "I was so tired of war and insecurity, I would have even worn a burqa to sleep if it helped."

She held up the embroidered garment and inspected it. The head-to-toe wrapping had no openings except a thick mesh-like covering for the eyes. As she put it on, the rocky dirt road, the brilliant mountain peaks, the rumbling motor were all snuffed out. Heela's world went black.

4

The Sewing Center of Khas Uruzgan

We walked uphill, my Afghan guide and I, stepping between the naked brambles, using the larger rocks as leverage. We continued until the larches thinned away, until the air cut cold and sharp. After a while there were no more camel thorns, no more boulders, just pure reddish soil straight to the summit.

At the top, lungs burning, we looked out. For miles and miles, nothing but the crumpled earth. Deep ferrous rocks and crimson-brown sand. It was as if we were the last two humans on the planet, as if we'd lost ourselves in some endless red emptiness. The only interruption was far off in the distance, a pair of mountains capped in pure white snow. The melted runoff dribbled down the sides, coalescing into five or six rivulets that merged into a tiny stream near the basin. And there, around the stream, nestled between the two mountains, was a tiny, solitary patch of green. People lived there.

Since the beginning, Afghanistan has been a country of valleys. Only 12 percent of Afghan soil is arable, just half of which is actually cultivated due to water scarcity, making the nation one of the driest, roughest-hewn patches of territory in the world. What water can be had is usually sourced from the mountains, the single immutable feature of country life. Life on the slopes themselves can be a struggle, so Afghans tend to live around the mountains or between them, huddled together in narrow dales. It can take days to travel from one valley to the next. Unsurprisingly, such conditions were not conducive to the development of a centralized state, either endogenously or through outside intervention.

(On the other hand, the conventional image of the wild, hirsute tribesmen of the Afghan frontier perpetually fighting back modernity and foreign invaders—which, in the eyes of said invaders, were invariably the same thing—doesn't tell the whole story either. Before the modern era, Afghanistan was not, in fact, a "graveyard of empires." Some foreign campaigners proved victorious, such as the Arab and Persian armies that, over centuries, brought Islam. And others regarded the country as nothing more than a convenient buffer, looking beyond it for riches. The British, for instance, may have fought, and lost, battles on Afghan soil, but the real prize was India.)

For a long time, the people of the Afghan valleys herded sheep and goats. Wealth in pastoral societies is a peculiar thing, because, being on the hoof, it can wander off or be pilfered or slaughtered. With too little to go around and no state to enforce property relations, fighting could be frequent and brutal. You adapted by leaning on those you trusted most: first your immediate family, then your cousins, your cousins' cousins, and so on. Clannishness, in other words, was not a symptom of Afghans' preternaturally backward ways, but rather a sensible response to harsh and precarious conditions. Over time, the mountain dwellers developed complicated kinship networks of trust and solidarity, organized into groups called "tribes" that they believed had descended from a common ancestor. Hundreds of Pashtun tribes, large and small, are scattered across the country.

In the lawless mountains, you needed strategies—conscious or otherwise—to survive. On the one hand, you had to stand ready to defend yourself against slights and intrusions, as there was no outside authority, no central government, to call upon. On the other, it was no less prudent to attempt to elicit the best in others, to promote generosity and hospitality. In fact, the two approaches tended to work in tandem, typifying what some sociologists call a culture of honor. Of course, Afghan tribal society, with its feuding clans and warm hospitality, is the prototypical honor culture, but to varying degrees you can find such societies wherever life is rugged, resources scarce, and the state absent, from the deserts of Arabia to the highlands of Scotland—and even closer to home, in the nineteenth-century Appalachian foothills of the Hatfields and the McCoys.

For the ancient Pashtun mountain families, anything that marauding rivals could plunder was worth protecting and controlling—and this included women. Females were a family commodity; in some cases, mountain clans even tattooed their animals and their women with the same markings. As pastoralists settled into sedentary agricultural life, the intimate clustering of village communities curtailed women's freedoms even further. A woman became the embodiment of her family's "honor," always signaling, through her behavior, the virtues of her parents and siblings. To safeguard this honor, families cloistered their women in the home, separating them completely from unrelated menfolk. Men inhabited the public sphere, women the private. This practice of seclusion, called *purdah*, became the dominant form of sexual organization in much of rural southern Afghanistan, varying in degree from village to village but almost always present in some form. If a woman needed to venture into the public sphere, purdah was preserved symbolically through the burqa. (Again, there's nothing quintessentially Afghan or Islamic about purdah; it predates Islam, and can also be found in non-Muslim contexts, such as in certain Indian Hindu villages.)

To mention all of this is not to say that purdah is the "natural" state of things. Indeed, there is no immutable natural state—Afghan societies, like all societies, are forever transforming themselves. By the twentieth century, purdah's emotional and symbolic power had driven urban elites into a culture war with traditional rural forces. Over decades, reformers campaigned to dismantle the system, their movement culminating in the 1959 decision that allowed women to unveil (and may have helped spark violent riots in Kandahar that left sixty people dead). By the 1970s, life in cities like Kabul, where women went to school, took jobs, and married relatively late, felt ages removed from the Pashtun countryside.

Following the Soviet invasion, the Communists, to their credit, passed decrees making girls' education compulsory and abolishing certain oppressive tribal customs—such as the bride-price, a payment to the bride's family in return for her hand in marriage. However, by massacring thousands of tribal elders, they paved the way for the "commanders" to step in as the new elite. Aided by American and Saudi patronage, extremism flourished. What had once been a social practice confined to areas deep in the hinterlands now became a political practice, which, according to ideologues, applied to the entire country. The modest gains of urban women were erased.

"The first time a woman enters her husband's house," Heela told me about life in the countryside, "she wears white"—her wedding dress—"and the first time she leaves, she wears white"—the color of the Muslim funeral shroud. The rules of this arrangement were intricate and precise, and, it seemed to Heela, unchanged from time immemorial. In Uruzgan, a woman did not step outside her compound. In an emergency, she required the company of a male blood relative to leave, and then only with her father's or husband's permission. Even the sound of her voice carried a hint of subversion, so she was kept out of hearing range of unrelated males. When the man of the house was not present, boys were dispatched to greet visitors. Unrelated males also did not inquire directly about a female member of the house. Asking "How is your wife?" qualified as somewhere between uncomfortably impolite and downright boorish. The markers of a woman's life—births, anniversaries, funerals, prayers, feasts—existed entirely within the four walls of her home. Gossip, hopscotching from living room to living room, was carried by husbands or sons.

In 1994, the civil war was in its second year. Every attempt to cobble together some sort of détente between the rival factions had failed spectacularly. The Russians and the Americans, whose interventions had brought this state of affairs about, had lost all interest in the country. Osama bin Laden was living in Sudan, and al-Qaeda as we know it today did not yet exist. Nor did the Taliban. Instead, a country of thirty million that had at once been the center of the Cold War was now quietly and anonymously devouring itself.

Late that summer, Heela settled into Musqinyar's ancestral home in a corner of Uruzgan Province called Khas Uruzgan (khas meaning "special," the district having been the provincial capital ages ago). Although fighting was less intense than in Kabul, here, too, rival warlords—chief among them Jan Muhammad—were locked in a bloody power struggle, leaving the road dotted with rogue checkpoints and militia posts.

But Heela's concerns lay closer at hand. In the countryside a woman was expected to work long and hard at keeping up her home, and in a way this was a blessing. Heela threw herself into the task of remaking their inherited house, which had sat empty for more than a decade. The squat, one-story structure was designed to honor the local virtues of family, privacy, and hospitality. A large compound wall of tawny mud bricks surrounded the property, with holes punched through to examine visitors. Upon entering you found yourself in a small courtyard, where weeds and crabgrass had edged onto the walkway. To the left sat a guest room, the quintessential mark of a southern home, set off by itself so that visitors might not inadvertently glimpse a female. A pair of apple trees stood near the opposite wall. It took about twenty paces to get from the main gate to the front door.

The house itself measured about fifty feet to a side and consisted of a number of narrow rooms arranged in railroad fashion. The living-room walls remained bare, because Heela hadn't been able to bring photos from Kabul. Beneath the house was a small cellar. In the backyard, a vegetable patch grew near the door and privet lined the mud walls. In the far corner stood a tiny chicken coop.

Had Heela been able to leave the compound, she would have found a bucolic hamlet of maybe fifty homes, each very much like hers. There was no main road; instead, a web of narrow dirt tracks ran between the farmers' fields, connecting one house to the next. The village was bounded on one side by a muddy stream, which ran just a few hundred feet from her house, and on the other by rock formations that rose rapidly skyward into a set of looming massifs. An old wooden footbridge crossed the stream to a grassy embankment, from which a gravel road led to the bazaar.

Heela's village was one among dozens that peppered the basin of the mountain range, which stretched as far as she could see. In total, some fifty thousand souls called Khas Uruzgan District their home, most of them farmers and herders. If the women rarely left their homes, the men did not venture much farther—some had never set foot outside the district in their lives.

Out here you lived by nature's rhythms, rising and returning with the sun, growing the food your family ate and sewing the clothes they wore. Without electricity there were no televisions or telephones, although by the late 1990s hand-cranked radios were making an appearance. To hear the latest news you headed down to the bazaar, a ramshackle row of windowless one-room shops fashioned out of old shipping containers, each with corrugated iron shutters and straw flooring. Out in front hung signs advertising Iranian colas, Pakistani biscuits, spare tires, and jerry cans of gasoline, which you could purchase once a week when the fuel truck came through.

The shops flanked an uneven dirt road, on one end of which stood the government office, where the local governor normally lived, and on the other an old schoolhouse. In 1994, both were vacant. When a car passed through, men and boys would step out of their shops and look. The nearest town, Uruzgan's capital, Tirin Kot, lay seven hours away, on a highway that ran through multiple militia checkpoints. Even in more peaceful times, however, news came slowly. When the Americans appeared in 2001, some villagers assumed that the white-skinned interlopers were the Soviets.

After selling some of his inherited land, Musqinyar opened a small pharmacy in the heart of the bazaar. At first, with roadblocks and bandits, it had taken weeks for goods to reach the village; by autumn, they were not arriving at all. Prices soared, and the family relied on Musqinyar's brother Shaysta, who had resorted to subsistence farming. Almost daily, bodies were being dumped in the mountains, victims of war and hunger. There were days when Musqinyar stood with Heela in the backyard looking at those snowcapped peaks as if they were some premonition of the winter and the hardship to come. As if death were now the common order of the land, the only principle binding country and city, men and women, holy warriors and Communists alike. And it may well have become so, if not for a new force that arose suddenly in the south to change everything.

Drive away from Uruzgan, taking the sole rutted pebble road running southeast. You'll cross miles of low open brush in Ghazni Province, then wheat fields and apricot thickets, and farther on dry scrubland again, leading up to the barren gravel hills of the province of Paktika. In three decades of war much has changed, but in this corner of the country you can still find a smattering of hill tribes clinging, against the odds, to their old ways of life. They make a good starting point for those looking to excavate Afghanistan's distant past. Surprisingly, however, they also carry a more contemporary relevance: a glimpse into the obscure origins of the Taliban. Most writing on the Taliban assumes that they originated in extremist Pakistani madrassas in the 1980s. In fact, the group's origins lie much deeper in the Afghan past.

Visiting Paktika in 2010, I came upon a small hilltop village where locals had gathered around a silent, downcast man. Nearby, a young herder paced back and forth, watching him intently, and, off to a side, tribal graybeards stood conferring. One of them approached, pushing his way through the scrum, and announced a verdict: for killing Rahim Gul's cow, Moheb Jan was to pay him two sheep and twenty days' worth of labor.

Afterward, I sat down with the elder, who explained that each transgression in his community carried a fixed fine. Break someone's nose in a fight, and you gave him a chicken. Break a bone, and you surrendered a sheep or goat. Murder, depending on the circumstances, could cost you a piece of land, your house, or even one of your women, who would go to the victim's family in marriage.

This was how the hillspeople had learned to live with each other in a world without a state or police or judicial system. Each tribe had its own set of intricate rules, decided by elders elected by the clan's entire male population. The elders derived their status from experience and the respect traditionally accorded to the aged. No man, however, outranked another in rights, and it was rare for one family to possess significantly more than any other. For men, at least, a deep egalitarian ethos ran through the tribal system.

For a long time, most of the Pashtun belt had functioned this way. Eventually, however, when some tribes moved down from the mountains into agricultural settlements, certain enterprising individuals developed ties with distant state authorities, and soon hierarchies sprang up. In eighteenth-century Kandahar, for example, the Safavid Empire of Persia had established suzerainty, incorporating tribal figures of their liking into their military or using them as intermediaries in dealing with the native population. The egalitarian system of the mountains slowly gave way to one dominated by tribal strongmen, and decisions were increasingly made not through traditional tribal law but on the whims and biases of a small clique of notables. It was not long before Kandahari tribes were the most thoroughly hierarchical in the country.

As a consequence, a different form of justice grew in popularity as an alternative to the tribal system: religious law, or sharia. Like tribal law, religious law expressed itself in a detailed set of punishments and restitutions for particular crimes. Its main practitioners were mullahs, who led Friday sermons and could adjudicate disputes. To become a mullah, you studied for up to twelve years in a madrassa, where you learned the intricacies of Islamic law, along with history, philosophy, and logic. In Pashto, such students were called taliban. Because a mullah was guaranteed employment for life, this was a course of study particularly well suited to those from the humblest backgrounds. It was in greater Kandahar, where tribal structures were the weakest, that the taliban were most fully integrated into social life.

In times of strife, taliban have usually mobilized in defense of tradition. British documents from as early as 1901 decry taliban opposition to colonialism in present-day Pakistan. However, as with so much else, it was the Soviet invasion and the US response that sent the transformative shock. In the 1980s, as guns and money coursed through the ranks of the Kandahar mujahedeen, squabbling over resources grew so frequent that many increasingly turned to religious law to settle their disputes. Small, informal bands of taliban, who were also battling against the Russians, established religious courts that heard cases from feuding fighters from across the south. Seemingly impervious to the lure of foreign riches, the taliban courts were in many eyes the last refuge of tradition in a world in upheaval.

After the Soviet withdrawal, intra-mujahedeen bickering exploded into outright warfare, but the talibs would have no part of it and put their weapons down, retiring to a life of preaching and study. They watched as Kandahar plunged into a civil war as brutal and rapacious as Kabul's, a near-total breakdown of society with rogue gunmen and militias running wild.

In the land of the blind, the one-eyed man is king—and in Kandahar, this one-eyed man turned out to be a small-time taliban preacher named

Mullah Muhammad Omar. A minor figure known only for his bravery (he lost his eye in battle against the Soviets), he was part of a burgeoning movement of talibs looking to end the terror. With an unfailing air of simplicity and modesty, Omar was seen as less politically ambitious than his colleagues, and was soon anointed by the movement as its leader. "The religion of God is being stepped on, the people are openly displaying evil," he said in a speech at the time, "and the evil ones have taken control of the whole area; they steal people's money, they attack their honor on the main street, they kill people and put them against the rocks on the side of the road, and the cars pass by and see the dead body on the side of the road, and no one dares to bury him in the earth."

Thousands of talibs rallied to the cause, and an informal, centuries-old phenomenon of the Pashtun countryside morphed into a formal political and military movement, the Taliban. As a group of judges and legal-minded students, the Taliban applied themselves to the problem of anarchy with an unforgiving platform of law and order. The mujahedeen had lost their way, abandoned their religious principles, and dragged society into a lawless pit. So unlike most revolutionary movements, Islamic or otherwise, the Taliban did not seek to overthrow an existing state and substitute it with one to their liking. Rather, they sought to build a new state where none existed. This called for eliminating the arbitrary rule of the gun and replacing it with the rule of law—and for countryside judges who had arisen as an alternative to a broken tribal system, this could only mean religious law.

Jurisprudence is thus part of the Taliban's DNA, but its single-minded pursuit was carried out to the exclusion of all other aspects of basic governance. It was an approach that flirted dangerously with the wrong kind of innovation: in the countryside, the choice was traditionally yours whether to seek justice in religious or in tribal courts, yet now the Taliban mandated religious law as the compulsory law of the land. It is true that, given the nature of the civil war, any law was better than none at all—but as soon as things settled down, fresh problems arose. The Taliban's jurisprudence was syncretic, mixing elements from disparate schools of Islam along with heavy doses of traditional countryside Pashtun practice that had little to do with religion. As a result, once the Taliban marched beyond the rural Pashtun belt and into cities like Kabul or the ethnic minority regions of northern Afghanistan, they encountered a resentment that rapidly bred opposition.

So the Taliban's history is fraught with complication. But the important point is that they, like so many other factions in Afghanistan, were never an alien force. Rather, they were as Afghan as kebabs or the Hindu Kush—a fact that US soldiers would learn the hard way.

When winter came to Khas Uruzgan, the meadows were left yellow and ruined, the mountain passes and roads buried under snow. Life retreated indoors, and no news from the outside would come until springtime. It had always been that way, until one winter afternoon in early 1995, when a neighbor came by to inform Musqinyar that the war was over. When Musqinyar reached the bazaar, he saw Toyota jeeps with rocket launchers piled in the back and some mullahs milling nearby. The big landowning families and the major warlords were surrendering their weapons to the new authorities. If the men of the bazaar rejected the rule of the Taliban mullahs, they did not show it. Instead, they approached, one after another, to kiss their hands and thank God for peace.

As the weeks passed, it transpired that life went on much as before, except that now you could drive the breadth of the district without worry, which meant that the shops were stocked once again and the prices settled back down to reason. Heela watched the events with little interest. There was no whip-wielding religious police because the men of Khas Uruzgan had beards and prayed regularly anyway. There was no shuttering of girls' schools or orders for women to stay indoors because there had been no such schools to begin with and women were confined to the home as it was. With no TVs or cameras, the ban on moving images meant nothing. Heela might have disliked the injunction against music, but the civil war had already rendered outdoor music parties obsolete, and no one would stop her from listening to her cassettes in the privacy of her own home.

In time, as Musqinyar returned in the evenings to relate the news of the day, she grew to appreciate her new rulers. She was pleased to learn that authorities were clamping down on the tribal practice of using females to settle feuds, for which they found no sanction in their version of religious law. They were even prepared to look the other way when the stubborn details of state making clashed with deeply held beliefs. When the wife of Mullah Abbas, the new Taliban minister of health, fell ill, he ran up against the prohibition of contact between women and male doctors and nurses, which had created a dire shortage of female medical practitioners. In response, he pushed for the creation of a nurse training program in Kabul. One afternoon in 1998, Abbas, a Khas Uruzgan native, called Musqinyar to explain that Heela, as one of the few educated women in the district, had been selected to participate.

Heela and two others, with chaperones, were taken in a van across a gutted country, along highways that lay ruined but bandit-free. They arrived in the city of her birth on a quiet spring day. From the car, she stared at what had become of her childhood streets: crippled beggars wheeling themselves about, roads torn seemingly beyond repair, almost no traffic anywhere, whole neighborhoods lying in apocalyptic ruins. She turned away, wondering how Muslims could have done this to themselves.

For six months, she trained under the watchful eye of her Taliban supervisors and was not allowed outdoors even once. But the work was engaging, and as she roomed with women from other provinces, it almost felt like her university days. She learned midwifery and basic nursing, and it filled her with hope that she might be able to make Khas Uruzgan her own, that she might carve out a future for herself there.

Back home, news of a woman with medical skills spread quickly through the village. Husbands started to bring in their pregnant wives or ailing mothers. For many women, it was their first trip outside in years. Some even feigned illness for the opportunity.

From her patients, Heela learned that extended confinement had varied psychological effects. For some, the compound walls so completely delineated the limits of their universe that they had developed something akin to agoraphobia. For others, especially those who'd had a taste of freedom in childhood, the internment of married life plunged them into depression. (One favored method of suicide was self-immolation; another was throwing oneself down a well.) A third group, certainly the largest, adapted to their confinement, if only because it was the sole world they had ever known.

Although she was a transplant, Heela herself had been slipping into this last category as the demands of the household and her growing family consumed her. After Omaid had come Jamshed, now rapidly turning into a sprightly toddler, and then Nawid and Walid, baby boys born just a year apart. Weeks and months bled into years, and the 1990s drew to a close. "We all thought," she said, "that life would just go on that way, forever."

The first snows had already set upon the lower slopes of the ranges behind Heela's house in the autumn of 2001 when Musqinyar heard a terse radio proclamation: the Taliban government was finished. At the bazaar, he saw some shopkeepers standing nervously about, and nothing more. The governor's house stood vacant, and village elders had gathered in a nearby home, preparing to elect a new government. Within weeks, the air began to throb day and night with the sound of helicopters. In December, a twelve-foot-high barbed-wire fence appeared in a desert clearing near the bazaar, curling around a set of massive camouflage tents. Sandbags were piled high out front, and a group of Afghans, whom villagers did not recognize, stood watch outside.

Heela greeted these events with as little interest as the previous change of power, eight years prior. Life began and ended within her compound walls, a life in which dreams and memories were lost or deadened, leaving only the incessant din of daily being. Her days started before sunrise: "In our area," she recalled, "if a woman doesn't wake up before the morning prayer call, they say she isn't really a woman." After praying, she headed for the tandoor, a clay oven dug into the ground used for making naan. She stoked the fire with wood collected the day before and then loaded the oven. Musqinyar and the boys rose at dawn and they all sat around a communal breakfast of warm bread and green tea. Sometimes she would watch Musqinyar as they ate. He was always dapper, his clothes unstained and freshly pressed; it never ceased to surprise her how meticulous he was, how fortune had graced her with a self-sufficient husband.

After he left for work, Heela tended the goats and chickens in the backyard, put out milk to set yogurt, tidied the house, peeled vegetables, and looked after the boys, the two oldest of whom were now of school age. Caring for Musqinyar's elderly mother, who had come to live with them, was an added responsibility.

In all of this, in every working day, Heela found a certain necessity to things, a growing conviction that these realities pressed upon her for a reason and that there was much that was good and even holy in them. She knew that she had mastered homemaking as few others transplanted from the city could have, and she only wished that the rest of the village could see it for themselves. One elderly woman who sometimes visited with vague medical complaints said that Heela's was the cleanest, most orderly house she'd seen in her years. But in general guests were rare. During harvest season women would be busy in their courtyards cleaning and drying the apricots and almonds that their husbands had brought home, and it was only during growing season that there was time for medical concerns. Patients dribbled in to Heela's house at a rate of about one per month. Usually they would complain of highly nonspecific ailments, but occasionally a pregnant woman would present with symptoms of anemia. Without access to a clinic, there was little Heela could do beyond offering dietary advice. Sometimes, in severe cases, she dispatched the patient's male blood-relative escort, her *mahrem*, to a mullah or a peregrinate Sufi saint to collect an amulet containing a Koranic verse suited to the problem at hand.

It was well into the springtime of that first post-Taliban year before she saw a sign of change: a shipment of medicines donated by the US government arrived at the new base and was subsequently parceled out to community leaders. Heela could now prescribe iron pills. Shortly after, an NGO showed up to remove mines left over from the Soviet war. It was the first time, as far as anyone could remember, that an international aid group had ever visited the area. Then, that summer, workers from another agency appeared, to distribute seeds to needy farmers.

Musqinyar began to see the world anew. Ex-Communists around the country were embracing the US-backed government—many were even working directly for the Americans—and he didn't want to be left behind. He began making trips to the base to meet soldiers, who were members of the US special forces, and he often took Omaid along. In the evenings, he would regale Heela with tales of his visits. Old dreams were dusted off and updated. For the first time in years, he spoke of traveling abroad. He promised that Germany awaited, and maybe even Mecca, too, where they would make their holy pilgrimage together.

And just like that, Heela felt the tug herself. That something inside her that had driven her to economics at university against her parents' advice, that something that had given her the courage to travel cross-country with Taliban officials to study nursing—it was pulling at her again. It had now been four long years since she'd last set eyes upon anything outside the main wall of her compound, four years of births and meals and quarrels: life lived, no doubt, but she wanted more. When Musqinyar came home in the evenings, she started to beg him to take her somewhere, even just for an afternoon. She had no idea how such a feat could be accomplished, but she didn't see why they shouldn't try.

The trouble was, Musqinyar did not have the slightest idea how to pull this off, either. If villagers caught Heela walking about outdoors, the gossiping and backbiting and the resulting shame could be enough to tear apart the strongest family. Not long before, there had been the case of a woman of marriageable age sighted walking alone near the bazaar, prompting folks to say that she was up to no good. Even Heela had assumed so, for what other reason could there be for a woman of that age? Sure enough, it was later learned that she had run off in an unsanctioned marriage or had turned to prostitution. She was not seen again, and the family left Uruzgan in shame.

But for Heela, there was also an obstacle much closer to home: her mother-in-law, the family's octogenarian upholder of tradition. Since marriage, Musqinyar's mother had left her house only a handful of times in her life, and she spoke with the stubborn authority of someone who knew that this was the way things had always been and would always be. She saw it as her duty to protect the family name, especially since her daughter-in-law had arrived with her Kabul ways.

Musqinyar thought hard for some days, and then he announced to his mother one afternoon that Heela had fallen sick and needed to be rushed to a nurse on the far side of the district. The old woman demurred, insisting that exposing Heela would do the family more harm than having her sick in bed for a few weeks.

"And if she gets worse?" he asked. "Do you want to be responsible?"

She had no reply. Heela, listening in the next room, ear to the door, could not believe the ruse was working.

After dinner, she fitted herself into a mud-green burqa and stepped outside, following Musqinyar and the children. She didn't know where they were headed, and she didn't care.

The sun sat low and fat and pink on the horizon. Through the burqa mesh, she could make out Musqinyar's sandals swinging into and out of view. They headed along the dirt path leading to the stream.

Holding his hand, she crossed the wooden footbridge and stepped into the backseat of the car, which was always parked on the far embankment. Musqinyar drove them to the bazaar, by now almost shut down for the night. Around this time, boys would bring their goats into town to feed on the garbage heaped by the roadside, a de facto sanitation service. The children working the shops would be busy pulling down the rusted iron shutters. Their sunburned grandfathers would be squatting nearby, repeating their tired tales. Yet even in its crumbling decay, the bazaar still showed some signs of the new era: a poster of a Bollywood starlet, a small satellite dish perched atop a shop.

They waited until the street was clear, Heela ducking out of sight, and then rolled slowly toward the shops. As they pulled up to Musqinyar's store, she could just make out through her mesh the flowing, cursive script on the window: KABUL PHARMACY. Inside, the dusty shelves were choked with Chinese- and Pakistani-made medicines. With no hospitals for miles, this was it. You addressed your health care needs here at Musqinyar's pharmacy, or you didn't address them at all.

"Today," he told her with a smile, "you are my guest. Take whatever you like." Heela shuffled through the rows of chalky white boxes as the boys scurried here and there. Six-year-old Jamshed hoisted himself onto a chair behind the glass counter and pounded his fist. "I'm a doctor!" he announced. Heela wished her Kabul friends could see her now, out again, reclaiming her place in the world. One of the boys knocked over a pile of medicines. Heela shrieked and spanked him, but Musqinyar burst out laughing. The muezzin crooned and the sky darkened. She selected a few boxes to take home, including a drug that cured headaches and another that protected against the evil eye.

The trip lasted less than an hour, but Heela felt like the luckiest woman in Khas Uruzgan. Although she would experience much in the years to come, this would be the only family outing she would ever have.

It was a summer's day in 2002, a day so hot that Heela was avoiding the garden altogether, when someone rapped on the front door. Musqinyar was at work and the boys at school, so she did not answer, but the knocking continued and finally the visitor called out her name. She pressed her face against the metal gate and carefully said, "Who is it?"

"Qudus Khan," said the voice. It was the district governor, one of the most powerful men in Khas Uruzgan. He was also in charge of an NGO that operated on foreigner-donated funds.

"I'm sorry," she said self-consciously, "my husband isn't here."

"No, we'd like to speak with you. We heard there's an educated woman in this house."

"That's me," she said through the closed door. "I can read and write."

The governor told her that they had received funding to establish a female vocational training center and needed someone to help oversee the project. Would she be interested? Heela stood staring at the door. It took a moment for the words to register. She knew that this sort of opportunity came along only once or twice in a lifetime. But turning around, she saw her mother-in-law—standing "with her arms folded like a warlord," she recalled.

"Thank you for your offer," she said, "but I don't want to work."

Qudus Khan insisted that she was the perfect person for the job, since they didn't know of anyone else who had experience "outside the house." Heela was at a loss. She glanced around to her mother-in-law, and finally said, "It isn't my decision. Please talk to my husband when he comes home."

As soon as he left, her mother-in-law walked up to her. "What's wrong with you? How could you let those men hear your voice? You're going to make trouble for my son, aren't you?"

Heela ignored her and went inside. She was feeling that tug again, and her mind raced with possibilities. Although she knew of no female in her village who had successfully worked outside the house, she didn't see why she couldn't be the first. Confidence was a rare currency, and ironically her stint working under the Taliban had endowed her with more than any woman she knew. That evening, Musqinyar jumped at the news. Nine years of village life had not yet eradicated the last vestiges of his former world. The two began conspiring to get Heela the job.

Fortunately, the position only required twice-monthly visits to the vocational center. The furtive trip to his shop had convinced him that if planned carefully, it would be possible to smuggle her to the center and back without discovery. The only challenge, as always, was his mother. After a day of discussion, he dreamed up a cover story: he would be taking Heela to "visit the village shrine." When he tested the idea with his mother, she shot back, "What good is a woman her age going to the shrine? The holiest work is here with me in the kitchen."

Musqinyar countered that, with his newfound religiosity, he preferred a more observant wife. And it was true that he had taken to the Koran, even growing out his beard like the rest of the village. Would she actually stand in the way of religion? There was nothing that could rightfully be said to this, and she knew it.

On the appointed day, Heela awoke earlier than usual and fished out her most respectable outfit, holding it up for inspection. The burqa was loose and flowing, sandy-brown like the earth. She set it aside and readied breakfast, then proceeded to finish her chores for the day. It was not yet mid-morning when she and Musqinyar and the children, along for effect, loaded themselves into the station wagon. As they drove the long back road around the village, she caught herself telling rambling stories, her habit when anxious.

The car pulled up to a nondescript house and Musqinyar scanned the area, then motioned for Heela to get out. She had taken only a few steps when a man on a bicycle appeared on the horizon, pedaling toward them. She jumped back into the car. He sped by without looking up.

Heela got out again and this time nearly ran to the gate. Inside, a group of women trainees were crowded together in a small room, hunched over sewing machines. Most were Hazaras, whose families tended to take a slightly more permissive approach to purdah than the Pashtuns of her village. Still, like Heela, they had all endured significant risks to come, and, as the machines sputtered along, the mood was tense. It was

2002, the Taliban had been gone for almost a year, and the Americans were busy building a new Afghanistan, yet in Khas Uruzgan these women had no choice but to work in secret. Everyone there knew the stakes: if word leaked, they would almost certainly be accused of prostitution—a charge that, under the strictures of village life, was usually punishable by death.

Heela was to be an auditor, ensuring that none of the students or teachers made off with the materials. As thrilling as it was, she was not happy to linger. She kept glancing at the door, expecting village men to burst in at any moment. She took down the inventory and hurried back to Musqinyar's waiting car.

At home, her mother-in-law asked, "Did you go to the shrine?"

"Yes," Heela replied.

"Did you pray for me?"

"Yes."

One evening a month later, Musqinyar arrived home with a wad of cash and handed it to Heela. She counted it: 8,500 Pakistani rupees—nearly $150. She looked at him.

"Take it," he said.

Heela knew that she'd be getting paid, but the amount still came as a shock. She handed it back, saying it belonged to him, the man of the house.

He pushed it right back into her hands. "It's yours," he said. "You've earned it. It's your right."

Heela hadn't gone to work for the money, but, holding the cash in her hand, she felt a gravitas like she'd never experienced. Still, she knew of no women keeping money they had earned. It belonged to the family, to the husband. But it was clear to her that Musqinyar was serious. Had something like this ever happened in the village before? That night, before bed, she sewed a pocket into her dress to hide the money, as if Qudus Khan might come to his senses and snatch it back at any moment.

Every two weeks Heela engaged in a ritual of deceit with her mother-in-law, and every month a new wad of cash arrived. It felt as if she were rediscovering her old self. On those rare occasions when elderly female relatives visited the house, she spoke more knowingly and confidently. She knew that despite their age, they would never understand the world the way that she did or see what she'd seen. "I stopped thinking only about my children and my four walls," she recalled. "I thought about my village and Afghans everywhere."

Occasionally she sent the boys out to the bazaar to buy small gifts for Musqinyar. Sometimes they made a game of it. "We got dice and made bets, me and him," she said. "The kids were always supporting him. I usually lost and would send the boys to buy him clothes. I think I pick out nicer clothes anyway, so this worked in my favor. Then once we played and he said, 'If you win, I'll buy you a necklace.' I finally won, and it was a gold necklace. I still have it."

Cut into the stream in front of Heela's house at various points were small canals and irrigation ditches, which fanned out to the farms of the village. Few households owned plots outright. Instead, most land belonged to the *khan*, who functioned as a feudal lord of sorts, with villagers working as sharecroppers. Nearly every village had at least one khan; some, like Khas Uruzgan governor Qudus Khan, were prominent district-wide, but most were known just in their own village. The khans of Khas Uruzgan had risen to power only in the previous thirty years, when the old elite fled or were killed off by the Communists, and they had climbed to their positions through expert management of CIA-sourced funds and landgrabs. Musqinyar kept up good relations with Hajji Abdo Khan, the khan of their village, as a matter of politics, but he and Heela knew that he was a cause of much poverty. And when the village received aid money, it was understood that Abdo Khan would take a cut. Still, only with his tacit approval was the sewing center able to function at all.

That small room with no windows and a dozen old sewing machines was the sole space where women regularly gathered outside their home anywhere in Khas Uruzgan save the Hazara areas. A girls' school existed on paper, but only to soothe foreign powers and Western aid agencies, as there was no actual facility. In fact, there had never been a girls' school in the village. When the Communists declared female education compulsory, they had toyed with the possibility of threatening recalcitrant families with jail time, but a series of uprisings in Kandahari villages against the idea led them to back off. The Communists may have believed that they were imposing modernization on the backward countryside, but from the farmers' point of view a household could not function without women doing the necessary work indoors. With no jobs waiting for high school graduates, villagers could only see potential ruin in allowing their daughters outside.

Not much had changed in the years since, except that two decades of jihadi war had left purdah with a thick Islamic gloss. So everyone involved in the sewing enterprise—Hajji Abdo Khan included—took great care to keep the effort under wraps, lest they be accused of abandoning their religion. It took nearly three months for talk to start bubbling up around the district of the strange building where women had been seen entering. Heela took the news as a sort of inevitability, as if freedom, like all things in a world forged by war, was fleeting by its very nature. Yet even after Qudus Khan shut down the center to avoid trouble, she held on to those three months and did not let them go. The tug within her was nearly constant. It occurred to her that she now understood how the sewing business worked better than anyone. She had spent hours checking machines and spool stocks and fabric supplies. She knew what risks the women were taking to learn the trade, what she was risking herself just to check on them. Why couldn't she run a center herself, right in her own home?

Musqinyar did not even need to hear the details of her proposal. "I'll arrange it with Qudus Khan in the morning," he said, "and get some machines."

The following day, under cover of darkness, Musqinyar and Omaid unloaded sewing machines from the car and carried them down to the cellar. In return for the donation, they had agreed to provide dresses for Qudus Khan to sell. The governor would quietly put word out about Heela's "medical practice."

On the first day of sewing class in that cramped cellar, fourteen women showed up. They would return once a month, each using her own brand of subterfuge. Nilofar, who might have been seventeen (though no one knew for sure), feigned illness to come. Mina snuck out in the afternoons, when her family was taking its midday nap, dressed in black—the color of the elderly, who were ordinarily allowed to pass without notice. Getting caught would likely have meant death, but she kept coming back. Nazo waited until the men in her house were asleep to cross the fields. At her advanced age she would not have been punished as severely as the others, but then she started bringing her two granddaughters. When her son-in-law discovered the excursions, he was incensed. With some effort, she convinced him that she needed help getting to the doctor. Nonetheless, after the third class, he began suspecting that education was involved and confronted her, shouting, "Don't corrupt my daughters!" Nazo swore that she was doing no such thing. "Look!" she insisted. "I don't have any books. I don't even have a pen. I have nothing. Come check my room."

The class, initially two hours, soon expanded to four. "At first, we didn't talk about sewing at all," Heela said, "but instead about how to maintain proper hygiene, how to take care of your house, keep your husband happy, time management, some useful kitchen skills, and so on. These were things I had learned in Kabul, but how could you expect these village women to know about them? I taught them about city life, about the Koran, and then how to sew. I also gave them a primary education, how to write basic things and do basic arithmetic."

By the sixth month, the students were learning how to operate the machines and measure cloth. Upon graduating, each was granted a table, a ruler, and, to their astonishment, a working sewing machine. This created another set of difficulties, as they had to conspire to sneak the machines into their houses. Eventually the governor awarded the materials to the men of the house, under the guise of a foreign grant. Musqinyar delivered the dresses directly to Qudus Khan, who passed them on to other district officials for sale.

Heela found that she had a way with the students. For women venturing outdoors for the first time, her words came soft and reassuring. Yet they also saw in her a striking model of modernity, bedecked as she was in Kabul's sartorial splendor: baggy trousers, ankle bells, and a daub of eye shadow. For many, she was the first woman they had ever met who had cast her eyes upon the outside world.

Class size dwindled during harvest season, when men would bring home fruit for their wives to clean and dry, and fluctuated unpredictably whenever domestic difficulties broke out: occasionally a woman somewhere in the district would get beaten or killed, scaring the students off for a month or two.

One of the students was a young woman rumored to have been kidnapped from Kabul during the civil war, and Heela was eager to learn more. During the first sessions, the woman sat in the back without saying a word. Heela couldn't help staring at her as she worked. Did she know anyone back home? How did she end up here? On her fourth visit Heela cautiously brought up Kabul, and the woman told her the name of her home neighborhood. Emboldened, Heela decided to ask her directly about her story at the next session. But she didn't return, and Heela never saw her again.

After harvest season the students returned and another class graduated, but the women were finding it ever more difficult to explain how they were mysteriously acquiring the skills to work the machines. And Heela lived with the constant fear that the sound of a dozen machines going at once could be heard from the outside. Worse yet, there was her mother-in-law, whom Musqinyar had sworn to secrecy. Although she hadn't impeded the classes—what, after all, could she do without leaving the house herself?—she had stated in no uncertain terms that she found the whole enterprise dishonorable.

One spring day in 2003, Heela looked up from her machine to see her mother-in-law standing at the top of the stairs.

"Someone is here for you," she said.

Turning to her students, Heela motioned frantically and they scrambled, noisily pushing their machines into a corner and taking cover behind curtains. She threw on a burqa and went upstairs. Standing glowering at the gate was Jamila, a relative of her husband—a woman "very clever and fat," as Heela shared later.

"I killed your chickens," Jamila said. The birds had evidently wandered into her yard. "All nine of them." She looked furious.

"Why are you angry? I should be the one that's angry."

"Those infidels gave you chickens, and they damaged my garden."

"Infidels? They were from a charity."

"A foreign charity. Infidels." She slowly scanned the yard. "Forget about the chickens. I heard you are working for the infidels as well."

Heela's mouth went dry. "I'm not working for anyone," she said. "Someone is lying to you."

"No, the whole village is talking about it. They're saying that you're working for the infidels. You better stop it. I know what you are doing."

"I've done nothing wrong!" Heela exclaimed. Her mother-in-law shuffled closer to listen. "And I have an education. I have a right to work if I want to."

"No, you don't," Jamila shot back. "Keep going on like this, and no one will see a single family member of yours alive."

Heela's mother-in-law chimed in. "Why don't you come inside for some tea?" Heela stared at her in disbelief. Before she could say anything, Jamila strode past and made her way inside. As she sat down, she spotted a pair of baby blue burqas, puddled onto the floor.

"Whose are those?" she asked. Her eyes swept the room. In the cellar, a dozen women held their breaths. Heela tried to change the subject. "Have some tea and let's talk. This is between you and me. It's got nothing to do with the village. It's my fault the chickens came to your garden. It's really my fault, I'm sorry." She waved her hand across the room. "Look around. Do you see a problem here? I'm just a simple housewife."

Jamila finished her tea and left. Heela's heart settled and she went back to her students. After a few nervous minutes, Heela continued her lesson, and the machines started up once again.

Suddenly the cellar door burst open. Jamila stood there, aghast, with Heela's mother-in-law standing beside her. The machines stopped; the students froze.

One of them broke into tears. "I'm just a widow. I have no choice," she sobbed, "I have no choice."

Another said, "Please, sister. We're poor. We just need money."

People started speaking all at once, begging Jamila not to say a word. Women's lives were at stake. Heela reminded her that since they were relatives, the news would put Jamila's family in an unfavorable light as well. This, finally, seemed to cool her down, but before she left she told Heela, "It's not just me. The whole village is talking. Don't be selfish. Think about your families, think about your religion." She paused at the top of the stairs and added, "I'm not responsible for what happens to you."

Heela canceled classes for the month. But the stoning started anyway. First, rocks rained down on the window and the roof. Then, when her boys left the house, village youths hurled stones at their heads. One month rolled into the next, and the students refused to return to class.

It was not long before Qudus Khan sent a delegation to Heela's house to investigate why dress production had stopped. Heela answered through the door, as usual, but then grew concerned that the visitors would accidentally be stoned, so she invited them in. The four men sat cross-legged on the living-room floor as she served tea and sweets. Zabit, a sweaty bear of a man, barraged her with questions about the use of the equipment. She hardly gave it a thought.

That evening, when Heela related the day's events to Musqinyar, he stared at her incredulously. She could see him becoming stiff with anger.

"I had to invite them in," she said. "I didn't have a choice."

Without a word, he got up and walked out. This was serious, and she knew it. He almost never lost his temper. She shouldn't have brought those men in or allowed them to hear her voice, but what else could she have done? Still, it would cause problems for the family. People would talk, bemoaning how her education had gone to her head, how she acted as if she still lived in Kabul. They would blame Musqinyar for not reining her in, question his manhood and the family's purity.

She found him in the front yard and tried to apologize, but he would have none of it. Heela had never seen him this way. She continued to press her case, and as she spoke he flashed with anger and suddenly kicked her hard on the legs. As she cried out, he managed to land two more kicks. She stormed into the bedroom and slammed the door.

It took more than an hour for her to cool down. Then she went to the kitchen and chopped up some vegetables and threw chunks of lamb into the pan. When the food was ready she walked a plate out to him, but he grabbed it and hurled it across the room.

For days after, she refused to speak to him. Yet even as she seethed inside, she considered herself lucky. They almost never fought, and not once had he brought up the possibility of taking a second wife, as permitted by Islam and local culture. Unlike most village men, he seldom laid a violent hand on her. This episode, in fact, would be one of just two serious fights they would have during their time in Uruzgan. Heela knew that it could be so much worse. Her neighbor Wazhma, for instance, had talked back to her husband after he took a second wife, which had so enraged his family that the women of the household held Wazhma down as her brother-in-law shot her dead.

The new government would no more intervene in such matters than it would if you had in some private rage killed your own oxen or damaged your own house. So Heela was grateful for her good fortune, even though in their other serious fight Musqinyar had broken her arm. "But that was my fault," she insisted. "I had talked back to him. Women out in the village don't talk back to their husbands, it's just a law. When men say something, women should just listen, and you should never talk in a loud voice, because a man outside might hear. I made that mistake, but I was lucky. In Tirin Kot, a man once beat his wife with an ax and she survived, but her head was split open. Husbands who only use their hands or feet are very kind."

Weeks passed before the pair could make amends, and by then the damage had been done, just as Musqinyar had feared. Zabit had started a rumor that Heela was running a house of prostitution, and Jamila swore to her relatives that she had seen the girls in action. It was only by the grace of God that her students survived their beatings, some only barely so. Musqinyar closed down the school.

For months Heela had been living in stolen moments, snatched from a social structure that yielded little to women of ambition. In the end, she realized, you surrender that which you have taken—at least in Khas Uruzgan. And for the first time in years, the tug was gone. She waited patiently but it did not return. In time, even waiting for it seemed foolish, reckless in fact, and she hated herself for having believed otherwise. She started skipping meals and letting housework go. Her slide into someplace dark was steady and perhaps irrevocable. Musqinyar, however, refused to accept it. One evening Heela went to bed and found new jewelry on her pillow. Another time, a Pakistani-type dress that had been all the rage in her Kabul life appeared in her wardrobe. Sometimes, a wife of one of Musqinyar's friends would be brought to the house for "treatment." Yet Heela could not brighten, no matter how she tried.

As always, Musqinyar, summoning a seemingly endless reserve of hope, refused to give in. Yet his optimism now faced challenges on multiple fronts: if life at home was trying, things around the district were not faring any better. It started in that summer of 2003, when a motorist was mysteriously gunned down not far from the village. Later, a farmer was kidnapped, and another was held up at gunpoint. Someone fired rockets at the nearby American base. Heela ordered the children to stop playing outside. Musqinyar ate his dinners in silence, brooding over things better left unsaid.

The war had returned.

PART TWO

5

No One Is Safe from This

In early 2008, I traveled across Maiwand, a desert district west of Kandahar city. Here, more than one hundred years earlier, a girl named Malalai had led Afghan tribesmen, in Joan of Arc fashion, to a stunning rout of imperial British troops. Or so the legend goes. To this day, the battle figures powerfully in the Afghan national imagination. Thousands of girls are still named Malalai, while Maiwand is invoked by schoolchildren in verse and song, and by the dusty signs above pharmacies and banks everywhere.

Yet as I drove down the district's lone highway, there were no traces of that past glory, only bare country running in all directions. Every mile or so, a culvert lay burst open, or a bridge railing mangled. Sad one-room shops clung to the roadside.

I turned south off the highway and followed a gravel road until reaching a river. The water was the color of sand and you could not hear a sound from it. Irrigation channels ran out to a few identical-looking terra-cotta houses off in the distance. The settlements were part of a stretch of countryside known as Band-i-Timor, the last human outposts before miles of trackless red desert.

I came to a small bazaar, a single lane flanked by shops selling motor oil, bicycle tires, cartons of eggs, and energy drinks. There were Coca-Cola bottles caked in dirt and signs obscured by dirt and windows crusted over with dirt. There were no cars. Near a water tank, a goat stood watching.

I passed the Band-i-Timor pharmacy, where a child sat behind a counter with his arms folded. Heading down the street, I came to a wooden stall selling freshly squeezed juices; behind it stood the proprietor, a boy who could not have been more than ten years old. Two figures approached from the far end of the bazaar walking a cow, and as they passed they looked at me and said nothing. They, too, were mere boys. They continued on and disappeared into a field.

It was as if I had stumbled into a frontier version of *Lord of the Flies*. Where were the adults?

"Some are in the mountains," the juice boy said, pointing to the flat scrubland stretching to the horizon. He meant, it seemed, that they had joined the Taliban insurgency. Others, he said, were off harvesting poppies in neighboring provinces or had resettled in Pakistan or Iran, leaving the women and children behind. They had all left because of the war.

I followed the road as it bent away from the shops and ran along dying meadows to another bazaar, this one with shuttered shops and mud homes slumping in decay. It lay perfectly silent, devoid even of children. The doors to some of the homes had been left open.

The road continued away from the river until the meadows thinned and succumbed to open desert, each village along the route lying abandoned. I returned to the first bazaar, where the boy explained that fighting between the Americans and the Taliban had grown so intense that one morning the villagers had collectively decided to vacate Band-i-Timor forever.

The Americans and the Taliban. It was their war that Heela and Musqinyar had seen hints of in 2003, a struggle for power once again lapping at the edges of their lives. To understand the sources of the conflict, I realized that I would have to go back even further, to the first months after the US invasion, when Band-i-Timor and Khas Uruzgan and the rest of the country were still at peace.

I thanked the boy and was about to leave when he grabbed my arm. "Listen, do you want to buy a generator? I have a really nice one—hasn't been used in years." I told him I was sure he could find a better use for it in his village, where electricity was so hard to come by.

"Oh, nobody uses generators here," he replied. "If we start them up,

the Americans think we're running a bomb factory and raid our houses."
He looked off to the horizon. "And the Taliban think we're using it to spy
on them. Better to live without."

The sky clotted gray and the winds gusted cold as the men crowded into
an old roadside gas station. It was daybreak in Band-i-Timor, early
December 2001, and hundreds of turbaned farmers sat pensively, weigh-
ing the choice before them. They had once been the backbone of the Taliban's support; the movement had arisen not far from here, and many had
sent their sons to fight on the front lines. But in 2000, Mullah Omar had
decreed opium cultivation to be un-Islamic, and whip-wielding police saw
to it that production was halted almost overnight. Band-i-Timor had
been poppy country for as long as anyone could remember, but now the
fields lay fallow and children were going hungry. With the Taliban's days
numbered after the US invasion, the mood was ripe for a change. But
could they trust the Americans? Or Hamid Karzai?

An enfeebled elder, Hajji Burget Khan, rose to speak. A legendary
war hero and a chief of the millions-strong Ishaqzai tribe, Burget Khan
commanded respect that few present could rival. "He was an inspiring
leader," a tribal elder told me later, "as pure as the rain falling from the
sky." He was also a consummate pragmatist, having forged alliances over
the years across the political spectrum, including with the Taliban. Now
he was extolling the virtues of the coming American order. There would
be jobs, he said, and there would be development. And, most important,
farmers would be left alone to do the work they'd always done.

A second elder then addressed the audience. A generation younger
and a few waist sizes larger than Burget Khan, Hajji Bashar was a leader
of the politically important Noorzai tribe, a frontier tycoon who had
made his millions smuggling opium. Like Burget Khan, he had a knack
for backing the right horse—he was an early financier of the Taliban—
and now he insisted that with American wealth and power on their side,
the future had never looked brighter.

For the first time in years, hope took hold of the poor farmers of
Band-i-Timor. The local Taliban council of religious clerics was declared
null and void, and in its place the attendees formed a council composed

of representatives from all Maiwand tribes. Hajji Bashar was elected governor of the district, prompting the former governor and police chief to flee overnight. It was, in effect, a bloodless coup, with the Taliban authority replaced by an America-friendly administration. Although Maiwand would have many governments in the decade to follow, only this one, farmers would say for years afterward, truly belonged to them.

The parched Maiwand desert began to show signs of life. Schools and clinics, long ignored and abandoned by the Taliban, reopened their doors. Aid workers arrived to repair water channels and irrigation systems. Step by step, elders worked to help the fledgling government stand on its own. Hajji Burget Khan persuaded hundreds of former Taliban foot soldiers to declare their allegiance to the Karzai government. It was a move as old as the wars themselves: just as these men had once flocked to the Taliban, they would now, for sheer survival, throw their weight behind the new power. Hajji Bashar delivered to the Kandahar governor fifteen truckloads of weapons, including hundreds of rocket launchers and anti-aircraft missiles, that he had collected from former Talibs. Bashar, in fact, harbored ambitions to become a national player and was quick to find his way to the Americans. He had initiated contact as early as November 2001—when the Taliban was still in power—via clandestine meetings with US officials. Then, in January 2002, he showed up at an American base and spent a few days telling officers everything he knew about the Taliban. His crowning achievement came the following month, when he helped convince erstwhile Taliban foreign minister and Maiwand native Mullah Mutawakkil to surrender to US forces, making him one of the highest-ranking Talibs in American custody.

In fact, Mutawakkil's defection was only the latest in a rush of Taliban officials looking to switch allegiances. Within a month of its military collapse, the Taliban movement had ceased to exist. When religious clerics in Pakistan launched a fund-raising campaign to get the Taliban back on their feet and waging "jihad" against the Americans, it was roundly rejected by the Talib leadership. "We want to tell people the Taliban system is no more," Agha Jan Mutassim, finance minister of the fallen regime and Mullah Omar's confidant, told reporters. "They should not give any donations in the name of the Taliban." He added: "If a stable Islamic government is established in Afghanistan, we don't intend to launch any action against it."

Khalid Pashtoon, spokesman for the new Kandahar government, declared: "Ministers of the Taliban and senior Taliban are coming one by one and surrendering and joining with us." The list included the Taliban ministers of defense, justice, interior, vice and virtue, information, health, commerce, industry, and finance—in effect, the entire Taliban cabinet; key military commanders and important governors; diplomats; and top officials who had worked with Mullah Omar. The avalanche of surrenders knew no bounds of ideology: leaders of the notorious whip-wielding religious police were among the earliest to defect. A group of former Taliban officials even announced that they were forming a political party to participate in future democratic elections. "We are giving advice to Hamid Karzai," said their leader. "We support him."

By surrendering, the Taliban were following the pattern that had marked Afghan politics for much of the previous two decades. After the Soviet withdrawal, many Afghan Communists had rebranded themselves as Islamists and joined the mujahedeen. During the civil war, factions shifted loyalties based on nothing more than bald pragmatism. Upon the Taliban's entry onto the scene, warlords across the Pashtun belt had either retired, fled, or joined them. Now it was the Taliban's turn, and as one member of the movement after another submitted to the authority of the Karzai administration, there emerged the possibility of a truly inclusive political order.

It had long been Karzai's desire to convene a *loya jirga*, a grand assembly of elders, to elect a transitional government. The idea took hold around the country. At Kandahar's soccer stadium (last used under the Taliban as an execution ground), thousands of farmers and dignitaries packed the stands to rally for the jirga. Delegates were to be drawn from each of the nation's three hundred–plus districts. In Maiwand, unsurprisingly, the revered Hajji Burget Khan was elected despite his advanced age. "We felt as if we were born anew," recalled Kala Khan, a fellow tribal elder. "There was nothing we couldn't accomplish."

Spring washed over Band-i-Timor and the acacias bloomed and pomegranate groves grew thick, and for the first time in years the fields were lavender bright with poppies. Not far from the main river, overlooking those fields, stood a large quadrangle of mud buildings, with cars and jeeps parked out front and dozens of farmers milling about. This was the home of Hajji Burget Khan, who was busy day and night receiving Ishaqzai tribesmen from other districts, other provinces, even as far afield as Pakistan. They came to pay their respects to the octogenarian leader, and Abdullah, the family driver, would usually be dispatched to ferry them in from the bus stop.

One hot May night, Abdullah was sleeping in the courtyard when a thunderous blast shook him awake. Looking up, he saw a blinding white light in the space where the front gate had been. Silhouetted figures rushed toward him. He ran for the guesthouse, shouting that the house was under attack. Inside, Hajji Burget Khan was already awake; he had been sipping tea with visitors before the dawn prayer. His bodyguard Akhtar Muhammad raced into the courtyard, firing his weapon blindly. Before he knew it, he was thrown to the ground. Two or three men were on top of him. He was shackled and blindfolded, and he was kicked again and again. He heard shouting, in a language he couldn't understand.

Hajji Burget Khan and Hajji Tor Khan, Akhtar Muhammad's father, ran into the courtyard with other guests, heading for the main house. It was then, as the first morning light shaped the compound, that they saw armed men standing on the mud walls in camouflage uniforms and goggles and helmets. American soldiers. Gunfire erupted, and Hajji Tor Khan went down. Before Hajji Burget Khan could react, he, too, was shot.

Nearby, women huddled in their rooms, listening. Never before had strangers violated their home—not during the Russian occupation, or the civil war, or under the Taliban. A woman picked up a gun and headed into the courtyard to defend her family, but the soldiers wrested it out of her hands. Then a soldier appeared with an Afghan translator and ordered the women outside. It was the first time they had ever left their home without a mahrem. They were flexicuffed and had their feet shackled, and some were gagged with torn pieces of turban. The group was then herded into a dry well behind the compound. As the day broke and village farmers stepped out into the dawn air, the women's cries rang out across the fields and mud houses, never to be forgotten.

The soldiers stayed for hours. House by house throughout the village, men were pulled out and marched to an open field. There, Hajji Burget Khan lay clinging to life. Then he and the rest—fifty-five of them in all, nearly the entire adult male population of the village—were loaded onto helicopters and trucks and taken away.

The central thesis of the American failure in Afghanistan—the one you'll hear from politicians and pundits and even scholars—was succinctly propounded by Deputy Secretary of State Richard Armitage: "The war in Iraq drained resources from Afghanistan before things were under control." In this view, the American invasion of Iraq became a crucial distraction from stabilization efforts in Afghanistan, and in the resulting security vacuum the Taliban reasserted themselves.

At its core, the argument rests upon a key premise: that jihadi terrorism could be defeated through the military occupation of a country. That formulation seemed natural enough to many of us in the wake of 9/11. But travel through the southern Afghan countryside, and you will hear quite a different interpretation of what happened. It comes in snippets and flashes, in the stories people tell and their memories of the time, and it points to a contradiction buried deep in the war's basic premise.

You can find this contradiction embodied in a sprawling jumble of dust-blown hangars, barracks, and Burger Kings, a facility of barbed wire, gunmen, and internment cages: Kandahar Airfield, or KAF, as it came to be called, the nerve center for American operations in southern Afghanistan, home to elite units like the Navy SEALs and the Green Berets. A military base in a country like Afghanistan is also a web of relationships, a hub for the local economy, and a key player in the political ecosystem. Unravel how this base came to be, and you'll begin to understand how war returned to the fields of Maiwand.

In December 2001, an American Special Operations Forces unit pulled into an old Soviet airbase on the outskirts of Kandahar city. They were accompanied by a team of Afghan militiamen and their commander, a gregarious, grizzly bear of a man named Gul Agha Sherzai. An anti-Taliban warlord, Sherzai had shot to notoriety in the 1990s following the death of his illustrious father, Hajji Latif, a onetime bandit turned mujahed known as "the Lion of Kandahar." (Upon assuming his father's mantle, Gul Agha had rechristened himself *Sherzai*, Son of the Lion. His first name, incidentally, roughly translates as "Respected Mr. Flower.") With American backing, Sherzai seized the airfield, then in ruins, and subsequently installed himself in the local governor's mansion—a move that incensed many, Hamid Karzai among them. Nonetheless, Sherzai brought a certain flair to the office, quickly catching notice for his fist-pounding speeches, tearful soliloquies, and outbursts of uncontrollable laughter, sometimes all in a single conversation.

Sherzai may not have had much experience in government, except a brief tenure as Kandahar's "governor" during the anarchic mid-1990s, but he knew a good business opportunity when he saw one. The airbase where the Americans were encamped was derelict and weedy, strewn with smashed furniture and seeded with land mines from the Soviet era. Early on, one of Sherzai's lieutenants met Master Sergeant Perry Toomer, a US officer in charge of logistics and contracting. "I started talking to him," Toomer said, "and found out that they had a knowledge of how to get this place started." After touring the facilities, the Americans placed their first order: $325 in cash for a pair of Honda water pumps.

It would mark the beginning of a long and fruitful partnership. With Sherzai's services, the cracked and cratered airstrip blossomed into a massive, sprawling military base, home to one of the world's busiest airports. Kandahar Airfield would grow into a key hub in Washington's global war on terror, housing top secret black-ops command rooms and large wire-mesh cages for terror suspects en route to the American prison in Guantanamo Bay, Cuba.

For Sherzai, KAF would be only the beginning. In a few swift strokes, he made the desert bloom with American installations—and turned an extravagant profit in the process. He swiped land and rented it to US forces to the tune of millions of dollars. Amid the ensuing construction boom, he seized gravel quarries, charging as much as $100 a load for what would normally have been an $8-a-load job. He furnished American troops with fuel for their trucks and workers for their projects, raking in commissions while functioning as an informal temp agency for his tribesmen. With this windfall, he diversified into gasoline and water distribution, real estate, taxi services, mining, and, most lucrative of all, opium. No longer a mere governor, he was now one of the most powerful men in Afghanistan. Every morning, lines of supplicants would curl out of the governor's mansion. As his web of patronage grew, he began providing the Americans with hired guns, usually from his own Barakzai tribe—making him, in essence, a private security contractor, an Afghan Blackwater. And like the employees of that notorious American firm, Sherzai's gunmen lived largely outside the jurisdiction of any government. Even as Washington pumped in funds to create a national Afghan army and police, the US military subsidized Sherzai's mercenaries, who owed their loyalty to the governor and the special forces alone. Some of his units could even be seen garbed in US uniforms, driving heavily armed flatbed trucks through the streets of Kandahar.

Of course, even in the new Afghanistan there was no such thing as a free lunch. In return for privileged access to American dollars, Sherzai delivered the one thing US forces felt they needed most: intelligence. His men became the Americans' eyes and ears in their drive to eradicate the Taliban and al-Qaeda from Kandahar. Yet here lay the contradiction. Following the Taliban's collapse, al-Qaeda had fled the country, resettling in the tribal regions of Pakistan and in Iran. By April 2002, the group could no longer be found in Kandahar—or anywhere else in Afghanistan. The Taliban, meanwhile, had ceased to exist, its members having retired to their homes and surrendered their weapons. Save for a few lone wolf attacks, US forces in Kandahar in 2002 faced no resistance at all. The terrorists had all decamped or abandoned the cause, yet US special forces were on Afghan soil with a clear political mandate: defeat terrorism.

How do you fight a war without an adversary? Enter Gul Agha Sherzai—and men like him around the country. Eager to survive and prosper, he and his commanders followed the logic of the American presence to its obvious conclusion. They would create enemies where there were none, exploiting the perverse incentive mechanism that the Americans—without even realizing it—had put in place. Sherzai's enemies became America's enemies, his battles its battles. His personal feuds and jealousies were repackaged as "counterterrorism," his business interests as Washington's. And where rivalries did not do the trick, the prospect of further profits did. (One American leaflet dropped by plane in the area read: "Get Wealth and Power Beyond Your Dreams. Help Anti-Taliban Forces Rid Afghanistan of Murderers and Terrorists.")

For several hours a day in a small Kandahar office, special forces and CIA officers pored over intelligence reports from the field, almost all of them originating from Sherzai's network. They worked closely with the head of the local spy agency, a Sherzai crony named Hajji Gulalai. An ex-mujahed, he had been tortured so badly by the Communists that he had acquired a skin condition for which an aide had to constantly scratch and massage his back. With such a history, your list of enemies ran long, and the Americans knew it. According to former special forces soldiers, the two sides had an informal pact. "He'd give us intel," explained one, "and then we'd let him do whatever he wanted." A group of soldiers in a special forces detachment wrote in a collective memoir that on operations, Gulalai's men "could get into places and exact payback for something that had nothing to do with their mission." They added, "It happened a few times. The detachment had a deal with him."

Whatever they had been before, Sherzai and his men were now creatures of a world where, as the Bush administration had proclaimed, you were either with us or against us. Sherzai's network fed intelligence—which in the absence of an actual enemy was almost all false—to the Americans, and reaped the rewards: a business empire strung across the desert, garish villas abroad, and unfettered control of southern Afghan politics. The Americans, in turn, carried out raids against a phantom enemy, happily fulfilling their mandate from Washington.

Amid this bounty, Sherzai's operatives homed in on one place in particular: a district not far from Kandahar city that they nicknamed "Dubai," a reference to the port metropolis of shopping malls and palm trees that represented, for Kandaharis, an oasis of unbridled wealth and opportunity. For Sherzai's men, their new land of opportunity, their new Dubai, was none other than the impoverished desert district of Maiwand.

Hajji Burget Khan and the other captives were brought to KAF and deposited in metal cages stacked side by side in the open air and flooded by bright white lights. They were forced to kneel there for hours, their hands bound behind them. Some passed out from the pain. Some lost sensation in their hands and feet. Then they were marched into a room and made to strip and stand in front of American soldiers for inspection, inspiring a humiliation that, in the Pashtun ethos, was difficult to even imagine. "When they made us walk naked in front of all those Americans," captive Abdul Wahid later told a reporter, "I was praying to God to let me die. If someone could have sold me a poisoned tablet for $100,000, I would have bought it."

In a final act of emasculation, soldiers appeared with clippers. One by one the captives' beards were shorn off, and many of them broke down in tears. Some, for resisting, had their eyebrows removed as well.

Hajji Burget Khan, tribal leader and war hero, would not be seen alive again. The truth of what happened in his final hours may never be known. One account has it that he died en route to KAF from his gunshot wound. Another version, a confidential dispatch from the Canadian Joint Task Force 2, part of the special forces team that carried out the raid, states that "an elderly father died while in custody" at Kandahar Airfield, "reportedly from a butt stroke to the head, which has caused much grief/anguish in the village."

For days, the prisoners were questioned. "We don't know who we have, but we hope we got some senior Taliban or at least some Taliban folks in there," Lieutenant Colonel Jim Yonts, spokesman for the US Central Command, told reporters. Yet it soon became apparent that the captives had all followed Burget Khan in embracing the new American order. After five days, they were brought to Kandahar's soccer stadium and released. A crowd of thousands, who had made the trip from Maiwand, was there to greet them. A few months earlier many of these farmers had packed the stadium seats waving the new Afghan flag and chanting in favor of the coming loya jirga. Now, for the first time, anti-American slogans filled the air. "If we did any crime, they must punish us," shouted Amir Sayed Wali, a villager elder. "If we are innocent, we will take our revenge for this insult." Tribal elder Lala Khan asked, "Is there any law? Any accountability? Who are our leaders? The elders, or the Americans?"

The raid would leave lasting marks on a number of levels. "If they touch our women again, we must ask ourselves why we are alive," declared villager Sher Muhammad Ustad. "We will have no choice but to fight." Back in the village, one woman was heard shouting at her male relatives, "You people have big turbans on your heads"—the quintessential accoutrement of Pashtun manhood—"but what have you done? You are cowards! You can't even protect us. You call yourselves men?"

Hajji Burget Khan's son, wounded in the raid, was left wheelchair-bound. Burget Khan's close friend Tor Khan, who had been shot four times, died a slow, agonizing death. Villagers did not take him to the hospital for nearly twenty-four hours, fearing that the Americans would find him and finish the job. Six-year-old Zarghuna, fast asleep when the soldiers arrived, awoke in a panic and, searching for her parents, fell into a well shaft. It took hours for her parents to find the body. "She was the laughter of the house," her mother said.

American officials declared the mission "definitely a success." As Major A. C. Roper explained, "It's all a coalition effort to help rid this country of people that stand against peace and stability." Roper's confidence was grounded in intelligence indicating that Hajji Burget Khan had been meeting with senior Taliban leaders. That charge, it turned out, was true, but only in the most literal sense: he had been trying to convince the Talibs to support the Karzai government. The brief against him had been written almost entirely from the accusations of Sherzai and his allies. "Burget Khan was too independent," said Hajji Ehsan, a member of the Kandahar government. "He was independently popular and Sherzai saw him as a threat."

In the weeks following the killing, Ishaqzai tribespeople from around the country descended on Maiwand to pay their respects. The large Ishaqzai community in Pakistan staged angry protests. In the years to come thousands would be killed on all sides, but it would be the memory of Hajji Burget Khan's murder that villagers would never relinquish.

The men of Band-i-Timor were no strangers to tragedy, and as the summer came they returned to their fields, gathering at the mosque on Fridays to talk about the work and the rains and the future. Then, one morning in August, three months after the death of Burget Khan, they learned that US forces had raided Maiwand again, this time arresting the entire police force—ninety-five officers—in one precinct. The government announced that the captives were "al Qaeda-Taliban." Locals were mystified. "They were part of the government," said the police chief of a nearby station. "The government paid for their salaries and food. I don't understand how they could do this." The policemen had, in fact, been appointed by Hajji Bashar, the Noorzai elder who had worked so assiduously to win support for the new government. Within days of the arrests, a new police unit took over the precinct—all of them Sherzai's men. Meanwhile, the captured policemen in US custody were beaten, some of them suffering broken ribs, and stripped of their possessions, only to be released eventually, with the government spokesman admitting that officials "never had hard evidence" of a connection to militants. Instead, the spokesman acknowledged that "these people were all tribesmen of Hajji Bashar and very loyal to him."

The mood in Band-i-Timor continued to harden. If the government could do this "to their own people," said Amanullah, a storeowner, "then there is no guarantee they won't come after regular people. No one is safe from this." Some weeks later US forces stormed Band-i-Timor once again, this time detaining Hajji Nasro, a local leader and supporter of Hajji Bashar who had also allied with the new government.

The noose was tightening around Hajji Bashar himself. At first he had met regularly with US military and intelligence officials. The goal, he later told a reporter, "was to make the situation in Afghanistan stable and also to help the Americans negotiate with moderate members of the Taliban to reconcile with the government." But now the writing was on the wall: the Americans were not fighting a war on terror at all, they were simply targeting those who were not part of the Sherzai and Karzai networks. Bashar fled with his family to Pakistan to wait for the dust to settle.

Bashar's story might have ended there, if not for his unquenchable ambition to land a position in the Afghan government. By 2005 he would rekindle contacts with American intelligence, who connected him with officials from the US Drug Enforcement Agency and the Federal Bureau of Investigation. Over tea in a series of meetings in Dubai and Pakistan, he opened up about some of his business activities in hopes of winning Western backing for his political aspirations. The Americans, however, had other plans. Bush administration officials had drawn up a list of the most wanted international drug barons who posed a threat to US interests. When Assistant Secretary of State Bobby Charles saw it, he asked, "Why don't we have any Afghan drug lords on the list?" This was, in fact, a thorny problem, because some of the biggest Afghan narcotics kingpins—Gul Agha Sherzai and Ahmed Wali Karzai, the president's brother, chief among them—were allied with Washington, and in some cases even paid by the Americans. Finally, US officials settled on a name: Hajji Bashar. He was a small-time player on a list of heavyweights, and potentially valuable to Washington as a peace broker, but political expediency sealed his fate.

Bashar was lured by the FBI to an Embassy Suites hotel in New York City. For days they spoke on intelligence matters, sharing meals and tea. When they finished, he was—to his astonishment—handcuffed and read his rights. A trial on drug charges followed, and he is now serving a life sentence at Brooklyn Metropolitan Detention Center.

The Noorzais and Ishaqzais, the two largest tribal populations of Maiwand, had lost key leaders, both of them bridges to the Americans, and now the communities felt cut adrift. "We felt decapitated," said elder Kala Khan. "How could we convince our people that the Americans were our allies after this?"

As the seasons turned, the raids continued. Band-i-Timor was also the home of Akhtar Muhammad Mansur, former head of the Taliban air force, who had retired and offered his backing to the new government. Watching the violence unfold, he repeatedly approached government officials, pledging his support to anyone who would listen. Finally, learning that he was on the American target list, he, too, fled to Pakistan. Unlike Hajji Bashar, however, he abandoned reconciliation. Years later, he would become one of the leaders of the Taliban insurgency.

To the Americans, Sherzai's "intelligence" rang true because the tribes populating Maiwand had supported the Taliban when the movement first appeared. But the exigencies of the war on terror meant that US forces were unable to recognize when those same tribes switched allegiances in 2001—which is precisely what made Maiwand so lucrative in Sherzai's eyes. There were weapons to be requisitioned, tribal elders to be shaken down, reward money to be collected—boundless profits to be made. For Sherzai and his allies, it was indeed the New Dubai.

Once, when soldiers had come through Band-i-Timor, locals would smile and call out in greeting, but now they only watched in silence. People started carrying weapons again. The raids continued and villagers began fighting back, and that meant some people were caught in the middle. Soon, for many there was no choice but to leave. Whole villages decamped to Pakistan, deserting their fields, returning to refugee camps. It was a development that officials in Kandahar city could not ignore, but they insisted that it was a necessary evil in the fight against terror. "Sometimes, the best way to catch a fish is to drain the pond," said Khan Muhammad, a high-ranking security official.

What if, however, there were no fish to begin with?

The air was cooling down and I knew the sky would darken soon, so it was time to leave Band-i-Timor. Three boys lined up to watch as the truck I was in pulled away, kicking up dust all around. I sat with a tribal elder, my guide, who had fled the area for Kandahar city years before. He pointed out the orchards of his youth, now standing wild and untended. Farther on, the road had disappeared under desert sand. Our truck labored across the gravel hills and onto the highway. We passed an empty police checkpoint, and then an armed man on a motorcycle appeared, his face covered in a bandanna. He gave our truck a friendly wave and rode on toward Band-i-Timor. By nightfall, we had returned safely to Kandahar city.

I would return frequently to southern Afghanistan, each time discovering new fragments of this lost history. On one trip I found myself in a roomful of tribal elders when a militiaman walked in and sat in the corner. When he learned that I was a foreigner, his face clouded. Throughout dinner, I could feel his eyes on me. Young boys came in to clear the empty plates and the elders walked out into the courtyard to stretch, and then, for a moment, I was alone with him.

"Tell me something," he said. "What do you think about Gul Agha Sherzai?"

Without knowing who the militiaman was or who he was connected to among the panoply of elders here, it was a question to dread.

"Well," I said, as diplomatically as I could. "I know he's a famous man. He's well known around here."

The man broke into a broad grin. "Yes, he's famous. Everyone loves him. He's a national hero."

It turned out that the man was one of Sherzai's commanders. He introduced himself as Sher Muhammad and spent the rest of the evening recounting his exploits as a Sherzai hit man, targeting "Taliban and al-Qaeda criminals" side by side with the Americans. Often, he told me, his team wound up arresting the same person again and again, and one day he had suggested to his boss that it might be easier simply to kill their captives.

"But Sherzai looked at me angrily and called me naive." Then, he said, Sherzai held up a hard-boiled egg. "You see this? There are two ways to peel this egg. One is to break it open forcefully, but then you make a mess, and you'll lose some of the yolk. The other way is to do it carefully, a number of small cracks one after the other—and you get as much as you can out of it. That's why we keep arresting them."

Later I mentioned my encounter with Sher Muhammad to Sharafuddin, an old man I had befriended who ran a small bakery in downtown Kandahar, and he replied with a story of his own. A banged-up war hero from the anti-Soviet jihad, Sharafuddin had a bullet still lodged in his arm, shrapnel in his back, and a prosthetic testicle. His mujahedeen unit had contained a number of future Taliban figures, but ever since the Russian withdrawal he had abjured politics, opting instead to tend his bakery. By 2002, deep into his twilight years, he was arising daily at three a.m. to knead dough.

That year, trucks rolled up to the bakery one morning and men surrounded the building with weapons drawn. Sharafuddin had seen them around town. They were Sherzai's people. As soon as he stepped out, they were on him. He was thrown into the back of a Toyota, his feet were bound, and the barrel of a gun was thrust at his temple.

"You're a terrorist," one said.

Sharafuddin was taken to KAF, where American interrogators accused him of being a member of al-Qaeda. When he denied it, telling them that this was all some horrendous mistake, metal hooks were inserted in his mouth. They twisted, and he screamed. Then the soldiers applied electric shocks.

"But compared to what happened next, this was pleasant," he told me. "The Americans had treated me like a real guest." Transferred back to Sherzai's intelligence team, Sharafuddin was brought to a nondescript government transportation office. In the basement, unknown to the office workers above, was a series of windowless rooms. It was a secret prison. There, his hands and feet were bound and he was hung upside down from the ceiling. "I was dangling like a goat in a butcher shop," he recalled.

For the next eighteen days, twenty-three hours a day, he hung there. "I even pissed on myself," he said. "I tasted my own piss. It tasted like battery acid." Twice a day the interrogators would enter the room. There were six of them, wearing civilian clothes, and they would take turns striking him. Hanging next to him was Hajji Muhammad, a tribal elder and landlord, who one day was beaten so badly that blood poured from his mouth, dripping down his jowls and into his nose. Through the whole night Sharafuddin listened to him moaning and sobbing. In the morning men came, untied him, and took him away.

Sharafuddin was accused of conspiring to attack the Americans, but everyone present understood the trumped-up nature of the charges. It took more than two weeks for his relatives to borrow 50,000 rupees—about $800—and buy his release. Upon returning home, Sharafuddin learned that Hajji Muhammad had succumbed to his wounds. He himself could hardly move for weeks. "I felt like my joints were severed," he recalled. "I felt needles all the time. Even my hands felt heavy."

Months went by, and then he was arrested again. The nightmare repeated itself, and again his family scrounged together funds to buy his freedom.

Over the years, it became a ritual of torture. Sharafuddin began planning for the arrests, putting money away monthly, the way someone might save for a new car.

Then one day in 2005, the Taliban—by then reconstituted—buried a bomb outside the home of the commander heading Sherzai's intelligence unit. The blast killed him instantly, and Sharafuddin was never bothered again.

6

To Make the Bad Things Good Again

One morning in early 2002, superintendent Abdul Ali approached the main schoolhouse in Khas Uruzgan. A fresh layer of snow blanketed the street and there was no traffic in sight. The building up ahead stood without commotion, just as it had during the Taliban years.

He walked up to the front gate and saw that it had been smashed in. The security guards were missing. The place smelled of something acrid, like seared metal. When Ali stepped inside and crossed the parking lot he saw the cars, every one of them torched. They looked as black as burnt bread. Near the door to the main building the soles of his shoes began to squish, and he glanced down and recoiled. It was blood. When he looked up he saw it everywhere, smeared on the walls, puddled on the walkway.

Carefully, he opened the front door. The building had served as a temporary headquarters for the new government, but now the hallways were empty and silent. He turned the knob of a classroom and stepped inside. There, lying on blood-sodden sleeping mats, were the bodies of Abdul Qudus—a pro-American government official—and his aides. It appeared that most of them had been slaughtered in their beds.

Feeling sick and unsteady, Ali headed out the back door onto the playground. Splayed out on the snow was another body. It was Shah Muhammad, a government official, a supporter of Hamid Karzai and opponent of the Taliban. A splintered femur protruded from his thigh, and he had a single bullet hole in his back. His hands were bound with plastic cuffs bearing markings that Ali couldn't understand. They read: "US Pat. No. 5651376. Other Pat. Pending."

"Justice," Jan Muhammad told me years later, "justice is the most important thing. You see, without it, you can't have stability. That was on my mind always—how do I ensure justice? How do I make the bad things good again?" We sat cross-legged on his guest-room floor, sipping green tea, on a warm spring day in 2010. With glass tables and gold-framed portraits of President Karzai, ornate curio pieces and finely crafted porcelain vases, the room was airy and clean—and he was proud of every inch of it. "I earned all of this," he told me, unprompted, "not like those warlords who steal land. I'm not a thief." Seated nearby were the hangers-on and acolytes you tend to accrue in Afghanistan when you are a man of means and power: a pair of bodyguards, two or three cousins, a secretary, someone who dealt with guests, and an old man with no discernible role. There was also a young boy whom Jan Muhammad liked to keep around. "He has beautiful eyes," he explained.

Since his release from prison, Jan Muhammad had found a new lease on life. In January 2002, he was appointed by Karzai as governor of Uruzgan—the post he had held before the Taliban days. For friends and supporters it was as if the world had been righted again, as if the Taliban years could be forgotten. But Jan Muhammad discovered that he could not forget. In meetings, at dinner, at night with his family, he found his thoughts wandering back to that darkened cell, to that open latrine. Still, he threw himself into the task of remaking Uruzgan as best he could. Unlike most other governors, he had received special dispensation from Karzai to directly appoint personnel in Uruzgan's ten districts. Each district had its own governor and police chief, who would answer to Jan Muhammad alone.

"When I started," he said, "I tried to fix the nightmare the Taliban had left us. I had fought ten years against the Russians. Nearly died. I lost seven family members, I lost my best friends, my home was bombed. Despite it all, I fought and led our mujahedeen and liberated Uruzgan from the Russians. Then I was forced to hand everything over to the Taliban." He laughed a breathy, bitter laugh. "The rest of the story you know, the story of our nightmare."

As governor, his job was to restore order to the land and return Uruzgan to the simpler times, when rulers cared for their subjects, when duty and honor mattered. He often discussed this vision with Karzai. "We knew we'd have to leave the old way of doing politics behind," he said. He drew close, garlic and onions on his breath. "The problem, you see, was that the Taliban were clever. Their spies were everywhere. They had supporters. If you took a nap"—he snapped his fingers—"they'd kill you."

Jan Muhammad knew that there was only one way to navigate through such intrigue: rely on those he already trusted. His tribesmen, the Popalzais, had stood by his side throughout the Taliban years. Some had been imprisoned simply for knowing him. Some had risked their lives to help spirit him away to Pakistan for his meetings with Karzai or had risked their freedom to smuggle money into prison for him. There is no community like the community of sorrow, and as far as he was concerned none had suffered more under the Taliban than the Popalzais. They had run things in Uruzgan for as long as anyone could remember, at least until the recent wars, and it was time to set things right.

So in every district Jan Muhammad appointed a Popalzai governor and police chief, or figures from closely related tribes. The trouble was, many of these communities had already chosen their own leaders during the waning days of the Taliban. In Khas Uruzgan, elders had elected as district governor an anti-Taliban personage from the mujahedeen era, a former school janitor named Tawildar Yunis ("Groundskeeper Yunis"). He was working out of the governor's house, along with a locally elected police chief and other officials, collecting weapons from surrendering Talibs. But they were not Popalzais and, even worse, maintained political links to one of Jan Muhammad's rivals from the civil war years. So Muhammad appointed a local Popalzai elder and friend of the Karzais, Abdul Qudus, as his governor. But Yunis refused to budge, the imprimatur of Khas Uruzgan elders lending his claims an undeniable air of legitimacy. Unswayed, Abdul Qudus then requisitioned the local school for himself and his coterie of followers, declaring that it was now the rightful governor's residence and that it was *his* job to collect Taliban weapons. In response, Yunis appealed to everyone from Gul Agha Sherzai to President Karzai himself, but none were willing to wade into the growing mess. Tensions rose by the day. Jan Muhammad's side began openly questioning Yunis's anti-Taliban bona fides, throwing him into fits of rage. He returned the favor by declaring Jan Muhammad's men soft on the Taliban.

The actual Taliban were perplexed. During the standoff, a trio of senior Taliban officials made their way to Khas Uruzgan to surrender to the new government: Tayeb Agha, an erudite, well-spoken twentysomething who had served as Mullah Omar's personal secretary and adviser; former finance minister Agha Jan Mutassim, who had publicly rejected calls from Pakistani clerics to wage jihad against the Americans; and Health Minister Mullah Abbas, the official who had been responsible for recruiting Heela and other women to study as nurses and midwives. All three had been members of the Taliban since the movement's inception. Their surrender should have been a political coup for the young Karzai government. But surrender to whom? Who was actually in charge?

It was late January 2002, and at the schoolhouse Abdul Qudus and his aides had settled into their rooms for the night. The building had a single narrow hallway with half a dozen dilapidated classrooms, a patio extending into the parking lot, and, as with all southern compounds, a mudbrick wall enclosing the premises. That evening, as an icy wind swept through the hallway, the security guards sat huddled together, wrapped in heavy pattus and dozing off.

Sometime during the night, a blast shook the front wall and startled them awake. It was a sound unlike any of them had heard before. A sudden white light flooded the compound. Rahim, a guard, ran into the parking lot. When he saw men in black balaclavas and boots, he did what he was paid to do, raising his weapon to fire at the intruders. They returned fire, and soon bullets were zipping past him. Abandoning his gun, Rahim fled through the back.

Inside the building, Abdul Qudus and the others lay listening in their beds. The voices outside were growing louder. Finally, Shah Muhammad, one of Qudus's bodyguards, loaded his weapon and stepped into the hallway, firing blindly into the darkness. Shots were returned and he was struck in the leg. Stumbling back into the classroom, he managed to crawl through an open window to the rear playground. Then a second and third Afghan official ventured into the hallway to confront the attackers. The identity of the assailants was still unclear.

Leading the charge, as it turned out, was Master Sergeant Anthony Pryor, a thirty-nine-year-old Green Beret, a member of an "A-team," billed in the trade as "door kickers" or "five-minute wonders" for their expertise in storming compounds and close-quarters combat. As Pryor later recounted it to a reporter, he was inching toward a classroom door when an Afghan struck him from behind, dislocating his shoulder and smashing his collarbone. Someone then dug his nails into Pryor's face, ripping off his night vision goggles. "He started sticking his stinking fingers into my eyeballs," Pryor said.

Neither side had the slightest idea who the other was. In the darkness, the Afghan government officials knew only that they were under assault, possibly from the Taliban out for revenge. Master Sergeant Pryor and the other members of the special forces team were convinced that they were up against hardened al-Qaeda fighters.

In great pain, Pryor was struggling to stand up when an Afghan jumped on him and the pair came crashing to the floor—a blessing for Pryor, since the impact popped his shoulder back into place. A solid man, Pryor had the strength of a horse and was quickly atop his adversary. He broke the Afghan official's neck and shot him dead with a 9mm pistol.

Then, crab-walking along the wall, he drew closer to the classroom where Abdul Qudus and other Afghan officials lay cowering in their cots. There are no witnesses to what happened next. Pryor claims that he acted in self-defense, but Khas Uruzgan residents point out that the bodies were found in their beds, handcuffed, and there were no signs of struggle. Either way, every official was killed. In twenty minutes, the violence was over.

Or so it seemed. A US attack on a group of pro-American officials would have been a shocking turn of events under any circumstances, but things would only get stranger. Down the road from the schoolhouse stood the governor's compound, a sprawling collection of administrative buildings including a police headquarters, a jail, and a weapons depot. It was home to Yunis and his allies, and their guards were sitting near the main gate when it, too, burst open and shouting men rushed through, the white lights glaring and explosions going off all around. Security guard Abdul Nafeh raised his weapon in defense, but a torrent of bullets cut him down instantly.

Inside a single-room police hut, the clamor awoke chief of police Malek Rauf. A large man with a hearty laugh, Rauf had been elected by a tribal council as part of the Yunis administration, a decision spurred in part by his anti-Taliban credentials and his renown from the Soviet days. He recognized the invaders' shouts as English and realized immediately that these must be Americans. "Don't worry," he said to one of his men, "they are our friends." As the soldiers rushed in, he threw up his hands and shouted in Farsi, "We're friends! Friends, friends, friends!" But he was seized and hurled to the floor, and boots kicked him hard. He heard his ribs crack.

Inside the governor's hut, governor Tawildar Yunis sat listening to the commotion outside. As the shouting drew closer, he squeezed out the back window, climbed over the compound wall, and escaped into the night. Others were attempting to flee as well, but not all were as fortunate. Sixteen-year-old Muhammad Karim was later found with a bullet in his head.

The survivors of both attacks were rounded up and loaded onto helicopters. As they flew off, AC-130 gunships sprayed the compounds with rockets, sparking an explosion in the weapons cache at the school and engulfing the parking lot in flames. It would be hours before the first villagers ventured into the charred sites. In the governor's compound, they found that the attackers had left behind a calling card. Emblazoned with the symbol of an American flag, it bore a handwritten message: "Have a nice day. From Damage, Inc."

The toll from the two attacks: twenty-one pro-American leaders and their employees dead, twenty-six taken prisoner, and a few who could not be accounted for. Not one member of the Taliban or al-Qaeda was among the victims. Instead, in a single thirty-minute stretch the United States had managed to eradicate both of Khas Uruzgan's potential governments, the core of any future anti-Taliban leadership—stalwarts who had outlasted the Russian invasion, the civil war, and the Taliban years but would not survive their own allies. People in Khas Uruzgan felt what Americans might if, in a single night, masked gunmen had wiped out the entire city council, mayor's office, and police department of a small suburban town: shock, grief, and rage.

Once again Police Chief Malek Rauf was forced to the ground. Looking up he could see bright lights and cages, men shouting from inside the cages, and American soldiers shouting back. Every few moments he was hit with something stiff, maybe a belt, and kicked with steel-toed boots. His friends were lying prone beside him, crying out, "We're Karzai's people!" as they were beaten.

They were in a hangar at Kandahar Airfield. Many hours had passed since the raids. Their hands and feet were shackled, each prisoner chained to the next. Soldiers "were walking on our backs like we were stones," Rauf later recalled. Another captive said, "I was so afraid, I did not expect to remain alive and see my family again."

When news of the massacre reached Jan Muhammad's ears, he could hardly believe it. Someone had falsely tipped off the special forces that Abdul Qudus and the others at the school building were Taliban fighters, pointing to their large weapons stores and the three high-ranking Talibs in the neighborhood. The Americans "know who is responsible," he fumed to a reporter. "People have died. Whoever is responsible should be executed." Muhammad couldn't prove it, but he was sure that it was Yunis and his cronies, looking to eliminate their rivals, who had tipped off the Americans. Yet someone else had also cast Yunis as a Talib, pointing to *his* large weapons stores and reports of high-ranking Talibs in the area. Muhammad swore for days afterward that his hands were clean, but elders in Khas Uruzgan who had backed Yunis believed differently.

What neither side could understand was how the two sets of allegations had made it to the Americans unreconciled. In fact, both pieces of intelligence from the rival camps had climbed all the way up to CENTCOM, the United States Central Command in Tampa, Florida. Specialists there had analyzed photos of the two sites and concluded that both were likely "al Qaeda compounds." CENTCOM had then issued an order to KAF-based Special Operations Forces to raid the two rival sites, a mis-

sion designated as AQ-048. In the weeks before the attacks a reconnaissance team had attempted site surveillance three times, in each instance
being thwarted by equipment malfunction or inclement weather. But
despite never having laid eyes on the sites, CENTCOM ordered the mission to proceed. Companies with the First Battalion, Fifth Special Forces
Group, took the job, splitting into two teams for the twin nighttime
assaults and bringing with them a New Zealand unit as well as FBI agents
to interrogate suspects.

The only sign that something might have gone terribly wrong came
after the killings, when troops discovered flags of the new Afghan government in both compounds. CENTCOM in Florida was radioed, and
the troops were assured that "no, there are no friendlies at the site."

It took weeks for the Americans to admit any error, at which point
Malek Rauf and the others were released from KAF—which American
soldiers had dubbed "Camp Slappy"—with an apology. The sixty-year-
old Rauf could not stand for weeks, and his skin bore the welts of torture.
To soothe tempers, he was reinstated as the district's official police chief.
Then, not missing a beat, Jan Muhammad maneuvered to install one of
his own allies, Qudus Khan—no relation to Abdul Qudus—as the Khas
Uruzgan district governor. (Half a year later, Qudus Khan would come
knocking on Heela's door to ask her about overseeing the vocational
training center.) Tawildar Yunis, meanwhile, fled town, never to be seen
again. The trio of top Taliban officials who had been trying to surrender
saw that they would be marked men regardless of their intentions and
left for Pakistan, where in coming years they would play a prominent
role in the anti-American insurgency. A year after the raid, despite
Washington's admission that it had killed only pro-American civilians,
seven soldiers involved in the attacks received a Bronze Star for valor.
Master Sergeant Anthony Pryor, for his part, was awarded a Silver Star.

"The greatest thing that ever happened to this country," Jan Muhammad
told me, "was the coming of the Americans. They're true friends." From
the beginning, he had reason enough to be grateful. The United States
had brought the business of counterterrorism to the Tirin Kot desert,
and Jan Muhammad would be just the man to oversee the new venture.

Like Sherzai in Kandahar, he leased land—which wasn't his—to the US military for a base and supplied fellow tribesmen as construction workers. The instant profits were reinvested in the buildup of a private army, another Afghan Blackwater, a force under his control but rented out to the US military. He diversified his portfolio to include development work and trucking and, like any good Uruzgani landowner, opium. Soon he had reclaimed his pre-Taliban honorific *khan*, the suffix of the rich and powerful. To the Americans, he became simply JMK.

By midmorning, the courtyard of the governor's mansion would fill with hundreds of turbaned men squatting ears to knees, waiting their turn for an audience. Many of them were tribal elders and district officials looking to petition JMK for funds and services. If you were a poor, sunburned farmer living where the soil was bone dry and you wanted the village to fix your irrigation ditch, you'd ask your *malek*, or village headman, for assistance. But the malek would have no discretionary funds of his own because local officials lacked the ability to collect taxes. So he would request aid from the district governor or other such authority, who, in turn, would appeal to the provincial governor or regional strongman, who ultimately sourced his wealth from the Americans.

The politician is a particular type of creature never found far from money, but in most societies he or she usually also bears the burden of legitimacy, of winning votes by articulating a program and selling visions of a better life. In Afghanistan, however, government budgets have long rested on the rickety edifice of international aid, so power has depended solely on one's proximity to that aid. For that poor, sunburned farmer, repairs for his irrigation ditch hinged entirely on whether his malek had the necessary connections in Tirin Kot and Kabul, the right access. There was no commodity more precious. Access meant the difference between breathing in gravel dust on broken macadam roads and coasting along a paved highway. It meant the difference between gainful employment at a construction project and watching the work from afar. Between having a clinic nearby and dying at home.

In this pyramid of patronage the access brokers, from JMK on down to district-level officials, were the true political elites. If you did not belong to their networks, through tribe or clan or friendship, you were out of luck. In Uruzgan, this meant that an expanding web of Popalzai tribal officials was effectively cutting off other communities—in particular, the Ghilzai tribes—from access. For many in the Ghilzai elite, the only solution was to try cultivating the Americans on their own.

It was so hot that Aziz Mansour was staying indoors, but even from there he could smell the stench. He left his shop and walked out onto the dirt lane past the market stalls, others soon joining him. The odor was overwhelming and it was everywhere. As he walked to the central roundabout, the heart of Tirin Kot, where the main avenues converged and the shops pressed tightly together, he saw that there were no cars and no donkeys, just a gathering crowd. It was a good minute before he pushed his way through and saw it: dead bodies piled in a heap, many stripped naked. Flies everywhere. One head had been mashed to a pulp. He could not bring himself to look at the others.

When people stepped forward to remove the bodies, a man with a Kalashnikov slung across his shoulder approached and asked, "Are you their friends?" They stepped back. A jeep arrived with more armed men, who shouted and kicked people and pointed their guns until the crowd dispersed. The bodies lay decomposing for two days.

The previous evening, JMK's militia had shown up at the house of an influential Ghilzai elder named Pai Muhammad. He and some relatives were ordered outside, shackled, and forced to lie in the dirt. A commander then called someone on his satellite phone. "We've got him. What do you want us to do?"

On the other end of the line was JMK himself. He wanted the issue of Pai Muhammad resolved once and for all. Although Pai Muhammad had briefly allied with the Taliban in the 1990s, after the invasion he had thrown his support behind the Karzai government. In JMK's drive to "make the bad things good again," however, such a change of heart mattered little, and he had taken to angrily, frequently, and publicly denouncing the wave of Taliban surrenders. Like the Americans, he found the notion of a Taliban pardon abhorrent. It was about justice—not just for him, but for all those who had been wronged.

Unsurprisingly, Pai Muhammad saw things differently and had gone to JMK to plead his case. Rebuffed, he had then collected weapons from ex-Talibs and delivered them to the governor as a sign of their sincerity. But JMK was unswayed. The need for revenge had consumed him so thoroughly, and the imperatives of power had shaped him so perfectly, that he could not accept the surrenders as real. In his mind, the "Taliban" had become a fixed and timeless category of people, not an ephemeral political allegiance like all the others in his country. "We don't negotiate with terrorists," he had said.

That morning, as the men lay prone, the commander listened to JMK's reply and said, "Hold on." He raised his weapon and shot Pai Muhammad in the head, then turned back to the phone. "Did you hear that?"

The others on the ground began shouting and struggling. Almost at once the militiamen were upon them, and soon the captives lay bloodied on the ground. Some had their clothes ripped off. One of the men was taken aside. Then a soldier climbed into his jeep, turned on the ignition, maneuvered the vehicle around to face the other captives, and drove over them. And then back again. The lifeless bodies were tossed into the back of the jeep, driven to the town center, and dumped at the roundabout, where they would lie for all to see and learn from. The survivor was released to "warn others what happens when you support the Taliban." It was early 2002, and throughout Uruzgan people understood: there was a new sheriff in town.

The killings shook the Ghilzai community. "Pai Muhammad was beloved," said Abdul Matin of the Afghan Independent Human Rights Commission. "You can make one hundred faces recoil with just one slap. Every Ghilzai knew that his tribe was under attack." When Mullah Manan, who had been living a quiet life on his farm since the battle of Tirin Kot, heard the news he felt sick. Worried Ghilzai elders convened a grand council and concluded that they should redouble their efforts to demonstrate loyalty to the new government and the Americans.

Key to this campaign was a bespectacled ex-mujahedeen commander named Muhammad Nabi. Unlike many Ghilzai elders, he had openly defied the Taliban—which had landed him in the same prison as JMK, until both men were saved by Karzai. Upon his release, Nabi had publicly endorsed Karzai and the Americans. Still, that did not stop US forces from raiding his home some months later, breaking his windows, destroying his car, and tossing his clothes about. Supposedly the issue was a set of weapons from the 1980s. Nabi turned them over immediately. A week later the troops returned, this time accompanied by JMK's men. Nabi pleaded that he had surrendered everything, but they ransacked the house again, and, when nothing was found, he was arrested anyway and locked up in the governor's private prison.

A man of means and influence, a key access broker for thousands of Ghilzais, Nabi reacted like an aristocrat mistakenly accused of petty theft. "It was a disgrace," he recalled. "In the old days no one would treat an elder that way." He was grilled by JMK's interrogators about hidden weapons, and, when he continued to deny their existence, they threatened to send him to Guantanamo. "I love Cuba!" he answered back sarcastically. "Better there than this hell."

It took the intercession of Karzai himself for Nabi to regain his freedom. Ten days later, a sharecropper was laboring in the cherry orchards of the Nabi estate when he spotted something odd in the distance, atop a hill overlooking the fields. He crept close to see. Giant wheels. Wires and guns and men. It was the Americans again.

He hurried back to warn Nabi. The old man had had enough. He called some friends, who showed up armed. "I decided," he said, "that they wouldn't take me alive."

Crouching amid the apple trees, he watched as a column of US troops made their way through his orchard. Then a farmhand arrived to tell him that JMK's forces were moving in from a different direction. The Americans drew closer. "Muhammad Nabi of the Tokhis, please surrender yourself," their megaphone blared, referring to his subtribe of the Ghilzais.

Just then, Nabi saw JMK's plainclothes agents stumble into the Americans' path. In the confusion, he made a break for it. By sunset he was in the mountains overlooking Tirin Kot, the same peaks he'd retreated to twenty years earlier to fight the Soviets.

Nabi's family members were arrested and yet again the house was ransacked, but no weapons were found. This time, however, Nabi chose not to return. He fled to Pakistan with his closest followers. Thousands of Ghilzais lost their broker, their point of access to Kabul and the Americans.

One by one, other Ghilzai elders also began decamping for Pakistan.

Those who remained made a last-ditch effort to connect with the Americans. Ghulam Nabi (no relation to Muhammad) was a well-regarded elder who had been harassed by JMK's men so frequently that one day he showed up at a US special forces base to plead for protection. Unsure what to do, the soldiers called JMK for advice. He promptly accused Nabi of being an insurgent mastermind, and the Americans shipped him off to their new detention facility at Bagram Airfield. Eventually released through President Karzai's intervention, Ghulam Nabi swore revenge and slipped away from home one night, never to be seen again.

By the end of that summer of 2002, Ghilzais across Uruzgan had been effectively squeezed out of access. "We never even spoke to Ghilzais in those days," recalled Dan Green, who worked for a US military Provincial Reconstruction Team in Uruzgan tasked with bringing development and aid to the province. "We had no contacts. We did everything through JMK and the big non-Ghilzai tribes."

Even as the Ghilzai elders were being rounded up, there was still no armed resistance to speak of. As in Kandahar, in Uruzgan the Taliban had surrendered and al-Qaeda had fled, leaving the Americans without an enemy to fight. Nonetheless, with JMK at the helm, targets were never in short supply.

When the Taliban had chased Karzai during his abortive 2001 uprising, he had taken shelter with an Uruzgani named Muhammad Lal. Karzai never forgot the kindness, and after winning the presidency he gifted him a model of an Air China 757. Months later, Lal openly criticized JMK, and without missing a beat US forces raided his home. Lal wasn't present, but they found the model airplane—proof enough for them of an al-Qaeda presence. "Two of the four aircraft commandeered by terrorists for last year's attacks on the World Trade Center and the Pentagon were 757s," the State Department noted. In the subsequent months, Lal's home was subjected to repeated raids, until he fled to Kabul for safety.

As winter settled across Uruzgan and people marked the first full year since the Taliban's downfall, tit-for-tat killings and feuds over access to the Americans continued. But a new political order was slowly, undeniably crystallizing, unwittingly enforced by American forces.

Away from the Pashtun south, the story was different. In the northern province of Balkh, for example, two warlords—Rashid Dostum and

Muhammad Atta—jockeyed for control, leading to multiple small-scale skirmishes. The possibility of open warfare seemed all too real, but things never came to a head. Instead, United Nations negotiators were able to preserve the peace, as Atta accepted a governorship and Dostum a post in Kabul. I asked Eckart Schiewek, then a political advisor with the UN mission to Afghanistan, why the outcome was so different, why the southern pattern of killings had never taken hold. "There were no American troops," he replied, pointing out that almost the entire US military presence was concentrated in the Pashtun south and east near the Pakistani border. "You couldn't call on soldiers to settle your feuds."

Anthropologist Noah Coburn found a similar dynamic in his study of Istaliff, a district near Kabul similar in size to Khas Uruzgan but with no regular US troop presence. "International military forces," he wrote, had "little interest in involving themselves in local politics" in Istaliff. Because none of the various Afghan factions competing for power enjoyed privileged access to foreign troops, no group could outmuscle the other, and no one "seriously considered trying to establish hegemonic control over town politics." The result was a tenuous, fragile stability—but stability nonetheless. No communities were severed from state access, nor were there cycles of bloody revenge. And, to this day in Istaliff, there is no anti-American insurgency.

In southern Afghanistan, the mix of American boots on the ground and strongmen itching to outflank their rivals prevented such détentes. Day by day, marginalized southern communities from one valley to the next were slipping out of the government's orbit. The Americans were beginning to wear out their welcome—and it was only going to get worse.

7

Black Holes

Noor Agha could feel the shackles digging into his wrists. First one arm was yanked upward, then the other. Blindfolded, he still knew what was coming. It was a familiar script. A nightmarish play. Arms reached around his waist, hoisted him up, and then released him. He dropped down until the dangling ceiling chains caught and he was left there hanging, waiting for the door to open again.

When it did, he heard footsteps and then a deep, low growl. The dog's teeth cut into his leg and he tried to cry out, but with his gag he could not. Soon, he was bitten again.

When he was finally untied and brought down, the blindfold was removed and he blinked at the American soldiers standing around him. They asked about al-Qaeda and the Taliban, about names he'd never heard. They were not at all pleased with his responses.

Noor Agha was in a quandary. He had served with the Afghan National Police in Gardez, a mud-caked town in the southeastern part of the country, in a unit with a well-known anti-Taliban history. He and his friends had opposed the Taliban during the 1990s, and when the United States invaded he had assured friends that "America will save us."

Nonetheless, one summer day in 2003 he had been arrested without explanation. By now, he'd been in captivity at a tiny US base for more than a week. Back in the interrogation room the following day, he found himself kneeling on a long wooden bar with his hands tied to a pulley above. He was then pushed back and forth, the bar rolling across his shins, as the interrogators asked their questions over his screams.

The following day, he was lying with his back against the wooden floor as soldiers stood over him. His mouth was pried open, and bottle after bottle of water was poured down his throat. He felt as if his stomach were about to burst, and then blacked out. When he awoke, he vomited uncontrollably. The questions continued.

It took another week for his transfer to the main prison at Bagram where, to his great relief, the interrogators came less frequently. He was never told why he had been detained. One day, just as mysteriously, he was handed a letter acknowledging his wrongful imprisonment and told to go home.

Noor Agha's path signaled the moral morass that the American mission was sinking into. At every step the United States may have been the hapless victim of Afghan strongmen, but it was also setting the rules of the game, and then following those rules through to their logical, bloody conclusions. The war on terror had become an end in itself, the ultimate self-fulfilling prophecy.

His story begins in the district of Zurmat, where the highlands of the southeastern Afghan-Pakistani border give way to the broad floodplains of the interior. With its neat bazaars and roadside soda vendors, its rectilinear farming plots and fields of apricot and apple, Zurmat had the look of an ideal summer destination for future Western tourists—had it not also been home to the Shah-i-Kot Valley, a rocky, imposing gorge that offered the perfect redoubt for retreating armies. After the US invasion, a few hundred Taliban and al-Qaeda fighters holed up in its snowy summits under the command of local Taliban leader Saif ur-Rahman Mansur. Far from home and fearful of traveling into Pakistan, the fighters were low on options, so Mansur sent a letter to the Afghan government offering talks to end his "armed defiance of the interim administration." Secret negotiations were launched, but with Kabul and Washington in no mood for reconciliation, the initiative quickly collapsed. US troops stormed the valley in a campaign dubbed Operation Anaconda, the American military's largest set-piece battle since the first Gulf War. In a decisive victory, Mansur was killed, along with dozens or perhaps hundreds of enemy fighters. Eight US soldiers, and an unknown number of civilians, also lost their lives.

After Anaconda, Zurmat was etched into American minds as a Taliban haven. And the small district had indeed produced more Taliban than any other outside the deep south, earning it the sobriquet "Little Kandahar." But much as in post-2001 Kandahar, the Taliban in Zurmat—with the sole exception of Mansur's crew—had retired to their homes. The most prominent to abandon the movement was Taliban cleric Khalilullah Firozi, who openly supported Karzai and was entreating others to do likewise. Early on, however, Firozi's home was raided and he was imprisoned by US forces. It would be the first in a series of raids over the coming year against anyone understood to have been even remotely connected to the ancien régime. American troops invaded the dwelling of a prominent pro-government preacher, Mullah Hayatullah, on the mistaken impression that he opposed Karzai. They stormed the home of Hajji Wodin, a popular philanthropist and comedian. They burst into the residence of well-known Taliban defector Abdul Ghaffar Akhundzada, who, assuming thieves had broken in, scrambled up to the roof and opened fire on the intruders. The Americans returned fire, prompting a neighbor—under the impression that the village was under attack from thieves or a rival clan—to run to the mosque and implore fellow villagers over the loudspeaker to rush to Akhundzada's defense. Neighbors started shooting from their homes; soon the Americans had a full-fledged battle on their hands. They called in air support, and only then did Akhundzada realize that these were in fact foreign troops. He turned himself in and was sent to Guantanamo Bay.

Through the decades of war, Afghans had survived by knowing where they stood, by calibrating themselves to power, the only sure bet in the frequent U-turns of Afghan history. In Zurmat, this was now proving impossible. "We didn't understand this new government or who it supported," said Aref, a local mullah. "We supported them, but they targeted religious people. No one could understand it. I myself fled to Pakistan. We lived every day in fear."

If reconciled Taliban were in the crosshairs, Dr. Hafizullah figured he would fare better. A distinguished tribal elder with a long anti-Taliban track record, Hafizullah had come to prominence during the anti-Russian jihad. Afterward he had established a small pharmacy, which in the education-deprived countryside was enough to earn him the honorific of "doctor." Under Taliban rule, he had been imprisoned and tortured for refusing to comply with their social edicts. After 2001, he won a tribal election and became Zurmat's first post-Taliban governor.

By all accounts a popular and competent official, Hafizullah was nonetheless an early victim of Kabul politicking, and in mid-2002 he was replaced with a Karzai flunky. Under the new administration, crime soared. Rogue police units terrorized the local highways, shaking down motorists and robbing merchants at gunpoint. As the district descended into open banditry, the government formed an emergency task force and called upon Dr. Hafizullah to head it. His commission established a criminal investigations team, the first of its kind in the area, and launched a crackdown against growing antigovernment sentiment, decreeing that anyone caught opposing Kabul would have his house burned down—a local tribal custom—and be fined nearly $50,000.

These were, to be sure, not the actions of a Taliban supporter—yet this was exactly how Hafizullah would be branded. The criminal investigations had turned over a stone too many to suit the powers that be, and things came to a head when his commission initiated a probe into a reported theft of $3,000 from local shopkeepers. Hafizullah tracked down the getaway car sitting brazenly by the main police station, a facility under the command of Abdullah Mujahed, a key American ally. He confronted the police chief—in public, no less—and forced him to repay the victims. Mujahed swiftly secured his revenge, informing the Americans that Hafizullah was a Taliban double agent. The ex-governor was promptly detained by US troops under accusations of providing "operational and logistical support for al Qaeda operations." A rash of wild charges followed, including an allegation that the $3,000 that he had recovered had in fact come from terrorists. He was banished to Guantanamo.

With Dr. Hafizullah out of the picture, Zurmat had lost a key point of state access. Fortunately for the district, another still remained. Commander Naim was an eminent tribal elder who had been elected security chief of Zurmat following the Russian departure, stayed on through the Taliban years, and was reelected in 2002. An ardent supporter of the Americans and one of the most popular figures in Zurmat, he nonetheless discovered one day that some men under his command had been detained by US troops. When Naim showed up to ask why, he, too, was arrested, blindfolded, and handcuffed. "They stripped me naked, out in the open, where everyone could see," he told a reporter. "I was thinking that these are infidels who have come to a Muslim country to imprison us, just like the Russians."

Taken from one base to the next, Naim eventually found himself shackled in the wire-mesh cages of Kandahar Airfield. "We were without hope because we were innocent," he recalled. "I was very sad because I could not see my children, family, friends. But what could we do?" Like Hafizullah, he was sent to Guantanamo.

Naim's downfall could be traced to Mullah Qassim, a longtime rival and Taliban follower who had reconciled with the new government and passed along the spurious intelligence that Naim was a terrorist. Soon, however, US military officials got wise to Mullah Qassim's Taliban past and descended upon his village to arrest him. The crafty mullah, however, had already fled to Pakistan. The Americans nonetheless detained a farmer named Qassim, mistaking him for the mullah. He, too, was shipped to Guantanamo.

With Zurmat's two most influential pro-government figures, Naim and Hafizullah, out of the way, the road to power was open to anyone who had the Americans' ear. For a time, Samoud Khan, a small-time commander who led a unit paid for by the US special forces, played this game as well as anyone. He was expert in picking off rivals left and right by branding them as al-Qaeda, while indulging in a variety of unsavory activities, not least his predilection for young boys. (He forcibly kept a pair—"tea boys," in the local argot—with his unit.) One day, however, he made the mistake of picking a fight with another local strongman who boasted ties of his own with the Americans. Soon, Khan himself was accused of supporting al-Qaeda and, in the usual turn of events, was arrested, beaten, and sent on to Bagram. Eight members of his unit, meanwhile, were rounded up and delivered to Guantanamo. Among them was one of those tea boys, Asadullah. At twelve years old, he became the prison's youngest inmate.

The US forces' conviction that the enemy threat was real—though there were no Taliban or al Qaeda to be found—deepened when Pacha Khan Zadran, an anti-Taliban warlord, turned against the Karzai government. Although he had been financed by US special forces, Zadran rebelled against Kabul when he was not awarded the governorship of three southeastern provinces. Soon his men were getting into skirmishes with US troops, even as he continued to denounce his own enemies as Taliban and al Qaeda. Rocket fire began to rain down upon American camps, and it grew even easier to manipulate US troops with spurious intelligence.

By the end of 2002, the twisted skein of alliances and betrayals had become impossible to disentangle. Take the case of Commander Parre, an anti-Taliban militiaman who controlled a checkpoint at a mountain pass near Zurmat. Parre cooperated with the Americans but ran afoul of Police Chief Abdullah Mujahed (the official who had stolen $3,000 from Zurmat shopkeepers) and other government figures. In short order, he was tricked into having tea with members of the Alabama National Guard's Twentieth Special Forces Group, who arrested him along with his entire unit.

At a nondescript US-run prison, Parre was forced to kneel on stones until he lost all sensation in his legs. At one point, his toenail was ripped off by an interrogator. He and the others were kicked, whipped with cables, and hosed with water. After a week, Parre's younger brother Jamal Nasir could barely walk. On a cold spring morning, complaining of intense abdominal pain, he asked to go to the bathroom. As two others supported him, Nasir's body suddenly went limp, and soon afterward his heart stopped. He had been tortured to death.

After two weeks of abuse, Parre and the others were dropped off at one of Mujahed's prisons. The police chief had consigned many a soul to American abuse, but the sight of those battered, near-death captives was too much even for him, and he petitioned for their release. In the eyes of the US special forces this constituted a grave betrayal, and a relationship that had already been souring took a dangerous turn. Almost overnight he was recast in the role of a man with questionable loyalties, a government official soft on terrorism. In a meeting attended by Mujahed and UN officials, an American officer threatened to kill him if he sided with those "opposing the Coalition."

The very structures that Mujahed had so ruthlessly exploited were about to turn on him. Soon he lost his post as police chief and was reassigned to a sinecure in Kabul. Months later, he was visiting home for a wedding when American soldiers dropped by and invited him to review intelligence at their base. Like so many others, Mujahed fell for the ruse of friendship and soon found himself locked up in a cage in Bagram. "They didn't allow us to sleep at all for thirteen days," he recalled.

Whenever he dozed off, a guard would strike his legs. Heavy metal music blared through the corridors. In the fleeting moments of silence, he could hear moans and cries but could not see where from.

One day soldiers appeared at his cage, and he was hauled outside and loaded onto an aircraft. They would not say where he was going. Many hours later the plane landed at another prison, where the air felt thick and wet. Mujahed was led through a row of cages as inmates in white and orange jumpsuits banged on the wire mesh and shouted, "This is Guantanamo! You are in Guantanamo!" In a sort of perverse poetic justice, he wound up in a cell near Dr. Hafizullah's.

While seizing Mujahed, the Americans also apprehended a number of his men, including drivers, cooks, and guards. Among them was Noor Agha. Years later, still battling memories of days spent hanging from a prison ceiling, he offered an epitaph for Zurmat and its environs: "There was no one left standing in the end. It was as if the whole system just devoured everyone."

Dr. Hafizullah, Zurmat's first governor, had ended up in Guantanamo because he'd crossed Police Chief Mujahed. Mujahed wound up in Guantanamo because he crossed the Americans. Security chief Naim found himself in Guantanamo because of an old rivalry with Mullah Qassim. Qassim eluded capture, but an unfortunate soul with the same name ended up in Guantanamo in his place. And a subsequent feud left Samoud Khan, another pro-American commander, in Bagram prison, while the boy his men had sexually abused was shipped to Guantanamo.

No one in this group had been a member of the Taliban or al-Qaeda. Some, like Abdullah Mujahed and Samoud Khan, certainly should have been brought to justice—but that was not Guantanamo's purpose. Others, like Commander Naim, were precisely the sort of pro-government figures that Washington had wanted to see at the helm of the new Afghanistan. Instead, Zurmat's mood of hope and reconciliation was rapidly giving way to one of rebellion.

Years later, Dr. Hafizullah and Commander Naim were finally transferred from Guantanamo to Afghan government custody, and then released following intense tribal pressure. Dr. Hafizullah returned to his pharmacy, while Naim resumed his role as tribal elder and mediator. But one winter night in 2009, the Americans came again for Hafizullah. He was led away in a hood and locked up in Bagram, where he still remains. He faces the usual set of charges, although Afghan officials and even some Western authorities vehemently deny their accuracy. The following year, Naim attended a meeting with the governor to discuss how they could convince insurgents to come in from the cold and support the government. Upon leaving, he was arrested by American special forces. Angry protests swept the province, and merchants carried out a three-day general strike in his support. But Naim, too, remains in Bagram to this day.

Far in the northeast, some 150 miles from Zurmat as the crow flies, in a deep valley of alder and white poplar dotted with small stone-and-timber houses, lies what was for a time one of the most dangerous corners of the planet for an American. The Korengal Valley was Afghanistan's Fallujah, a crucible for every flavor of radical Islamist the world over, an insurgent stronghold where more American soldiers met their end than almost anywhere outside the deep South. When I first heard about the Korengal I had, like most observers, chalked up the trouble to obdurate mountain folk and their preternatural hostility to foreigners. After all, the people of Pech, the broader valley system in which the Korengal lies, had been among the first to rebel against the Russians. But then I learned that they had resisted the Taliban as well, partly because, in addition to the usual excesses, the Taliban had clamped down on the timber trade, the lifeblood for these logging communities. It turned out, in fact, that Pech had actually welcomed US forces with open arms and that elders and community leaders had once jostled for access to the Americans.

When things changed, it began with a single man. The venerable Rohullah Wakil was a tribal leader who followed the ultraconservative strain of Islam found in Saudi Arabia. With sharp, thoughtful eyes, an aquiline nose, and a head of thinning salt-and-pepper hair, Wakil exuded distinction. Indeed, *wakil* ("lawmaker") had been appended to his name upon his election to Kunar's "parliament" in 1993, when the province briefly broke away to form its own ministate. Although he came from a line of fighters—his uncle was a locally renowned mujahed—Wakil had a softer edge, opting for a politician's life.

Despite his conservative background, Wakil had fiercely opposed the

Taliban and al-Qaeda, in part because his uncle had been assassinated in 1991 by an Arab at the behest, Wakil believed, of Osama bin Laden. (The al-Qaeda leader was at the time friendly with the family's bitter enemy, radical Islamist Gulbuddin Hekmatyar.) When the Taliban swept through the province in the late 1990s, Wakil's tribesmen were among the first to rally against them, taking to the mountains in a bloody guerrilla campaign. Wakil soon joined the pro-Western Northern Alliance and later took a job with the United Nations. In 2002 he was elected to the loya jirga, where he delivered an impassioned speech in front of thousands championing Karzai and the new government.

With the Coalition forces on the ground in Pech, the contracting money began to flow in. Wakil drew his share: hundreds of thousands of dollars from the British to help eradicate poppies. With such sums sloshing around, however, entrepreneurs and carpetbaggers of all shapes and sizes soon found their way to the Americans. Among these was Malik Zarin, a timber baron and tribal elder with an eye for whatever the foreign troops happened to be looking for, who quickly maneuvered his way into their good graces. With his starched vests and jet-black, tightly cropped beard, Zarin must have cut an impressively modern figure for the Americans in the backwaters of Pech, an impression no doubt bolstered by his special connection to US troops: his English-speaking sons. In a heartbeat, he became a key supplier of materiel and logistics as the Americans built up their presence in the area.

A not-so-subtle rivalry sprouted between Zarin and Wakil for contracting dollars and American access. With their sizable tribal influence, the two elders might have been a rich source of stability in the new Afghanistan. Wakil, in particular, was a striking image of exactly the type of ally Washington said it sought: reliably anti-Taliban, no trail of human rights abuses, and popular enough to bring America's message to the hinterlands. But the system in place did not reward stability, legitimacy, or popularity. Instead, it rewarded those who could serve up enemies, and that was Zarin's game.

On an August evening in 2002, Wakil hosted a gathering in his home that included the governor of Kunar Province and other key power brokers. The first grumblings of discontent with the Americans were already surfacing: patrolling US troops had twice shot and killed local Afghans carrying Kalashnikovs, mistaking them for enemy fighters. Wakil had convened the meeting to convince the local elite to placate their followers and redouble support for the American troops, who represented, in his words, "Afghanistan's only hope." The following day, he went to the nearby American base, asking the soldiers there to cooperate more closely with him to avoid such missteps in the future. As he left, he and his aides were stopped and cuffed. "Nothing made sense," he said later. "I just couldn't understand it."

In Bagram, following the usual pattern, they were interrogated and abused. Wakil was then shipped to Guantanamo. There, he was accused of supporting the followers of Hekmatyar (who, by 2002, had turned against the Americans)—an allegation ignoring the fact that a large part of the province's recent history had consisted of a long, bloody campaign against Hekmatyar by Wakil's party. He was also accused of opposing the Karzai government, of which he was actually a member; of being, on the one hand, a Wahabi, a member of a hard-line Islamic sect associated with the Saudis and al-Qaeda, and yet simultaneously of being part of a secret movement opposing the Wahabis; and of taking, along with his rival Zarin, $12,000 from Pakistani intelligence in order to "finance military operations" against the government and to disrupt the loya jirga, the grand assembly to which he'd been elected and at which he had spoken so stirringly.

Wakil appeared before a tribunal in Guantanamo to answer these byzantine and bizarre allegations. "If somebody is a leader of a tribe and that person is a bad guy, maybe the tribe would trust him one time. The tribe would not trust him again and again and again," he said, according to the transcript of his testimony. "I had been representative of my tribe since the Soviet Union left Afghanistan." He told the panel how he had been elected nearly a dozen times, and how he had worked with the Coalition forces. "I am so upset about the first court," he said, referring to a previous tribunal at Guantanamo, "because they called me an enemy combatant. I do not accept that. I do not believe that. The court told me that I was a threat to America and that I would remain a detainee. Now I am facing you and I assure you, I give you my word, I have been wrongly judged. I am not an American detainee. I am not an Afghan detainee. I am a detainee because of my personal [rivalries]."

In the end, the evidence looked so flimsy that even the Guantanamo tribunal members were apparently left bemused. "I just cannot help but ask," an official said in a hearing, "why are you here?" Nevertheless, Wakil remained in Guantanamo for five years.

Wakil's friend and colleague Sabar Lal, who had many brushes with death in the mountains fighting against the Taliban in the 1990s, also found himself in Guantanamo. In a similar tribunal hearing, he noted the paradox of his predicament: "All I can tell you is that I fought for six years against the Taliban. I killed a lot of them." It was "so ironic that I see a Talib and then I see myself here too. I am in the same spot as a Talib. I see those people on an everyday basis. . . . They say, 'See, you got what you deserve, you are here too.'"

I asked Michael Semple, then a senior United Nations representative for eastern Afghanistan, about Wakil. He replied, "It was utterly preposterous. He was calling us every day giving us intelligence. He was working with us. And all of a sudden he was declared an enemy?" As a UN official, Semple dealt with "delegation after delegation after delegation of people coming to say, 'Tell us what is Hajji Rohullah's crime, so we can go home. Otherwise, release him.' If you really want to get an idea of our powerlessness, and the powerlessness of the host authority"—the Afghan government—"this is a great example. None of us could do anything to get him. He just disappeared into a black hole."

During Wakil's absence, a vital link between his tribal community and the government was severed, the first in a series of steps that pushed them out of the political marketplace. "Wakil's faction was fully engaged, part of the political process," Semple told me, "but after he was taken off the scene, his followers all ended up inside the armed resistance." Within weeks of his arrest, the first rockets started to fall on US outposts in the area. Tit-for-tat shootings between Americans and angry villagers mounted. Then one day, again acting on Zarin's intelligence, US forces bombed the home of a prominent timber baron in the Korengal Valley, killing his family members. The deaths came just as the Afghan government was starting to clamp down on illegal logging. Soon, one village after another turned to open insurrection.

Meanwhile the profits continued to pour into Malek Zarin's coffers, to the point where a US embassy cable could describe him as "one of the

wealthiest men in eastern Afghanistan." In the new Afghanistan, however, war had a way of catching up even with the winners. In 2011, Zarin,
by then in his seventies, embraced a guest at a tribal meeting. The man
had hidden explosives underneath his waistcoat; the suicide blast killed
Zarin instantly.

Rohullah Wakil was finally freed from Guantanamo in 2008, returning to assume the role of tribal leader and mediating in Kabul on behalf of
his constituents. But in 2009, amid debate in Washington over the possible closure of Guantanamo, the Pentagon leaked a report to the *New York
Times* claiming that Wakil was one of seventy-four former inmates suspected of having "returned" to terrorism—even though he was living
openly and peacefully in Kabul, advising President Karzai. Leaving nothing to chance, everywhere he goes, Wakil now carries a sheaf of legal documents detailing his innocence. "For six years, I was ready to go to court
and defend myself. They should show the world their proof against me,"
he told a reporter. "I am ready to answer any question."

There was reason enough for him to worry: on a similar Pentagon list
were Dr. Hafizullah and Commander Naim, the two wrongfully
imprisoned—and subsequently rearrested—Zurmat elders. And then
there was the fate of Sabar Lal. Because of Taliban threats, upon his
release from Guantanamo he was forced to relocate from Pech to the
eastern city of Jalalabad. Whenever I visited him, he spoke ruefully of
the years he'd lost to Guantanamo's island cage and vowed to stay away
from public life altogether. Late one night in 2011, however, US soldiers
stormed his home and dragged Sabar Lal out of his bedroom. What happened next is unclear. Relatives and the night watchman claim that he
was blindfolded and executed, while a Coalition forces spokesman said
that he was shot dead because he was carrying a weapon. Afterward, the
Coalition announced that a "key affiliate of the al Qaeda network" had
been killed. It was a curious charge against a man who had complained
often to me about the militants' threats on his life.

If you were unfortunate enough to get caught up in this universe of
rivalry and intrigue and then fall into American hands, you would first
find yourself at one of a series of small US military outposts deep in the

countryside, known as Field Detention Sites. Interrogators there typically would have a limited grasp of Afghan politics, and intelligence would be poorly shared, so epic confusions usually ensued. The unit apprehending you might have a relationship with one strongman, for instance, while you worked for another strongman tied to a different wing of the US military or the CIA. In this way, hundreds of Afghans working for pro-American commanders wound up ensnared by one of the Coalition's many tentacles. And once branded as a terrorist, no amount of evidence or good sense could save you.

From the Field Detention Site, you would be shipped to one of the main prisons at either Bagram or Kandahar Airfield. You would then be questioned by a new set of interrogators, who made little attempt to reconcile existing intelligence with any fresh information that they obtained. Your journey would likely end here, locked away for months or even years—unless you were one among the two hundred Afghans destined for Guantanamo. There you would be assessed by officials ever farther removed from the battlefield, with even foggier knowledge of the country's politics. A result of this cascade of bureaucratic inefficiencies was that only a handful of Guantanamo's Afghan inmates would turn out to be Taliban members of any import.

Reading the official list of charges against the rest gives a sense of the farce the system had become. One inmate was accused, among other crimes, of supporting the political organization of Ahmed Shah Massoud, the pro-Western Northern Alliance leader murdered by al-Qaeda. Another was alleged to have been a member of Herakat-i-Inqilabi—an anti-Soviet mujahedeen group, backed by the United States, that had been defunct since the mid-1990s.

Inmate Muhammad Nasim arrived at Guantanamo accused of working as a deputy to Rashid Dostum, the pro-US warlord and former Gelam Jam militia leader who, prison authorities mistakenly believed, had "defected to the Taliban in 1998"—or so Nasim's classified file stated. In fact, Dostum had been a member of the Northern Alliance and a staunch anti-Taliban fighter, even winding up on the CIA payroll during the 2001 invasion. Nasim was also accused of being the former Taliban deputy minister of education, even though records indicate there was no person by that name in that position.

Abdullah Khan found himself in Guantanamo charged with being Khairullah Khairkhwa, the former Taliban minister of the interior, which might have been more plausible—if Khairkhwa had not also been in Guantanamo at the time.

Swat Khan's internment stemmed from an accusation that he was a high-ranking member of an "anti-coalition militia" known as the Mujahedeen Union. In reality, at the time of his arrest the union was a collection of pro-US militiamen in the pay of the CIA. "We worked for the Americans," said Malem Jan, one of Khan's comrades. "We met them regularly to get instructions and give intelligence." Khan's charge sheet also alleged that he worked simultaneously for a pair of commanders who were in fact long-standing rivals. In his initial questioning, Khan was hung by his wrists from the ceiling. Later, in Guantanamo, he attempted suicide. "It's all there when I close my eyes," he told me after his release. "The nightmare never leaves me."

Hajji Bismillah, the director of transportation for the government of Helmand Province, found himself in Guantanamo because of his close ties to Sher Muhammad Akhundzada—the province's US-backed governor. According to Bismillah's classified detainee file, American authorities mistakenly asserted that the governor was "originally the Taliban's second in command in the Helmand province." In fact, the Akhundzada family had been the Taliban's principal enemies in Helmand during the 1990s, precisely the reason why he became governor after their overthrow. This was open, public knowledge, but evidently no one along the chain of detentions from Helmand to Guantanamo bothered to check. Meanwhile, certain US units were detaining scores of Helmand farmers on precisely the contrary charge: *opposing* Governor Akhundzada, who was working closely with the Americans to consolidate his power. Bismillah's file stated that his intelligence value came not from any possible details that he could furnish about terrorists but from his knowledge of "biographical data on political figures in the new Afghan government"—just the sort of information that should have saved him from Cuba in the first place.

Nine Guantanamo inmates claimed the most striking proof of all that they were not Taliban or al-Qaeda: they had passed directly from a Taliban jail to American custody after 2001. Abdul Rahim al-Janko, a Syrian, had arrived in Afghanistan in 2000, fleeing a troubled home. His plan was to claim asylum in a Western country as an Afghan refugee. Being an Arab, he was directed in Afghanistan to an al-Qaeda camp, but, upon showing reluctance to train or fight, he was arrested on the suspicion that he was a Western spy. At the hands of al-Qaeda interrogators he was beaten and electrocuted and nearly drowned in a water tank. Eventually he confessed to plotting to kill Osama bin Laden on the orders of the CIA and the Mossad, Israel's intelligence service. This landed him in prison in Kandahar, in a cell not far from Jan Muhammad. Following the US invasion, al-Janko was handed over to US soldiers, who consigned him to Guantanamo. Eventually, a videotape surfaced of his coerced confession under al-Qaeda torture. Yet Attorney General John Ashcroft, eager to demonstrate progress in the war on terror, played an excerpt of the tape to journalists—without audio—as an al-Qaeda martyrdom propaganda video.

Most Guantanamo Afghans have by now returned home, but some still remain. Perhaps the unluckiest of this lot is Hamidullah, who has been accused of such a litany of misdeeds that you might conclude he is the world's most dangerous terrorist. American authorities asserted that he was aligned with "extremists" linked to the National Islamic Front—which was, in reality, a moderate pro-US mujahedeen party of the 1980s that counted Hamid Karzai as a member, and which was largely defunct at the time of Hamidullah's arrest. He was also alleged to have associated with Gulbuddin Hekmatyar, the Taliban leadership, Pakistani intelligence, Iranian intelligence, and al-Qaeda. He was said to harbor ties to Mullah Izzat (a pro-US commander), warlord Samoud Khan (from an entirely different part of the country), and Zulmay Tofan (another pro-US commander). He was accused of supporting the Afghan king, whose very post the Taliban and al-Qaeda strongly opposed; of being linked to warlord Ismail Khan (Karzai's US-backed electricity minister); and of meeting with Taliban leader Saif ur-Rahman Mansur, who, you may recall, was killed in Operation Anaconda in 2001, two years prior to the alleged encounter.

The prize for the most outlandish accusation of all, however, should go to the charge that Hamidullah maintained links to a commander named Hajji Almas. This was, in fact, true. But Almas was no terrorist; he was a major US contractor who played a key role in building Bagram Airfield and earned millions in the process. Thus, Hamidullah gained the ironic distinction of having been imprisoned in Bagram in part on charges that he was linked to a man whom Washington had paid to build the very prison in which he was held.

In Kafka's "In the Penal Colony," a savage tale of detention on a tropical island, the condemned are forced to lie prone on an extravagant execution machine that etches such commandments as "Honor Your Superiors" into their backs. Prisoners are never told the charges against them. "It would be useless to give him that information," an officer explains. "He experiences it on his own body."

The process was no less surreal for Afghans like Mohebullah, a bus driver detained in Uruzgan Province, whose Guantanamo file says:

> Reasons for Transfer to JTF GTMO: To provide information on the following: Detainee's file does not indicate why he was sent to JTF GTMO.

In fact, US soldiers had mistaken Mohebullah's home for that of a Taliban leader. When they stormed it one night, Mohebullah had fired into the darkness, thinking that they were thieves. Nonetheless, his internment remained a continuing mystery to all sides. Appearing before a panel to present his case, he said, "I am very happy to be in the Tribunal, because for the past one-and-a-half years, nobody asked me any questions. My father keeps writing me and asking why I am not coming home. What should I write him?"

The tribunal president responded: "I'm sure it would be difficult to answer that for you. The people that knew you that could say you weren't Taliban would not be relevant. Right now we have no accusation against you that says you were Taliban."

Mohebullah would remain in Guantanamo for nearly three more years.

In the vagaries of this system, you survived one way and one way only: through the ruthless exploitation of everyone around you. There was no getting around it. The broken alliances, the faltering hopes, the rude exposure of foreign agendas all dictated a certain logic of duplicity if you planned to remain alive and free. Warlord Hajji Zaman spelled this out for me one evening poolside at the Intercontinental, one of Kabul's two luxury hotels. He wore rimless gold glasses and sported a pristinely coiffed beard, a look that belied his adventurous past as a commander in eastern Afghanistan. In December 2001, when Osama bin Laden and hundreds of other Arabs fled to the Tora Bora Mountains along the Pakistani border, Zaman had pocketed huge sums of money from the United States for his services in hunting them down.

"The Americans came to me because they knew only I could get the job done," he said, raising a glass of scotch to his lips. He sat stiffly straight, a Kalashnikov leaning on one leg. On either side lolled a pair of bodyguards, who seemed to have had a few too many. The tinkling of a piano filled the air, and Western women dangled their feet in the pool. "This whole land," he said, sweeping his hand across hundreds of tiny house lights studding the mountains around the city, "this whole land is filled with thieves and liars. This is what you Americans have made." He ordered another round. "I know this game, I know how to survive." He was slurring his words by now. "I went to the Americans and said, 'I can find bin Laden.' I told them, 'Give me $5 million and I'll bring you his head.' So they went and talked to their bosses and arranged it, and I got $5 million. Then, a few days later, I went to al Qaeda and told them, 'Give me $1 million or I'll turn you over to the Americans.' So they gave me $1 million, and I convinced the Americans to stop the bombing for a little while. I told them we could use the time to find Osama, but really it was so those Arab dogs could escape to Pakistan. Then I went to the ISI," the Pakistani intelligence agency, "and said, 'Give me $500,000 and I'll give you al Qaeda.' They pulled a gun and told me to get out of their face." Zaman laughed, a long, raspy laugh that pushed his bodyguards into peals of delight. "You see, they don't play this game. You can't buy them."

I asked Zaman whether he worried that all the conniving would catch up with him. After all, he had accrued his fair share of enemies, including the family of the late vice president Abdul Qadir, whose assassination he was widely believed to have plotted. He clasped his hands. "I have nothing to be ashamed of! I fought for my country. Only cowards and foreign agents have to fear. Not patriots. Not the people who survived all of these wars. We are true patriots."

A few months later, a suicide bomber entered a crowd of government officials and dignitaries, worked his way up to Hajji Zaman, and blew him to bits.

PART THREE

8

Election Day

One day, a letter appeared at Heela's home bearing an impressive blue seal of a type she had never before seen. When Musqinyar arrived, he read the message aloud. "Afghanistan's first presidential elections are upcoming. The United Nations Assistance Mission in Afghanistan is seeking individuals to work in the forthcoming voter registration drive. Women are encouraged to apply."

Heela and Musqinyar stared at each other. It was mid-2004, about a year since her neighbor Jamila had discovered Heela's underground school and forced it to close. Since then, Heela had lost herself within the four walls of her house. It had been a particularly trying few months after her mother-in-law had passed away, for though the old woman had been a thorn in her side, the loneliness was oppressive. Now, this opportunity jolted her like news from a long-lost friend.

So she and Musqinyar began to plot. This time, they would have to be doubly careful. Jamila's words—"Keep going on like this and no one will see a single family member of yours alive"—still rang in her ears. To pull this off, Heela knew, she'd have to work somewhere far from her village.

As the only educated woman in huge swaths of Khas Uruzgan, Heela had no trouble landing the job. Musqinyar was enlisted as well, and since Heela could not be trained directly, he was coached and passed along what he learned. One evening, he came home with a stack of voter registration cards that they were to distribute to poor villagers across the district.

Most of the villagers had never voted for anything in their lives, but an unending stream of radio news and public service announcements had everyone thinking about the elections. People had started speaking knowingly about politics, the way they spoke about the coming rains or the year's crops.

It was warm outside on their first day of work, and Heela was up earlier than usual. Climbing into the back of the station wagon, she waited until Musqinyar appeared, dressed as usual in a crisp white salwar. They set out before the sky dawned to avoid the neighbors. After an hour of driving on a broken gravel road that wound through the dusty mountain country, they reached the far side of the district, home to a different clan, where their family was not known. Heela sat in the car and watched Musqinyar speak to the malek, the village headman. After some time he gathered all the menfolk in front of the mosque. They thronged around her husband, kissing his hand, and she could hear them pleading for better roads and clinics. For these villagers, who had never met a representative of the government or the United Nations before, it was as if he were an emissary from President Karzai himself. As dozens of curious faces looked on, Musqinyar explained that his only job was to register them to vote. He described the registration process, which required each person to fill out a card. Since few could read or write, he ended up completing most of the cards himself. And because most lacked proper identification, he created makeshift IDs with a Polaroid camera he'd brought along.

After the crowd dispersed, Musqinyar walked the malek out of earshot. They spoke and then turned and looked at Heela in the car, and continued the conversation. Eventually Musqinyar shook the malek's hands and hugged him, and he returned to the vehicle alone. Women getting caught up in politics, the malek had told him, would be like men going into the kitchen. Like men raising babies and women fighting war. There would be no female registration here.

They drove on to other villages, and in each the result was the same. Back home, Heela and Musqinyar put their heads together. She wasn't ready to give up.

It was Musqinyar who first struck upon the ruse: medicines. The next day, as he discussed voting with the men of another village, Heela was escorted from house to house to hand out cheap medications from their pharmacy. Once inside, alone among the women, Heela delivered her speech on democracy and voting. She filled out cards for them and explained that, unlike for the men, a photograph wasn't required. Some women, fearing their husbands, refused to accept a card. Others clutched them as if they were precious gifts. In some houses she met women who knew a thing or two about Kabul from the radio, and she spoke at length with them about the candidates. Although she wasn't supposed to favor one contender, she couldn't imagine anyone but Karzai for the job, and she never met anyone who disagreed. She explained that a woman's vote was hers alone, not her husband's; some housewives scoffed and said that it was wrong to divide a man and woman in this way, but others nodded in agreement.

During those weeks, Heela wondered for the first time if she might have a future in politics. Working for a candidate, perhaps, or continuing on with the United Nations if they'd allow her. To be out in the world, teaching, connecting—she felt that tug again, that force inside her that had led her to risk so much already. At home she pored over the constitution and studied up on the candidates' profiles, then lectured the women on what she'd learned. If only she could convince them that they, too, belonged to the public world, those small flashes of confidence she sometimes noticed in their eyes might grow into something of meaning and value. Just as they had for her.

Still, she had moments of doubt. In one hillside village she gave a card to a woman married to an Afghan who was living in Pakistan. "Sometimes a village is so small," Heela recalled, "that when someone gets a card, everyone knows, and so even her husband in Pakistan heard about it. People started talking—'so and so's wife received a card, she must be going out of the house on her own, she is getting involved in men's affairs, maybe she has taken a lover,' and so on. It was a big shame for her husband." When two of the woman's relatives escorted her back to Pakistan, they found her husband livid. A shouting match erupted between him and the relatives, whom he held responsible for his wife's indiscretions. Physical threats followed, until the husband pulled out a pistol and shot them, killing one and leaving the other critically wounded. "This was all from a card I gave," Heela said.

But for every story like this, there were others that filled her with hope: women tearfully promising to vote, girls asking about life in Kabul, and even, in a few cases, husbands encouraging their wives to register. "The registration cards were like little bricks," she said. "We wanted to build Afghanistan." The election, scheduled for October 2004, was to be the showpiece of Western efforts over the previous three years. The candidates included Gelam Jam leader Rashid Dostum; warlord Muhammad Mohaqeq, who had commanded Hazara militias during the civil war; and twenty-one other figures from around the country. But in Heela's estimation, Hamid Karzai, a fellow southern Pashtun, was the runaway favorite. Musqinyar agreed, and he could not find a soul who would speak ill of the interim president. Karzai had, after all, launched his uprising against the Taliban right there in Uruzgan, and the economy had blossomed since the Americans arrived.

The summer came and registration slowed, as the men were busy in the orchards and the women with their dried fruits. The fields abutting Heela's house had grown tall with the season, and it was in those fields that a boy from her village wandered one day, following the labyrinth of donkey trails that connected one plot to the next. He stepped through reeds up to his eyes and waded across tiny streams, and then he stopped cold. Lying in front of him, facedown, was a body. There was a single bullet wound to the back of the head.

The dead man was not from the village. No one could quite say where he had come from. There had been sporadic killings elsewhere in the district, but something like this had not happened here in the village since the civil war. The body was buried in an unmarked grave. For days, it was all anyone could talk about.

A week later, a man working for an NGO in a neighboring district went missing. Musqinyar had known him well, having served him often at the pharmacy. Shortly after, the UN issued a warning to employees: the security situation was worsening as the elections neared, although no one in Heela's village could figure out whom to hold responsible. As the mood shifted, men in the bazaar began speaking vaguely about "the situation."

Musqinyar concluded that it was just too dangerous for a woman to be moving about in far-flung villages. At first he said nothing, but Heela knew what he was thinking. When he finally told her, some days later, that "it's better for you to stay home from now on," she was unsurprised. And she knew that her husband could be a stubborn man, that once he made up his mind even the Prophet himself could not change it. But she tried anyway. She had been preparing a defense for just such an eventuality, and over dinner and the next morning she laid out her case. Without her, Khas Uruzgan's women would be cut off, effectively disenfranchised. If they gave up at the first sign of instability, how could they expect to accomplish anything? And the money—they were now earning more together than ever before.

He listened quietly but refused to budge. "If anything were to happen to you," he said, "I would not be able to live with myself."

One summer afternoon a year earlier, Qudus Khan, the governor of Khas Uruzgan, had been sitting in his office speaking to village elders when the district chief of police, Muhammad, pulled up in front of the building. He greeted the security guards out front, then strode briskly through the corridors and into the governor's office. He aimed his Kalashnikov at the governor. The men looked up. Muhammad squeezed the trigger. The governor's body jerked backward, and he fired again. The elders sat staring at the bloody mess. Muhammad turned, walked out, and drove off in his Ford Ranger police truck, lights flashing. He phoned officials in Tirin Kot to boast about his exploit, then continued on to another district and disappeared.

It was then that the killings had started to become a regular occurrence, and bodies began turning up around the district. But the genesis of the bloodshed could be traced to much earlier. After US forces assaulted the school and the governor's house in January 2002, wiping out most of the district's pro-US leadership in a single night, local politics were changed forever. The tenuously balanced forces that had ruled the district for a decade were swiftly replaced by one man: Jan Muhammad. Shortly after the killings, he had appointed his ally, Qudus Khan, as district governor. The scion of an elite family, Qudus Khan owned ample tracts of land and commanded the allegiance of thousands from his tribe, the Alizais. Having survived the civil war with relatively clean hands, he enjoyed popular support, and under his reign Khas Uruzgan remained largely at peace. He worked closely with US forces, landing lucrative contracts for reconstruction and security.

Such success did not go unnoticed in Tirin Kot, and JMK began to fear that his gilded position atop the province's patronage pyramid was in jeopardy, that his own appointee was perhaps *too* popular. It so happened that Qudus Khan's tribe was locked in a decades-long rivalry with the Karimzai tribe, so JMK replaced Malek Rauf as Khas Uruzgan's chief of police with a Karimzai named Asadullah. Jealousy and mistrust followed, as each man jockeyed for influence and access to the Americans.

Unsurprisingly, this did not end well. In the summer of 2003, Police Chief Asadullah was mysteriously gunned down as he drove to meet friends for dinner. The attack, the first political killing in the district since the American massacre, shook the authorities. But they chose not to conduct an investigation, and soon the bazaar was bubbling with speculation that Qudus Khan was the culprit. JMK, keeping with his divide-and-conquer approach, then appointed Asadullah's grieving brother Muhammad as the new police chief for Khas Uruzgan. Muhammad wasted little time in securing his revenge. (Years later, he, too, would be mysteriously shot to death.)

Upon Qudus Khan's death, tribal leadership passed to his son Naqibullah, who had also inherited a bit of his father's sense of stature. Suspecting that JMK was behind the whole affair, he denounced the governor publicly—a reckless move in Jan Muhammad's Uruzgan if there ever was one. Naqibullah was promptly arrested by the Americans as a "Taliban agent" and shipped off to Bagram. JMK then appointed a close ally, Hajji Obaidullah, to the governorship. For police chief, he chose Commander Zahir, the son of erstwhile police chief Malek Rauf. Unlike his father, whose affable ways had won him community support, Zahir proved notoriously ill-tempered and combative. He was built like a cauldron, with an enormous wedge of a nose to fit his bulbous face, and wherever he showed up trouble usually followed. The district's once effective police force became an open bazaar: drug traffickers bribed policemen, officers auctioned extra weapons on the black market, and criminals paid their way to freedom. Under the guise of security, Zahir established checkpoints and forcibly extracted a "tax" from motorists. For the first time since the civil war years, people felt insecure. In one area residents formed a pro-government militia for protection, but Zahir, viewing them as competition, informed the Americans that they were Taliban, and US forces killed them all.

The venality felt "like a sickness," as Heela put it. Finally, local elders convened a meeting of tribal leaders and educated people to address the ballooning sense of discontent. Musqinyar sat quietly through the discussion, listening as the graybeards considered how best to convince Tirin Kot to remove Zahir. He was not the type to speak up in meetings—in fact, he hated crowds of any sort—but he found the conversation excruciating. "You're all avoiding the issue," he finally said. "We can't change anything around here so long as Jan Muhammad is running things." The room went cold silent. As he proceeded to describe what everyone knew, the men stared into their laps or thumbed their prayer beads. When he finished, the elders continued to sit wordlessly, until one of them finally spoke and changed the subject.

Afterward, people whispered that it was a brave thing he had done. But there wasn't much more to be said, for JMK had informers everywhere. Everyone knew what had happened to Naqibullah—and he was from an illustrious family, no less.

Still, it seemed that the entire village had heard of Musqinyar's remarks. Gossip reached the bazaar and government offices, and soon enough hit the ears of Zahir himself. He said nothing and did nothing, but everyone knew that he had a long memory for such things.

Heela arose early, long before sunrise, on the morning of October 9, 2004. Outside, under an indigo sky, she could make out the silhouettes of several hulking men in the front yard. They wore large turbans and had rifles slung over their shoulders. "Our security for today," Musqinyar said.

It was the day of the first presidential election in her country's history. Musqinyar had done so well during the registration drive that he had been hired to oversee election day for the entire district. It had meant late nights for weeks, traveling with US forces to help survey potential polling sites, hiring and training local staff, coordinating ballot distribution—sometimes using donkeys—and arranging for the results to be safely and accurately counted. Now, the UN also needed a woman to manage the sole female polling station, and Musqinyar allowed Heela to work on the condition that she was provided security.

By sunrise they arrived at the polling center, the main schoolhouse. A curtain down the middle of the compound separated the male and female voters. As Heela proceeded to her section, she could see a crowd of men gathering near the gate a good hour before polls opened. She helped erect the booths and gather the documents, and then the gates opened and people rushed in. Khas Uruzgan's sunburned farmers flashed toothy smiles and waved to UN photographers as they presented their registration cards and dipped a finger in purple ink to prevent multiple voting.

On Heela's side, however, the story was starkly different. "I didn't see a single woman vote," Heela said. "I was the first and last woman to cast a ballot that day." At one point, men arrived with sack loads of registration cards. "They told me, 'The women in our village don't know anything about politics, so they asked us to vote for them.'"

Still, by day's end, initial results from around the district were already coming in—and the polls were proving to be a resounding success, with a turnout that even Musqinyar hadn't expected. There were boxes from villages so far-flung that he had never heard of them. For a country just a few years removed from civil war and brutal dictatorship, the election seemed a watershed. As election workers hugged and congratulated each other, Musqinyar stood by watching quietly, his eyes brimming. Even Heela took heart. Changing villagers' attitudes might take years, even generations, but she knew that their team had planted the first thoughts of equality in people's minds.

Karzai would go on to a landslide victory, the first popular mandate of any ruler in Afghan history.

That autumn, Musqinyar found himself thinking often about the future: about staying on with the UN, working the following year's parliamentary elections; about his children and Kabul and the possibility of returning when the time was right, when they'd be ready for university. Omaid, his oldest, wanted to be a doctor when he grew up. He was coming into the pharmacy daily as a sort of apprenticeship, and for Musqinyar the company was a blessing.

It was a quiet day at the shop one Saturday afternoon when a customer stopped by and conversation turned to the elections.

"I don't think they were a good idea," the man stated.

"Why?" Musqinyar asked.

"They're expensive. Who can pay these days?"

Musqinyar did not understand.

"They charge you money for not voting, but it wasn't even my fault. I was traveling," the man said.

Musqinyar still did not understand and probed further. Slowly, the truth came out. Police officers were going from village to village announcing via loudspeaker that whoever hadn't voted had to pay a fine.

Musqinyar could not believe it. He visited other shops and everywhere the story was the same. You had to prove you'd voted, or cough up the fine—and an ink-stained finger did not suffice, only a punched voter registration card would do (a step some polling centers had neglected).

For all his diffidence, Musqinyar did not conceal anger well. He strode over to the compound of Hajji Obaidullah, the district governor, stormed past his secretary, marched through the antechamber with its waiting supplicants, and barged right into the governor's office. "You need to do something about these police! They're out of control!" he shouted. The men seated around the room stared up at him, astonished. There were stacks of registration cards on the floor and a few farmers waiting in a corner. A police officer had a hole punch in his hands. Musqinyar had caught them red-handed.

"How does this concern you?" Governor Obaidullah snapped. "We weren't bothering you in your election work."

The two broke into a shouting match. A second official joined the fray. The farmers, there to surrender their fine, looked on, perplexed and fearful. Men from the hallway came to check on the commotion. The two sides were near blows when finally Musqinyar said, "If you don't stop this, I'll go to the UN. I'll go straight to Kabul."

Governor Obaidullah shrank back. "Look, you're making a big deal out of this. Don't worry, we'll take care of it." He waved his hand. "It's just a misunderstanding."

Musqinyar stormed out. As he left, he noticed a man sitting in the corner watching him. It was Police Chief Zahir.

When Heela heard about the fracas, she was beside herself. "Do you *know* what they do to people who cause problems?" It was true, and Musqinyar couldn't deny it. As soon as he'd reached his car he had realized his mistake, but it could not be undone. Or could it? Heela begged him to go and apologize, but he thought it would seem cowardly, unmanly. No, he would let the matter rest, without reporting anything to the UN. It would all go away.

The next morning, a friend who worked in the police department came by the pharmacy to see Musqinyar. "Zahir's been asking about you," he said quietly. "You need to be careful."

That evening, Captain Andy Brosnan, head of the American forces stationed nearby, invited a number of officials, as well as Musqinyar, to dinner at the base. Zahir was there, and Musqinyar could feel his eyes on him the entire night. When Brosnan asked Musqinyar about his plans for the coming week, Musqinyar replied directly in English, so that no one else could understand. Zahir chewed silently and watched.

After dinner, Musqinyar climbed into his old white Corolla and headed for home. The wind was strong outside, the sky already dark. As he pulled away from the bazaar, there was not a light anywhere for miles. No cars, either. He pulled onto the shoulder near the turnoff to his village and sat thinking. He couldn't get Zahir's stare out of his mind. Suddenly he turned his car around and headed back toward the pharmacy. Better to play things safe, he told himself.

He slept that night in the pharmacy. Early the next morning, he headed out over the cratered dirt road running toward the village. Nearing a culvert, he spotted a white station wagon, almost identical to his, sitting by the roadside. He pulled up to take a look. The car had been shot up like a sieve, its windshield spiderwebbed. Inside, lying in their own blood, were three bullet-ridden bodies.

He glanced around. Not a soul in sight. He jumped back in his car and sped home.

"That was meant for you!" Heela said. Musqinyar didn't say anything.

Finally he told her to ignore it, that it was just a coincidence. Trying to put it out of her mind, she went into the kitchen to chop vegetables for dinner. Busying her hands, giving herself a task, had always put her at ease. It was then that the realization struck her: after Musqinyar had denounced JMK at that meeting of tribal elders, he had mentioned to her that Zabit had been present—the same Zabit who had spread rumors that Heela was running a prostitution center. Could *he* have informed Zahir of Musqinyar's comments? He was also linked to a group of Afghans who had a long-running dispute with the family over land. A constellation of thoughts lit up as she jumped from one possible enemy to the next. Again Jamila's warning echoed in her head: "No one will see a single family member of yours alive."

She went back to her husband and stood in front of him. "We have to get out of here."

Musqinyar demurred, insisting the car shooting was a tragic fluke. Heela burst into tears. "What if something happened to you? What would I do? I couldn't live."

They ate dinner in silence. Then Heela grabbed him once again and pleaded that he flee now, even if she and the boys couldn't. Musqinyar threw up his hands. "Leave? You want me to leave? You want me to catch a flight out? Is that what you'd like? Fly to Kabul? Are you crazy? How can I leave? There's no airport here, there's nothing."

"Then drive!"

"You want me to drive away? After what I saw on that road?"

That evening a neighbor knocked on the door. For years Musqinyar had parked his station wagon on the neighbor's side of the river that ran through the village, since there was no room on his side. Now, the neighbor politely asked him to remove the car.

The ground shook. Heela was standing in the front yard, tending to her apple tree, when she heard a roar. It was nighttime, but she could see a faint white light from the southwest, the direction of Mecca. It grew brighter, and then a second explosion rocked the whole landscape. A yawning chasm opened in the earth, and from it emerged swarms of men running toward her. Now she stood alone in the desert. She ran desperately fast, but the men were gaining ground. They drew so close that she could hear their panting. She turned. "There were armed people coming from all directions," she said. "Some of them had American uniforms, some of them had a terrible scowl. One of them was so thin he had no flesh on his cheeks. His face was just a skull. I screamed and screamed to dear God, looking for my husband. I couldn't find him. One of the men reached out and grabbed me."

She snapped awake, panting, lying in her own sweat. Next to her, Musqinyar lay fast asleep. She muttered a *kalima*, an Islamic prayer. Her thoughts returned to those three unfortunate people murdered by the roadside. The Taliban had officially been denounced as the perpetrators, but she knew that wasn't the case.

She headed for the front yard. Looking to the horizon, she traced the outlines of the dark mountains that stretched far in both directions. She hated them. They were a reminder of the unconquerable distance to Kabul, of the unforgettable fact that this would never be home.

It was now three days since Musqinyar's outburst, and she knew that she'd have to do something. In the moonlight, she started filling empty wheat sacks with sand and soil and stones, lining them up against the windows. Then she piled one sack atop another in the front yard, the beginnings of a bunker. *I won't let anyone touch my family*, she told herself. *I won't. I won't.*

In the morning, Musqinyar laughed off her paranoia. He wasn't just any old farmer, her reminded her. He was a paid employee of the United Nations, a friend of the Americans, always welcome at their base. An all-around well-regarded member of the community. "You have too much imagination," he said. He took the children to school and Heela decided to busy herself with housework.

Musqinyar returned at sunset. As the family seated themselves around a dinner of broiled lamb and rice, there was a knock on the door. It was his uncle. Someone had stolen a gun from his house, and he asked Musqinyar to come investigate. Heela asked him not to go, but he promised he would return soon.

Now alone with the children, Heela cleared the dishes and put the boys to bed. It was about eight, and the sun had slipped behind the mountains.

She set about lighting candles and the oil lamp, then went to check on their new dog, leashed in the front yard.

A little past nine. Heela was reading by candlelight when the dog started barking. She had forgotten to feed the poor thing. She stepped outside and tossed it some bread and set aside a bowl of water.

Ten o'clock. The dog was barking again. Musqinyar had still not returned. Running low on oil, she snuffed out the lamp and the candles, letting the darkness settle. Her eyes adjusted and she used the moonlight to make her way around. The barking was incessant. Was the leash too tight? She would have to let the dog run loose.

She pushed the door open and went for the animal, then stopped. Something was moving in the front yard. Next to her, the dog stood with its back roached, staring into the darkness. She scanned the yard. The gate was a good twenty paces away. To her right sat the small stand-alone guest room, to her left the tiny thicket of apple trees. Something dark and amorphous appeared to be lurking near the guest room.

It moved again.

Somebody's out there, she thought. She backed into the house. She had no phone, no way of leaving. The children were asleep.

Musqinyar kept his automatic rifle in the bedroom. The thought seemed crazy, but she was desperate. When she found it, the weight surprised her. She had never handled a weapon before. She came to the living room, where an open window offered a view of the yard. The dog continued to bark.

At first, she could see nothing. Then a shape—a silhouette—emerged from the guest room. There was no mistaking it. Then she noticed another figure, crouching under an apple tree. And a third near the wall. And another? She picked out four shapes—*right in her yard.*

One of them started walking toward the house. The dog whimpered. Now all the shadows were moving. One passed directly by her window. He wore a large black turban and his face was covered. His eyes shone under the moonlight.

The shadows drew closer. Another one passed the window. Then a third. The fourth, the one crouching by the apple tree, suddenly stood up and walked toward the house.

Heela gripped the trigger. The shadow turned and paced back in the direction of the front gate.

She placed the gun on the windowsill and aimed. The frame rattled beneath her hands.

The figure turned and stared and headed back toward the house again. Straight toward her window.

She squeezed her eyes shut and pulled the trigger.

Village life is normally draped in silence. There are no cars, no generators, no televisions, no pedestrians. The shot rang through the valley and shook the whole house. Cakes of dirt from Heela's mud ceiling fell to the floor. The children came running from their rooms. And somewhere in all of this commotion, Heela heard the sound of footsteps fleeing. When she peered into the yard, the men were gone.

Musqinyar returned home around two in the morning to find Heela ashen-faced. Scouring the front yard by flashlight, he found footprints and cigarette butts everywhere. He looked shaken.

Heela implored him to leave that very night. He seemed lost in thought for a while, then agreed—but he needed time. "Give me two days to figure this out," he said. "We'll find a way to Kabul."

In the morning, Musqinyar loaded the boys into his Corolla and drove to work. Alone again, Heela threw herself into housework. She couldn't bring herself to look at the front yard, however. Not even in daylight.

Before noon, a group of women arrived at the house seeking medical attention. Their mahrem waited in the yard while the women, with a gaggle of coughing, sneezing children, pressed inside. As Heela examined them, one of the women struck up a conversation. They were, it turned out, Commander Zahir's wives. Heela looked up, struggling to control herself.

"How are things?" she asked timidly. "How is your family?"

"We're all fine, thanks," the woman replied. "But you know how things are in the village these days, with security. It's getting worse."

"I heard that a carful of people was attacked yesterday," Heela said.

The woman clucked. "The situation is very bad." She leaned forward and stared a long moment at Heela. "Why are you and your family still here? You're such good people. Why don't you leave until things get settled?"

"Why?" Heela nearly whispered. "Do you think we might have problems?"

Another wife interjected. "We just think it'd be better for you and your husband to spend some time away, that's all."

Then the oldest, Zahir's first wife, clasped Heela's wrist with her bony hand and said, "Our husband beats us. He's a cruel and angry man."

When Musqinyar arrived that evening, he brought news of his own. His friend in the police force had told him about a rumor that Zahir and Jan Muhammad had drawn up a list of "troublemakers" that included "some good people." It was all he would say.

There was no getting around it. Musqinyar now knew that they would have to find a way out of Khas Uruzgan immediately. There were three routes from the district. The roads west and north passed through police checkpoints, which meant that the eastern road, through Hazara territory, might be the only option. First, though, he had to contact friends in Kabul who could take them in. He would need a satellite phone, so he'd have to lean on friends in the UN, or the Americans. He would have to work on it.

The next morning, October 21, was the sixth day of the Islamic holy month of Ramadan, and the fifth since Musqinyar had confronted the governor. Heela had been up since two in the morning, as she had been every day that week, because women prepared the predawn meals. Musqinyar appeared in a pressed salwar and plaid black vest, and the family sat down for breakfast. They ate in silence. The muezzin called, and he rose and gathered his belongings for the pharmacy.

"You aren't going to work, are you?" she asked.

He stared back, as if to say, *Where else would I be going?*

"You can't go out there!" She nearly screamed the words. Not in twelve years had she spoken so loudly. Musqinyar ignored her and moved toward the door. Heela stared in disbelief. Stubbornness was one thing; this was too much.

"No!" she yelled. She threw herself in front of the door. "You have children! You have a son—he's almost eleven." She was now in tears. "What will happen to him?"

Musqinyar grabbed his firearm theatrically and stuck it to his temple. "Do you want me to sit in the house all day like a woman?" he shouted back. "I have a family to support. If I can't do that, what kind of man am I?"

He calmed himself. "Look, I need to find a satellite phone so we can get to Kabul." He swore that as soon as he could arrange everything, they would escape. But it might take a few more days, and until then they needed all the money he could garner.

After driving the children to school, he headed to the UN office. They did not, however, have a satellite phone for him to use. He then asked if they could at least assign him bodyguards, but they said that with the elections over, he was no longer their employee or their responsibility.

Meanwhile, Heela unclipped his clothes from the drying line. After months of effort, Musqinyar had managed to read the entire Koran, muddling through the archaic Arabic with an accompanying modern Farsi translation. "I want to wear fresh clothes tonight to celebrate," he had told her. "And cologne."

Musqinyar had also asked her to make *halwa*, a sweet carrot dish, in honor of the first anniversary of his mother's death. Families would distribute sweets to the poor as a way of blessing the departed's soul. When she finished, she stepped into the backyard to tend to the garden. She was still avoiding the front yard.

She kept herself busy until the sun started to slide behind the peaks. It was nearing *iftar*, the ritual breaking of the daylong fast. A chilled wind gusted across the house, and she wondered if winter might be coming early this year. Lounging in the garden, she listened for the sound of Musqinyar's tires crunching the gravel of the village road. He had mentioned that he might bring his brother Shaysta to dinner to discuss the plans to flee. Heela had always disliked Shaysta, though she could never put her finger on why. She was hoping, instead, for a meal alone with her husband and children.

After twelve hours of fasting, Musqinyar was eager to get home. Earlier than usual, he locked up the shop and pulled the iron shutter closed. He was with Omaid and Jamshed, and they proceeded to the mosque to offer prayers before iftar. There Musqinyar ran into Shaysta and invited him along for dinner, and then the four set out in the Corolla down the village's gravel road. Musqinyar parked the vehicle in a clearing not far from the house. After stopping at a small bakery to pick up steaming naan for dinner, they made their way along a donkey path until they reached an opening in the trees. Ahead lay the footbridge home.

Just then one of the children pointed to some bushes. "Father," he asked. "Who are they?"

There, in the shadows, were three men none of them knew.

Dinnertime neared. A gray overcast dusk rolled out over the land and Heela retrieved a shawl to keep herself warm.

Suddenly, a series of gunshots rang out. "From the moment I heard those bullets," she recalled, "it felt like they were hitting my heart." She raced to the front yard. An icy wind rushed in from the direction of the stream, carrying with it the unmistakable scent of discharged firearms. She thrust her head out the main gate but saw nothing. Then she scrambled up a ladder resting on the side of the house and balanced herself on the roof. Standing on tiptoes, she could just see across the stream, a good one hundred yards away. At first the landscape looked blissfully empty, nothing but acacias and fruit trees and farmland stretching for miles—and then she saw it. Just barely visible around a bend, near the ravine, was the glint of Musqinyar's white car.

She flew down the ladder. *This can't be happening to me*, she said to herself. *What sins have I committed?* Cracking the front gate open, she waited for a passing villager. Nothing. She retrieved a headscarf and wrapped it around her head and, in a moment of despair, darted out into the open. For the first time in ten years in Uruzgan she had left her house without permission, without her face protected. She felt naked.

She ran toward the stream just as a couple of elderly women were coming from the opposite direction.

"Stop, daughter! There are men there—you can't go."

"I don't care!" she sobbed. The two women tackled her and kept her back.

"Are you crazy? They'll kill you for wandering out there. Get back in your house. We'll let you know what happened later."

"No!" she cried, trying to pull free, but she knew they were right. She crumpled to the ground, wailing. "Just tell me, are they gone? All of them? Is my family gone?"

"No, daughter, everyone is fine," one said, caressing Heela's head. "Everyone is fine."

— 9 —

The Far End of the Bazaar

It was pitch-black when Heela awoke. The room spun. She wasn't sure how long she'd been out. Tiptoeing to the bedroom door, she could hear the two elderly women chatting in the hallway.

"God should destroy Commander Zahir," one said. "What problem did he have with these poor people? He's ruined so many lives."

Heela tried to piece together the preceding few hours. She had been dragged back home by the two women, who then shoved her into the bedroom. She was told to get some rest, that they'd look after Nawid and Walid. Musqinyar and the boys would be okay, she had said to herself. After all, if something was wrong, wouldn't someone tell her? She had then closed her eyes for just a moment, yet somehow hours had passed.

A knock at the door. Heela rushed to open it, and she saw Shaysta standing there, unscathed.

"Brother is injured, and the kids are a little bit injured," he said. "I just want to make sure you are all right."

The questions tumbled out of her. "Who was it? How did it happen? What are their injuries?" He wouldn't answer. "Where did they take him? There are no hospitals here. A hospital in Kandahar? If they need blood, I'll give blood. Take me to the hospital—anything. I just want to see them."

He waved his hand. "This is enough. We'll talk tomorrow. Get some sleep."

Sometime in the middle of the night, Heela awoke to a loud knocking at the front gate. Walid, her youngest, sat up next to her. "Mama, I think Father has come."

"No!" she said. "They're coming to get us. They are going to finish it." She corralled the children and the women in the bedroom and locked the door. The knocking continued, on and off, for nearly twenty minutes, as Heela waited, clutching an ax. Eventually, the visitor went away.

At first light, Heela heard Shaysta calling out from behind the front gate. She hadn't eaten in more than twenty-four hours, and the room lurched as she struggled to sit up. She fit herself into her burqa and made it to the gate, the boys behind her.

"Your husband is here," Shaysta said. "Come see him."

"How did he get here?" she asked. "What happened?"

"This isn't the time for questions."

"He's back from the hospital? Where are Omaid and Jamshed?"

Shaysta said nothing as he led them down a path toward the stream. A crowd had gathered ahead.

"You must be exhausted," she continued. "Last night was so—"

She stopped in her tracks. Lying neatly on the dirt road, on a bed of flour sacs, was her husband's body.

"Mama, why are there so many holes in his shirt?" Walid asked.

Heela stared. Then she dropped to the ground and started examining the body. "He must be in pain!" she said. "What's wrong? What's wrong? Don't worry, I'm here." She began unbuttoning his shirt to check for wounds.

"Enough!" Shaysta snapped. "He's no longer a mahrem!" Heela started sobbing uncontrollably.

Shaysta bent over to her and whispered fiercely, "What's wrong with you? Don't cry so loudly—you're a woman! Do you want people to hear your voice? Have you no shame?"

But there was no stopping her. "I was just drowning," she recalled years later. "I just kept crying. I couldn't breathe. I held on to my two sons, thinking I had no one else in the world."

Shaysta and other men brought the corpse inside, where, according to local Islamic custom, it would need to be washed and interred as soon as possible. Heela felt somehow disembodied, as if she were watching the events unfolding in her own house from above. When Shaysta asked her for money for the funeral, she mechanically handed over almost everything she had. Relatives were foraging through her husband's personal effects and taking what they wanted.

At some point during the day, Shaysta approached with news that her two older boys were being treated by the Americans in one of their field hospitals. Then he said, "Your husband told me that no matter what happens, you shouldn't cry. You need to be strong. It's in God's hands now." She nodded. He continued, "You should always cover your face, do you understand? You should remember him and never, ever uncover your face outside. Okay?"

She nodded again.

She retreated to her bedroom and shut the door. She needed time to think, away from the guests, away from the living-room clamor. She wondered if her boys were awake in the hospital. What kind of care were they receiving? Doctors made mistakes all the time. In fact, she knew of a few cases where, because of the need to bury bodies quickly, they had mistakenly pronounced patients dead. Suddenly she thought of Musqinyar's body.

Returning to the living room, she saw men wrapping up her husband for removal. "No!" she screamed. She clasped his leg with all her might. As relatives struggled to pry her loose, she fell back, her head hitting squarely on a wooden shelf.

Hours later, after dusk, she awoke with an excruciating headache. The house had grown quiet, as everyone had left save for one of the elderly women, Musqinyar's aunt. Heela ruminated on the days ahead. She had never heard of a woman living alone in Uruzgan, or even in Kabul. It simply did not happen. Here, widows were expected to marry their brothers-in-law. She shuddered at the thought of marrying Shaysta, or even spending time with him, or with anyone at all. But where could she go? Her parents had fled the country and she'd lost contact with them ages ago.

Single women were a radioactive commodity. She'd heard stories about women who had run away from home and been locked up on charges of prostitution—even in Hamid Karzai's relatively cosmopolitan Kabul. There was just no getting around it: you needed a man's sponsorship.

Lying in bed, she tried to force sleep to come. How would she support herself? There would be no more election work, no more sewing centers. It all seemed so ridiculous now, so reckless. Musqinyar would never have taken that elections job if she hadn't pushed for work for herself. How could she have been so selfish?

At least God had spared the children. Would Zahir come for them, too? She went out and gathered the two remaining boys and the auntie and brought them into the bedroom. Then she dragged a heavy chest in front of the door, put her husband's gun nearby, and waited. It took more than an hour for them all to doze off.

Sometime after midnight, Heela awoke to see the children and aunt sitting up in ashen silence. She could hear thuds. Footsteps. She looked up. *Someone is on the roof,* she thought. The old lady fingered prayer beads and muttered Koranic verses. Walid looked at Heela, his eyes pooling, and she grabbed him and covered his mouth.

The four watched the ceiling for a long time. At one point Walid had to go to the bathroom, but she could not bring herself to open the door, so he relieved himself in a small dinner bowl.

Only with the sunrise did the noises cease. Heela sent out the boys to plead with Musqinyar's male relatives to come spend the night. Upon news of a death, villagers were usually gracious beyond their means. Women contributed food and looked after children, men helped out in the fields, families donated money and clothing. But Heela was quickly realizing that her case was different. People were avoiding the house as if it had fallen victim to the evil eye. Spending the night seemed to be out of the question. Heela wondered if they all knew something she didn't.

Later that afternoon, a contingent of Captain Brosnan's soldiers visited, bringing news: Jamshed was convalescing seventy miles away, at the base in Tirin Kot, but Omaid, in critical condition, had been flown to Kandahar Airfield.

One of the Americans promised that they would solve the crime. "We have reason to believe that one of the following men may have been responsible," he said, and proceeded to list the names of top Taliban figures. "We're working with Police Chief Zahir," he assured her. "Do you have any idea who might have wanted to harm your husband?"

Heela was stunned. *Police Chief Zahir killed my husband!* she wanted to scream. But the Americans were supporting Zahir. How could she say anything? She would be arrested, of that much she was sure.

"I don't know who did this," she said.

That evening, Heela fell asleep at sunset. Around three in the morning, she and the aunt roused themselves to prepare the midnight meal ahead of the day's fast. As they passed the kitchen window, they heard the crackle of what sounded like a walkie-talkie. The women stared at each other, then circled back to the bedroom. They blocked the door with a crate and sat listening.

At first light, Heela ventured into the kitchen and looked into the yard. Nothing. Had she been hallucinating? But they had both heard it.

She woke the children and tried to go about her day. In all her years, she could not remember feeling so exhausted. The toll was apparent in her reddish eyes and hoarse voice, and the aunt worried that she was falling sick. She encouraged Heela to break her fast, but she refused. She didn't feel much like eating anyway.

In the afternoon, Shaysta showed up to inquire about her husband's land. Under tribal law, a woman did not enjoy property rights, and he was eager to relieve her of the family's acre of good soil. Under Islamic law, however, property in such cases belonged entirely to the woman.

That afternoon, a mullah arrived to inform her that she could choose between tribal and Islamic law. As Shaysta looked on, she announced that she was choosing the latter.

Retreating to the bedroom, Heela opened the drawer and fingered Musqinyar's salwar kameez. She looked at his watch, his prayer beads, his photographs. It took thousands of tiny acts to nurture a life. She thought of the women who had bathed and fed him as a child, the men who had taught him. All this labor, all the struggle that was required from so many for a person to become himself, and to what end? It struck her now as absurd. *What was the point?* she thought to herself.

But what choice did anyone have? Her thoughts turned to the children, to the future they had plucked from them when she and Musqinyar fled Kabul. Pointless or not, she had a duty to see that even in their consignment to this wretched place they would survive the best they could. And it was clear that there was only one course open to her: surrender. She'd capitulate to Shaysta, become one of his wives, and at least have someone to care for the children.

But the thought nauseated her.

It was then that she first contemplated suicide. In the village, the favored method was throwing yourself down a well. It was an honorable end, and she could think of no better way to ensure that her children would be taken in, that her family would be spoken well of. Shaysta would raise them as his own, and they would grow up in a better world.

That evening, the first stage of her submission commenced. Shaysta returned, demanding that she agree to hand over half of all future harvests from Musqinyar's land. He had even drawn up a contract. Heela signed the papers. Shaysta promised to return the following day. He told her, "We have other matters to discuss."

After sundown, Heela, the two boys, and Musqinyar's aunt once again barricaded themselves in the bedroom. It was the sixth night since the murder, and Heela knew that she'd have to make a decision soon. As she lay turning in bed, the dog started to bark. She pressed her ear to the window. Voices. She slowly opened the shutters, and the undeniable smell of cigarette smoke wafted in. The voices grew louder. Someone coughed. The two children were now clinging to her.

The old woman broke down. "I'm sorry," she sobbed. "I just can't do this anymore. You are brave. So, so brave. It's just too dangerous here. I'm sorry, I have to leave in the morning."

Heela said nothing. She sat looking at the wall for a long time. So this was it, the final turn, the last in a series of ineluctable steps by which the world would abandon her, leave her to the mercies of criminals through no fault of her own.

And then, for the first time since losing her husband, a new emotion welled up: anger.

She hated the woman.

She hated Shaysta. The very sight of him.

She hated her neighbors, the village, her relatives, everyone. She was alone in the world but for her children.

And something within her turned. She didn't know what it was but felt it growing inside. It was not the old tug; that was gone. This was a new feeling, one she hadn't felt before, something akin to private rage, but not quite. She couldn't give her children away. She couldn't let Zahir do this to them. She thought back to her parents' home in Kabul, with its musty tea smell, and her first days at the university, and all the times she had stolen away with Musqinyar. She thought about the civil war: so many had perished, so many lives ruined. But not hers. She recalled her miscarriage, and her flight to Uruzgan, and the Taliban.

At every step, she had survived. And at that moment, sometime past midnight on October 27, 2004, she decided that she would survive this, too.

Escape was the only option. But where? Peeking out the window she saw the outlines of fat mountains, sitting rudely against the night sky. She looked back at her red-eyed, hollow-cheeked aunt, and immediately felt sorry for getting angry with her. No, she wouldn't get angry—she would get out. And to do that, she needed every last bit of help she could find.

It took an hour for the cigarette smoke to dissipate and the voices to disappear. Then, turning to the old woman, Heela said, "We have to go somewhere, now."

"Where?"

Heela pointed into the blackness. "Out there."

The old woman looked at Heela as if she had gone mad. But Heela fitted on her burqa and led the children outside. The aunt scrambled after them into the frigid night. As Heela stood there, in the darkness, she realized that she had not the slightest clue what to do next.

"What's wrong with you?" the old woman repeated. "Are you crazy?"

"Just trust me," Heela replied. She knew that to get around outside, she'd need a mahrem. But who? How? She stood thinking, and then whispered, "Follow me." She led the group along a donkey trail heading to Shaysta's house. She rapped on the door, and when Shaysta appeared, blinking off sleep, she revealed her face. He gaped at her.

"Are you crazy? What are you doing here?"

"I have money for you," Heela replied.

"What?"

"I have money for you. Don't ask. It's an emergency. Follow me."

"You've really lost your mind. This is unbelievable."

But she moved on, heading back toward her house with the children in tow. He was forced to follow. Asking them to wait outside, she headed for the bedroom, where she took what remaining money she had, stuffed it into a small change purse, and tucked it underneath her burqa. She gathered her property documents and her faded voter registration card and stuffed them into the purse as well. Then she grabbed her husband's Kalashnikov, switched off the safety, and slung it over her shoulder, also under her burqa. Just before leaving, she took a copy of the Holy Koran. This she placed in a small burlap bag that she hung around her neck. It rested close to her heart.

Reappearing outside, she said quietly but firmly, "We need to go to my husband's pharmacy."

"*Now?*" Shaysta asked. "Are you sick? Are you losing your mind? What if someone sees a woman walking around at this time?"

"I have money there. My husband's money. I'll give it to you. Just take me there."

Shaysta stood thinking. "Okay, let's go. But quickly, before sunrise."

They walked toward the stream in the darkness. A full moon hung in the sky. No one spoke. When she stepped onto the footbridge, it creaked, and the old woman and the children jumped.

At the clearing on the opposite bank, Nawid said, "Mama, this is where they found father." Heela stopped. She felt an overwhelming urge to crumble right there. She peered through her netted eye covering, so desperately wanting to see, to understand.

"Go, go, woman!" Shaysta whispered. "Are you crazy? Let's go!"

As they passed the aunt's house, the old lady asked her grown son to join them for more protection. The group then proceeded along a narrow trail. Heela focused on Shaysta's sandaled feet ahead of her, just as she used to do with Musqinyar.

Passing the last house of the village, they emerged into the open country. The gravel road heading to the bazaar stretched out before them. From here, it would be a good hour's walk.

Shaysta stopped and stared ahead into the darkness. "There's a police checkpoint along this road sometimes. We can't go any further. Let's go home."

"No!" Heela said. "I can't. There's money—I promise." She was whispering loudly. "I promise in God's name."

She added, "We get it now or someone else might get there first."

Shaysta stared ahead, then looked at an adjacent field, waist-high with wheat. "Well, then this is the only way."

They stepped carefully through the farmer's field. Around them, the silence was complete. The fields were packed with mud and they stopped now and then to pull their feet free. The old lady wanted to rest, but Shaysta moved her along. It occurred to Heela that despite living in a farming community for ten years, this was the first time she had ever set foot in a field.

After some time, the wheat thinned and they were back on the gravel road. Still in single file, they walked until they came upon the dark rectangular outlines of the bazaar. There were no lights, no animals, nothing but a quiet wind wheezing through the narrow street. They approached the pharmacy.

When Heela cranked open the old shutters, the echo went caroming out over the buildings and the fields. For a moment everyone stood waiting. She stepped inside, and the memories—her surreptitious trip here with Musqinyar and the children, the years he had put into the business, the merciless pointlessness of it all—rushed back. She collapsed, sobbing.

Composing herself, she retrieved a few hundred dollars' worth of Afghan currency, everything the family had left, and handed it to Shaysta.

Now what? The enormousness of what she was hoping to do dawned on her. She had never heard of a woman successfully running away. But what choice did she have? She would rather die than return to the village. And at least she would die trying to survive.

Outside, she considered the darkened bazaar. Somewhere out there, Zahir's policemen were patrolling. She'd have to be quick, wherever she went. The trouble was, there were no neutral sides, nowhere to seek refuge. Everyone had lined up in one way or another. Zahir had spies everywhere.

She considered fleeing to a Hazara village. But was such a thing even possible? Shaysta would never escort her there.

Then she looked through the bazaar, past the governor's building, to a small hill overlooking the fields. She looked back at Shaysta and wondered. The idea seemed absurd, even reckless. She looked back at the distant hill.

"We have to go in that direction," Heela said, pointing toward the far end of the bazaar. "There's a man there who owes my husband money. You can have some."

Muttering under his breath, Shaysta slowly led them down the narrow road. She approached the very last building of the bazaar, looked at it, glanced back at Shaysta, and kept walking—right into the open desert.

Shaysta stopped. "What are you doing?"

She kept walking.

A dark compound loomed ahead up on the hill. The children clung tightly to her.

"*There?*" Shaysta exclaimed. "You want to go *there*? Are you crazy?"

She kept walking.

The elderly lady refused to budge another step. Her son and Shaysta chased after Heela, who kept walking up the gentle slope. Bright lights came into view.

"Are you sick? What is happening to you?" Shaysta asked.

She kept walking.

Soon she was close enough to see the concertina wire twirling up from the ground. Large cement barricades sat nearby. Floodlights drenched the clearing.

It was the American base.

"Heela, this is serious," Shaysta exclaimed. "Think about the village. What kind of person are you?"

She turned and asked, "What do you want me to do?" Tears streamed down her face. "Do you want me to go back to my enemies? Do you want me to live among those people who destroyed my life?"

"This is madness," he said, no longer whispering. "You'll bring shame upon the whole village. What will people say? A woman ran off to live with foreigners?"

She kept walking toward the base.

"You're a whore!" He was screaming. "You're a dirty prostitute. I swear to God, I will kill you!" He reached over and grabbed her.

She pulled back and revealed her gun, pointing it directly at him. "I am going."

Everyone stood speechless.

She kept moving.

A few dozen yards away, the US guards looked on as a man with a large turban engaged in a heated discussion with a woman holding a Kalashnikov.

Light shone down upon the group. Afghan militiamen working for the Americans trained their weapons on Heela.

"For God's sake, put your weapon down!" Shaysta screamed. "They're going to kill you!"

She stopped in her tracks and looked around, not knowing what to do next. Something was being said over the loudspeaker.

"Raise your hands!" Shaysta shouted. "They're telling you to raise your hands. Put them in the air!"

She held her hands aloft, and the gun and her documents dropped to the ground. Moments passed as everyone stood watching. Finally, a translator for the Americans spoke over the megaphone.

"Sister, what are you doing here? Why do you have a gun?"

Heela's two children identified the translator immediately from his frequent visits to the pharmacy over the years. They darted toward the sound of his voice, waving their hands. He recognized them and advised the Americans to open the gate.

The first thing Heela saw inside the base was her husband's old Corolla. She found herself staring at it, unable to approach, but the children ran over immediately. For them, it was a sort of homecoming.

When the Americans began questioning her, she knew that this was her chance. She wanted to tell them everything from the beginning: how she had fled Kabul, her underground schools, Musqinyar's dispute with Jan Muhammad's people, the corruption, the killings, everything.

But she stopped herself. If she had learned anything in her decade in Uruzgan, it was that politics out here didn't work that way. Her story would not be one the Americans wanted to hear. It might, in fact, be taken as indirect criticism of them. After all, who was Commander Zahir but their close ally? And Jan Muhammad, likewise? Her life now depended on the Americans, and there was no escaping the fact that she had to choose a side, like everyone else around her had done. The neutral ones ended up buried; the shrewd survived. She had to speak in a language that they would understand.

She said, "The Taliban killed my husband. I need your help."

Through a translator, an officer asked what exactly they could do for her. "I want to leave here," she said. "I can't ever come back. And I want to see my sons."

Over the next few days, the soldiers made her comfortable, gave the children candy, and explored ways for her to go somewhere else, somewhere safe. Then early one morning in November, after nearly a week on the base, she and the two boys were loaded onto a Chinook helicopter. The chopper lifted off the ground, hovered for a moment above the maze of mud walls and corrugated iron roofs, and carried Heela away.

PART FOUR

— 10 —

Back to Work

For a while, all Mullah Cable could do was play video games. Morning, noon, and night. It was January 2002, and while it would be some years before hope would erode from villages like Heela's, Mullah Cable had already lost faith in the future. It had been nearly two months since his ignominious retreat from Afghanistan, and he had hardly a clue what to do next. He and his family were living in a cramped cinder-block apartment with relatives in a working-class neighborhood of Karachi, Pakistan. He hated everything about the city: it was too big, too noisy, too crowded. The food was too spicy. And you couldn't trust anyone. Not long after his arrival, a Pakistani businessman had used a phony marketing scheme to swindle Mullah Cable out of a significant portion of the money he'd brought from Kabul. Some days later, he was robbed in a restaurant.

At first he had ventured out daily in search of work, but it was hard enough for Pakistanis to find jobs, let alone illegal Afghan immigrants. So he abandoned his quest, and for days on end he would retreat to an arcade parlor, playing virtual pinball and chatting up the Afghan owner.

Life now was a matter of keeping down the past. Mullah Cable was no more; indeed, if he could have had his way, Mullah Cable would have never existed. There was only Akbar Gul, and he told everyone that the previous five years were a diversion, merely a job that had to be done, a job he hadn't put much thought into. Privately, however, the bitterness clung to him. It was impossible to forgive the Taliban, Mullah Omar, all those who had left him in the lurch. He couldn't shake off this rancor, so he learned to live with it, fixing his mind on the days ahead.

Those were months of one job or get-rich-quick scheme after another. The nadir came when he opened up a delivery service with an acquaintance—and his partner absconded with the start-up funds. The truth was, you simply couldn't make ends meet in Pakistan, not honestly, not if you didn't know someone. Iran, on the other hand? Now there was a country. Akbar Gul had heard about it since boyhood, and it had always been the plan to get there, somehow. Now the war was over, and he knew that the time was right to make the trip.

Borrowing money from a cousin, he paid for a smuggler escort and was guided with other migrant workers through the hot open country of the Pakistani-Iranian border. They came to Shiraz, a towering city, bright and clean like nothing he'd ever seen. Every morning he showed up at the muster zone and sometimes found a day's work at a marble factory. Always gifted with his hands, he now put them to good use, making marble figurines for rich collectors in Tehran and further afield. He was a quick study and in short order was promoted to full-time employment.

Soon enough, however, Iranian authorities swept through the industrial zone to clamp down on illegal immigrants. Akbar Gul ended up hiding in a migrant camp on the city's outskirts. The spring months came and he continued to pick up occasional employment sculpting figurines, sending the earnings back to his wife and daughter in Pakistan. But the work was never steady, and he was left with ample time to think. Some evenings he stood across from the mall, watching the lights and the gleaming new cars and the men and women with their children. There were days when he went to the ice cream parlor, not for the ice cream but just for a look.

At nighttime, in bed in a shared room at the migrant camp, he would think back to Afghanistan, longing to be among his people, to hear Pashto spoken in the streets. He missed the food, the hospitality, the mountain air. He wanted to be near his family again. It was true that folks back home could never even dream of the sort of life Iranians enjoyed, with their trains and glass buildings and grand multilane highways. But what good was it all if you could be locked up or deported at a moment's notice?

That summer, he was listening to the radio when he caught a voice speaking Farsi with an Afghan accent. It was President Karzai. All refugees should return immediately, the president urged, to help rebuild their country. It was exactly what Akbar Gul was waiting for. That very night he arranged to leave for Pakistan to collect his wife and daughter. This time, he told himself, he wouldn't make the same mistakes. He would follow his brothers' footsteps. He'd get a job, maybe join the police force. It would be a new beginning, a quiet life.

When Akbar Gul and his family stepped out of the taxi in Kabul on a bone-dry, dead hot August day in 2002, he hardly recognized the city he'd left behind nine months earlier. It was a place reborn. There were returnees everywhere, living up in the mountains around town or squatting in abandoned homes. At an intersection, he saw a man in a pressed uniform and white hat directing traffic as cars flooded in from all directions. There were schoolgirls and bicyclists jockeying for space on the sidewalk, and vendors selling music openly on the streets. That very day, he picked up a cassette player.

With money saved up from Iran, he rented a small apartment at the edge of town. In a corner of one room he placed his other new acquisition: a television set. Over the weeks that followed, he reconnected with his old comrades, all of whom, like him, were settling into civilian life.

Early one morning he walked through downtown to a narrow street with low, red-painted cement walls and came to a large gated entrance. It was the Ministry of the Interior. A line of people had already formed, spilling out into the street, and a pair of men in pakols carrying Kalashnikovs stood watch. Akbar Gul sat down along the wall with the others. An hour passed, and then a second. The waiting men pooled money together and bought some *bolani* turnovers, which they parceled out among themselves and ate. A third hour passed, and still no one came out to address the line. Word was that only a few men would get interviews on any day. Finally, a man in a white-topped visor hat appeared and announced that they would not be taking inquiries today but that people should come back the next morning. Akbar Gul walked home, caked in dust from the broken asphalt roads.

He returned every day, and it took him a good week to make it into the waiting room. Applicants and police officers crowded in together, and he stood there for hours. A picture of Ahmad Shah Massoud hung on the wall, under it the words NATIONAL HERO OF AFGHANISTAN.

He came back for weeks more, but the waiting room was the farthest he got. The problem was that he didn't know anyone in the ministry, and without access you were out of luck. He tried other government agencies, construction firms, even aid organizations, but the story was always the same. "The situation became very bad," he recalled. "We had nothing. I came home one day and saw my daughter sleeping on a flour sack. There was no carpet or anything else—she was just on the ground." As the last of his Iran savings dried up, he started collecting old bread discarded from the bakery and soaking it in water for dinner, just as he had during the civil war.

Returning refugees were pouring into Kabul in part because so many had lost claims on their land out in the provinces. During the war years, squatters or warlords had occupied the vacant land, and without documentation it was impossible to prove ownership. Akbar Gul was more fortunate: relatives had stayed behind in his ancestral home of Wardak Province to guard the family property. They owned a plot of good soil, a small section of which had been apportioned to him. It had always been his intention to hold on to it for old age, but it was now clear that he would have to sell it, or at least part of it, just to survive the winter.

The property lay adjacent to his father's house, which had been empty for the better part of a decade. So in late September 2002, Akbar Gul and his family packed up their possessions once again and relocated to Wardak Province. Their new home, in Chak District, was only fifty miles from Kabul, yet it couldn't have seemed more remote. The village was perched on a broad gravel hill overlooking sagebrush slopes, and down in the valley below were wheat farms and apple orchards with small houses amid them, like tiny mud castles. The water that fed the soil was itself the color of mud, as was the road running across the valley to the bazaar. The mud-splattered shops there were converted shipping containers, with felt mats or tarpaulins covering their entrances. They all sat in the shadow of a gargantuan dam, which in better times had provided electricity for Kabul but had by now fallen into disrepair, its waters muddy and still.

After selling a portion of his land, Akbar Gul finally felt himself again. His daughter was eating, and he even had enough money left over to purchase a used station wagon, which he planned to put into use as a taxi. The winter came and went, and he busied himself meeting people around the village. His life was now made up of mornings chatting up shopkeepers in the bazaar, lunches of rice and naan, afternoons in slumber, and evenings back at the bazaar. For the first time since Iran he had money to spare, and he took to making improvements to the house. It gradually occurred to him that his worst fears about the Taliban collapse had not been realized. Maybe the coming of the Americans wasn't so bad after all. Maybe it was exactly what his people needed—help, stability, a chance for a decent life. Sure, there were problems. The Northern Alliance seemed to control everything, leaving Pashtuns like him impotent. But what country didn't have issues? Certainly this was better than what he'd suffered in Pakistan and Iran.

The trouble was, he needed to keep himself busy. Village life moved slowly, and a man with Akbar Gul's tastes couldn't keep still for long. Casting an entrepreneurial eye around the village, he saw opportunity everywhere. At the bazaar he would poke his head in at one shop after another, in no time assuming the role of occasional butcher, tire salesman, or grocery vendor as he filled in for his new friends. He spent most evenings behind the counter at an electronic goods stall, which sold everything from hand-cranked radios and flashlights to the newest addition to village life, the cell phone. He was there one day when a young man strolled up holding a broken phone.

"Can you fix this?" he asked. The phone wasn't turning on, even when fully charged.

"I don't know," Akbar Gul said, turning it over. In fact, he hadn't the faintest idea how such a machine worked.

The man said he'd pay whatever it took.

Never one to refuse a challenge, Akbar Gul agreed to take a look and told the man to return in a few days. He wasn't sure why he did things like this. It usually just landed him in trouble, but he couldn't help himself. He pried the phone open with a screwdriver and stared at the circuit board, with its strange knobs and pathways and wires. *There has to be a logic to it—it doesn't run on magic,* he told himself. He thought back to the automobiles he had retooled on the front lines. This couldn't be that different.

Yet it was. Everything was tiny, and you couldn't simply pull parts out. Or could you? He followed the pathways to a flat square with miniature wires emanating from its side like some sort of strange centipede. He took his screwdriver and slid the tip under the square. Suddenly, it snapped. Akbar Gul stared at what he'd done. *It had come clean off the board.* He tried to fit it back on, in the process mangling two wires. Struggling to fix those, he damaged others. In the end, the phone appeared beyond repair.

He jumped into his car and drove an hour to Kabul. At the electronics bazaar there, his fears were confirmed: the phone was ruined.

The was only one way out of this. On the spot, he purchased a phone of the same model and then replaced the damaged interior with the new one.

The next day, when the man found his phone working as good as new, he was stunned. "You're a genius!" he exclaimed. "I've been everywhere—no one could fix this."

Akbar Gul beamed triumphantly.

Over the next few days, as news of Akbar Gul's cell phone prowess spread, more villagers showed up with broken phones. With a reputation to uphold, he couldn't turn them down. He tinkered with each phone until it broke, then drove to Kabul and replaced it with a brand-new one. Within days, he earned renown across Chak as a cell phone wizard. "It wasn't a very profitable business," he admitted to me.

He began avoiding the bazaar. But the customers always found him.

With each phone he ruined, however, he learned something new about the way they worked. Eventually, he found that he had to rush to Kabul less often. In time he became something of a genuine cell phone expert, or at least more expert than anyone in the nearby countryside. Borrowing money from friends, he erected a stall of his own and began fixing phones.

Akbar Gul had finally found his métier. He started visiting electronics bazaars in Kabul to study the latest imports. There was so much to discover. In the newest phones, you could store snippets of songs as ringtones. Some could even play video clips. When he introduced these innovations in the village, they proved to be a big hit. People came with their favorite Pashtun tunes and Bollywood numbers, and he installed them for a modest fee.

By the summer's end, he had amassed a small fortune by village standards. It had been a year since his arrival in Wardak Province, and Mullah Cable was now known everywhere in Chak as Mobile-Phone Akbar Gul. Even customers from neighboring districts sought him out. He abandoned his plans to run a taxi business and decided that he would branch out into radios and televisions. The latter hadn't made it into the village yet, but they were spreading rapidly through Kabul, and he knew that it would only be a matter of time.

It was high noon and the earth baked and the bazaar was shutting down for sleep when a pair of men showed up at the shop. They both wore neat blue-gray uniforms, with Afghan flag patches on their lapels. One of them handed a phone to Akbar Gul and ordered him to fix it.

He had long feared this day would come. These were members of the brand-new Afghan National Police, and they descended like hungry dogs on anyone making good money.

"You'll need to pay like everyone else," Akbar Gul said.

Soon they were in a shouting match. It ended with the officer raising his hand and striking Akbar Gul, hard. The other one kicked over the stand. Then they walked away, leaving Akbar Gul standing there dazed. He watched them get into their police truck, kick up dust, and drive away.

That Friday at the mosque after prayers the shopkeepers gathered around bowls of fruit and swapped stories, and Akbar Gul recounted what had happened. The men nodded and told their own tales. Everyone agreed that the police chief and the district council and the governor himself were in on the racket. They traded stories from around the province of police checkpoints that would rob you dry and of officials in Kabul who would do nothing about it. They spoke of the Taliban's collapse and how locally elected councils had initially functioned as the replacement government until the Northern Alliance marched in and took over. A power struggle had ensued, with the Alliance commanders labeling their opponents as "Taliban" to secure their elimination by the Americans.

It was common knowledge that the men now controlling Wardak had grisly records. The police chief, for one, was a member of the Sayyaf militia—the same group that had participated in the massacre of Hazaras in Kabul during the civil war. But the most damning fact about the "new" police force, the thing that angered the shopkeepers the most, was that it actually wasn't new at all. It was simply an amalgamation of old militias and gangs. In Wardak's multiparty, multiethnic district of Jalrez, for instance, all sixty-five members of the police force hailed from a single pro-Sayyaf village.

Akbar Gul had heard some of these stories before but had never paid them much attention until now. When the police showed up at the bazaar a few days later asking for a "tax," he thought back to his friends' stories and paid without complaint. It was clear that refusing to pay would get him beaten or jailed—or, worse, delivered to the Americans as a member of al-Qaeda. It was not long before the police started showing up at the bazaar every week or so to collect their tax. But even then they were not satisfied. Sometimes they would forcibly enter homes and help themselves to whatever they desired. Once they broke into a house not far from Akbar Gul's and robbed a newly married couple at gunpoint of the equivalent of $50,000. The precinct headquarters became drug trade central, and most of the time the police themselves seemed high.

The biggest shock came when the police raided Karla Schefter's clinic. A sixty-year-old German nurse, Schefter had been running her humanitarian medical facility for more than a decade, to everyone's approval. The police, however, stormed the clinic in an ostensible search for "criminals" and made off with thousands of dollars' worth of equipment. "It depressed me," Akbar Gul recalled. "What did she ever do to anyone? She only helped us."

A few weeks later, a female neighbor who left her house without permission was abducted and raped. Although everyone knew that the police were responsible, nothing could be done. The victim later committed suicide to restore her family's honor. That autumn, the police kidnapped a young boy and took him to the mountains, where they gang-raped him and left him to die.

It was not long after these incidents that Akbar Gul received a call from Abbas, an old friend from the Taliban days.

"You know the situation," Abbas said. "What do you want to do about it?"

Akbar Gul certainly knew the situation. By now, everyone did. In addition to the news from his district, stories were flooding in from around the country. People were being taken away by helicopters during the night and never seen again, and there was not a law on earth to protect them. Tribal elders were being sent to Guantanamo. Guns and money were ruling the land.

"Of course I know. But what can I do?"

"We've started work. You interested?"

Work. So that was what they called it. Around the country, he knew, incidents were cropping up here and there. The odd shooting of a policeman, or a bomb buried in a road detonating when an American vehicle passed over. They were few, but noticeable. Akbar Gul was surprised that his former comrades were actually contemplating fighting. No matter how bad things were getting, he felt in his bones that there had been enough bloodshed. Now it was embarrassing even to admit that he had once been in the Taliban, and friends knew that it was a subject you didn't bring up in his presence.

Undeniably, the Americans and the police seemed to be no alternative. But could anyone actually take on the United States? The thought seemed absurd. He would never forget the bombing up in the mountains, or his trek through the forests of Waziristan.

"No," Akbar Gul replied. "Look, I've got my shop. I have a family."

Abbas insisted that the time was now, and Akbar Gul countered that the movement was over and for good reason. "I'm done fighting," he said. "And I think life will get better. We just need to be patient."

For many Taliban members who had abandoned the movement, however, life was turning out to be more complicated than anyone anticipated.

Muhammad Haqqani, a former Taliban deputy minister who fled to Pakistan during the American bombing, later recalled those initial post-Taliban years to a reporter: "When I was visiting my daughter one night, she asked me about our Kabul home, why we didn't have a car anymore. She complained that it was too hot in the refugee camp, and that she wanted to move back to the cool climate of Kabul. I couldn't answer her. But she could tell from my eyes how sad I was. I was a wreck—nervous, worried, and almost panic-stricken." Under such duress, it didn't take long for Taliban leaders to flock to the proverbial bargaining table, hoping to cut deals with the new government.

It was a replay, in their minds, of their own rise to power, when they had struck accords with anyone willing to submit to their authority. "We expected that if we offered no resistance, they would accept us and we could live in peace," said former minister of defense Mullah Obaidullah, one of the movement's most senior figures. Obaidullah, a confidant of supreme leader Mullah Omar, attempted multiple times to engineer deals with the new authorities. In January 2002, he contacted Kandahar governor Gul Agha Sherzai with a compelling offer: in return for amnesty, he would pledge loyalty to the Karzai government, forswear political life, and submit to regular government monitoring. Joining him were six other leading Taliban officials, including the notorious one-eyed, one-legged Mullah Turabi, who as minister of justice and head of the religious police had been a zealot's zealot, an architect of edicts outlawing everything from kite flying to music. The group now accepted the US-backed government's legitimacy, and after Sherzai signed off on the deal, retired quietly to their home villages. "They planned to take up a life of preaching, just like they did after the Russians left," reported Ahmed Shah Achekzai, a lawmaker who visited them at the time.

The Obaidullah group, and the three top Taliban officials who went to Khas Uruzgan in January 2002 in search of a pact (only to be stymied by the standoff between the district's competing governors) were far from the only ones looking to make arrangements. In fact, from Washington's list of the twenty-seven most wanted Taliban, a majority attempted to engineer similar deals. Mullah Abdul Jalil, the deputy foreign minister and one of Mullah Omar's trusted advisers, drew up a settlement with Uruzgan elders; top Taliban military commander Mullah Qaher surren-

dered his weapons and pledged support for the new administration; former Taliban spokesman Abdul Hai Mutmain reached an agreement with
Kandahari tribal elders—and so on down the line.

No sooner had the olive branch been extended, however, than it was
withdrawn. When news of Sherzai's deal with Obaidullah and his comrades surfaced, US officials were furious. Responding to Washington's
pressure, Sherzai reversed his position, announcing that all Taliban would
be detained and handed over to the Americans. Obaidullah and company fled to Pakistan. The new Afghan system quickly reorganized
around the logic of serving up "enemies" to the foreign forces, and one
attempted pact after another was thwarted.

Khairullah Khairkhwa, for instance, a onetime Taliban interior minister, was a Popalzai tribesman like Karzai and had been friendly with
the president's family. In early 2002 he contacted representatives of
Ahmed Wali, the president's brother, in the hopes of securing amnesty
and perhaps landing a post with the Karzai administration, and the two
sides met in a safe house in the Pakistani border town of Chaman. But
Pakistani authorities caught wind of his presence, arrested him, and
turned him over to the Americans. He was sent to Guantanamo.

Ex-Taliban governor Naim Kuchi was a leader of the Kuchis, Pashtun
nomads who number in the millions and crisscross the country with the
seasons. In 2002 he sided with the Karzai administration and functioned
as an access broker for his people. He was en route to a meeting with
government officials one day when he was detained by American soldiers, sparking bitter demonstrations across Kabul. He, too, was shipped
to Guantanamo.

Mullah Abdul Razaq, the Taliban minister of commerce, had surrendered to Afghan authorities and retired from political life. Nonetheless,
he was arrested by US forces—on Sherzai's suggestion—and dispatched
Guantanamo-ward as well, even though a subsequent military assess-
ment determined that "there was insufficient evidence to connect detainee
to any kind of involvement with the al Qaeda terrorist network." Razaq
also faced accusations of being a leader of the "Taliban movement in
exile." In fact, the Americans had confused him with the similarly named
Abdul Razak, a former interior minister who indeed was active in the
movement. But that Razak, in fact, had also initially sought to reconcile,

fleeing to Pakistan only after he was nearly arrested for his efforts. From there he had attempted to broker a deal directly with the CIA, but in this, too, he was unsuccessful.

By the summer of 2002, nearly the entire senior Taliban had sought refuge in Pakistan, leaving behind only midlevel figures lacking clout in the organization. Occasionally there would be talk of returning home, but the plight of many junior comrades inside the country loomed large over the deliberations. There was, for instance, the case of Mullah Ahmed Shah. When Sherzai's intelligence agents had come for him, Ahmed Shah was living quietly in his home village in Kandahar, having surrendered his arsenal and retired from life as a minor Taliban commander. Nonetheless, he was accused of harboring weapons; when none were found, he was hauled off to a secret jail in Kandahar city anyway.

There, Shah found himself in an underground cell crammed with farmers, tribal elders, and ex-Taliban figures, none of whom had seen the light of day for weeks. Despite his Taliban past, Shah was so widely respected in his community for his skills as an arbitrator that tribal elders mobilized for his release. "We met the prisoners in jail and saw that their feet were swollen," elder Fazel Muhammad recalled. "Their hands and feet had been tied for days. . . . They also beat them with cables. They were begging us to tell the guards to just kill them so that they could be put out of their misery."

Shah was told that if he couldn't produce weapons he would never step outdoors again, so desperate family members resorted to purchasing arms on the black market. A week after being released, though, he was thrown into the same dungeon on the same charges. By now, everyone understood the game—bribes—so the family pawned their livestock to raise funds for his freedom. As with Sherzai's egg, however, once cracked you were marked for life. Within weeks, Shah was dragged out of his home yet again. This time his liberty proved too expensive for his penniless family, so tribal elders demonstrated until their protests were heard all the way in Kabul. Shah was let out, but he had been back home for only a few weeks when he caught wind of rumors that they were coming for him yet again. Broken and fearful, he collected his family and fled to Pakistan, where he rekindled contacts with his old comrades. The Taliban, he realized, was where he belonged.

Not far from Ahmed Shah's village stands the simple mud house of Feda Muhammad, a former schoolteacher and popular Taliban commander. In 2002, like Shah, he surrendered his weapons and retired to his home to become a respected tribal elder in the community. Not long after, he was turned over to the Americans by Sherzai's agents. Upon his release, the normally warm and gregarious Muhammad refused to participate in the local village council and rarely left home. An intelligence agent working for the Karzai government, who had maintained a friendship with him, paid Muhammad a visit and tried to coax him out of the house.

He was "too ashamed to come out and talk to people," the agent told me. "Finally, I convinced his son to let me see him. He looked like a disaster. He hadn't been sleeping well. He started to tell his story of how he was humiliated, stripped naked, beaten, and how they put dogs on him when he was in that state. He was crying and asked how he could possibly live in Afghanistan with any dignity." Not long afterward, Muhammad, too, fled to Pakistan and reconnected with old friends in the Taliban.

Across the country, in one village after the next, the story repeated itself. In a way, the mood of retribution should have been expected. After all, the Taliban's human rights record and their sorry attempt at governance inspired no sympathy. The problem was not so much that the Taliban were targeted but that they were *uniquely* targeted: the men now allied with the United States harbored similarly deplorable records from the civil war era, yet their crimes went unpunished. A true reconciliation process would have required either bringing to justice people from across the entire political spectrum, or else pardoning them all. To the Taliban, justice unequally applied felt like no justice at all.

For the top Taliban leadership, the apparent inequity of a "war forced upon us," as Mullah Obaidullah put it, was so great that there seemed no choice but to organize some sort of resistance. Yet as they regrouped in the Pakistani city of Quetta, there was widespread disagreement about whether anything could actually be done. In late 2002, the leadership met in Karachi and voted in favor of a last-ditch effort to come to an accord with Kabul. Emissaries were sent to meet Karzai's representatives, but with reconciliation still a toxic idea in Washington and in Northern Alliance circles, the effort fizzled.

The course now seemed set. Mullah Omar organized a group of about a dozen top Talibs—almost all of whom had attempted to reconcile—as a new leadership body that came to be known as the Quetta Shura. Mullah Obaidullah took on the task of resurrecting dormant Taliban networks in Afghanistan. He and others reached out to communities in places like Jan Muhammad's Uruzgan and Sherzai's Kandahar, where resentment was steadily building over the killings, the night raids, the abductions, the torture, the broken alliances, and the fractured hopes. In these communities, the American presence was coming to be seen as an occupation, and Karzai's government increasingly regarded as Washington's venal and vicious puppet.

From this point on, there would be no turning back.

In Wardak Province, the defining event of those days was the defection of Ghulam Muhammad. A hulking man with a shrubby black beard, Muhammad had been a key Taliban provincial commander and an important tribal elder. Akbar Gul had long admired his family, and now that Muhammad was joining Kabul's side, he hoped that government jobs might open up for people like him. In 2003, Muhammad's brother Musa Hotak, who had also been a Talib, was elected as one of the delegates to draft Afghanistan's new constitution. The following year, the two brothers handed over their remaining weapons in a well-publicized ceremony attended by US forces, UN representatives, and the media.

Unsurprisingly, the move upset the balance of local politics, pushing Northern Alliance figures to view Ghulam Muhammad as a rival. You can undoubtedly guess what happened next: they fed the usual false intelligence to the Americans, who raided Muhammad's home in July 2004, a mere two months after his weapons surrender.

"I still get flashbacks," Musa Hotak recalled to a reporter. "They broke down doors, smashed every window. I was clubbed and bitten by dogs. My sons and nephews were hooded and shackled. My aged father was dragged out. No human being would do the things those animals did."

Ghulam Muhammad was taken to Bagram prison. When Akbar Gul heard the news, he simply could not understand why the Americans would do such a thing to their own ally. He started to wonder aloud whether the foreigners were in fact bent on colonizing us, like the British."

That summer, a police truck drove up to his cell phone stall. Two officers got out with drawn Kalashnikovs and ordered Akbar Gul to lie flat on the dirt. He was kicked in the head and jabbed in the small of his back, and he could hear them rummaging through his stall. As he was forced into the back of the jeep, the policemen informed him that he was in arrears on his car payments and that there was no bribe or elder that could save him. The jeep headed down the open highway in the direction of Kabul.

An officer turned and looked at him. "When we get there," he said, "we'll put heavy stones on your back. We'll keep adding them until you pay what you owe." When Akbar Gul protested that he owed nothing, they jabbed him again with their rifles. The jeep drove on, and the policemen wagered among themselves how many stones it would take to break him. It was then that he blurted out that he had savings. The jeep turned around. When they arrived at his home, Akbar Gul went into a closet, fished out a small cash box, and returned to show it to them. The men helped themselves and then said he was free to leave.

He went back to his shop in the afternoon, two years' worth of labor gone. He worked diligently that summer, long into the night, fixing phones and radios. He traveled to other districts for business. He had not made up even a fraction of his savings by autumn, but he had money to eat, and that was enough.

Then one day he saw the police truck driving up the street, sending him indoors into a friend's shop. Through the window slats, he watched as the policemen approached his stall. They milled around it, talking to each other, gesturing at the cell phones. One reached over and collected them and his tools. Then another raised a foot and kicked the stall hard. A third took his turn. Blow by blow they continued, until only wood shards were left. They returned to their vehicles and drove away.

Akbar Gul stood staring for a long while. A fellow shopkeeper came to console him, but Akbar Gul did not say anything. After some time, he went home.

Akbar Gul knew certain things: that Afghanistan wasn't a normal country, that to survive you should expect to exert yourself harder than anywhere else he could imagine, and that even then everything could vanish in a moment. He had gone from fearing the new order to embracing it. That, he understood, was how history moved. All ideas had their time; whatever life had been like before, under the new order everything would be different. "I believed it," he said. "No one could have convinced me otherwise. I believed it in my heart."

Now, he realized that things *were* different—but in all the wrong ways. Whenever he turned on the radio it was all hope and anticipation, but more and more that seemed like a cruel joke. The truth was, something appeared to be happening right there, in Chak District of Wardak Province. He noticed it in the way that people spoke about the future, about their children. Everyone seemed to be waiting for some sign that change of another sort was on its way.

To Akbar Gul, there could be only one explanation for what the Americans had wrought. They were the world's sole superpower, capable of toppling the Taliban government in two months with their fantastically sophisticated technology. If they were now siding with the Northern Alliance, arresting the wrong people, unleashing a predatory police force on his people, it could not have been by accident. No, he reasoned—it was by design. In the mosque on Friday, he would listen to sermons explaining that the Americans were bent on colonizing his country and converting the whole population to Christianity—just as the Russians had attempted to enforce Communism.

One day, Akbar Gul received another phone call from Abbas. "Business is good," he said. "We've been back to work. What about you? What do you think?"

This time, the answer seemed obvious. Or, as he explained to me years later, the answer had already been decided for him. And so it was that on that winter day in early 2005, Akbar Gul decided it was time to go back to work.

11

The Tangi

Spring had come early to the Tangi. The landscape was lush with wild almond and blooming acacias and flowering privet, and the fields were a brilliant green. Wheat fields and fruit orchards crisscrossed the narrow watershed basin between the two mountain chains that formed the valley's walls, no more than half a mile apart at their widest. Those mountains rose thousands of feet, dense and interlocking, a rock fortress. During the 1980s, the Soviets could never bring the Tangi to heel. Now, in 2005, it would prove the perfect place for a nascent Taliban insurgency to germinate.

It had been nearly a month since Akbar Gul had spoken to Abbas, and on a warm March day he had received a second call, with instructions to head to the Tangi. Early the next morning he drove his station wagon through the valley basin into a green thicket, pulling up to a house standing alone among the trees. The wall enclosure had partially crumbled away, exposing the yard. Weeds had edged over the walkway leading to the guesthouse, and trash was strewn everywhere. The windows were fractured, the walls pitted with the marks of some forgotten battle. No one was at home, so he let himself in.

The guest-room carpet smelled of onions and was imprinted here and there with boot tracks. Soiled linens were heaped in a pile. In one corner, he noticed a brand-new Panasonic TV and DVD player. He settled down and waited. More than an hour passed, and then Abbas walked in, followed soon after by a pair of armed men and a large gentleman with a well-manicured beard wearing a stately black turban. Akbar Gul recognized him at once as Mufti Abdul Latif, an old friend from the Taliban days. They exchanged greetings and sat down for tea.

"We aren't rich people," Abdul Latif explained. "We have nothing. We live by the grace of God. We'd like you to work with us."

"I'm ready," Akbar Gul replied. But he had many questions. "Where is Mullah Omar? Is he alive?"

"Praise God, Mullah Omar is alive and safe. He's in Pakistan."

"And everyone else?"

"They are all in Pakistan. They're busy working."

"Who is funding us?"

"We're getting money from Saudi Arabia, from Pakistan, from al-Qaeda."

"Where is al-Qaeda? Bin Laden?"

"No one knows. But their friends give us money sometimes."

"What do you want me to do?"

Abdul Latif knew Akbar Gul well. He also had an eye for human weakness, for pride in particular. He said, "I want you to be governor of Chak District. You'll be responsible for all of it."

Governor. Akbar Gul liked the sound of that. It was something he could get behind, put his efforts into. He wasn't the lowlife that the police had treated him as—he was smarter, more talented than almost anyone he knew in the village. A man of his caliber was destined to lead. He would be governor of Chak.

Of course, he knew that Chak District had a Karzai-appointed, US-backed governor. But it was clear to him that the new Taliban were already thinking of themselves as a government-in-waiting. And he wasn't about to be left behind.

Mufti Latif handed him a Kalashnikov and about $330 in Afghan currency. "Everything else," he said, "is up to you and God." Akbar Gul would be responsible for fund-raising, recruiting men to fight under him, arming them—all on his own. Luckily for him, resourcefulness was his strong suit.

He carefully wrapped the Kalashnikov in a flour bag and tied it to the underside of his car. As the sun grew faint, he drove out of the valley onto the highway, passing police checkpoints, and arrived home in the darkness. He hid the weapon in an old outdoor tandoor and went in for dinner.

Later that night he phoned his village friends. By midnight, eleven of them had assembled at his house. Young and unemployed, they had found little to savor in the post-2001 world. "It was good to put these sorts of people to work," Akbar Gul said.

There was Yunis, his closest friend, who had lent him money to set up his cell phone shop and had grown so fed up with the police that he was ready for anything. Habib Rahman was a driver who, when he did find work, was regularly shaken down by the police for bribes. Walid was unemployed and looking for money and excitement. Sayed Muhammad, the most religious among them, was also out of work and looking to make ends meet. Hamidullah toiled over a small plot of poor soil, frustrated by just about everything from the police to his lazy cousins. A couple of friends had shown up because Taliban from *other* villages were harassing them and they were looking for a group of their own for protection. Everyone shared an intense disgust with what the Americans had done to their country, their tribal elders, and their customs.

Akbar Gul addressed the room. "I don't want to be like other Taliban groups. We aren't going to do hit-and-run attacks and spend our days in the mountains. I want us to be strong and open. Out there. I want to control the roads and attack them in broad daylight." People sat listening in admiration. "We're all afraid of the enemy nowadays. My goal is to change that. I want to make the enemy afraid of us."

He divided up the $330 among the men. "God is merciful," he said. For the moment, at least, he knew he had their loyalty. And for the first time in years, he felt like himself again. To hold court, to fill men's minds with visions of your own, to matter—that was what he'd been missing.

Just one issue remained: weapons.

A year earlier, halfway across the country in Uruzgan Province, a similar story had unfolded for Mullah Manan. It began one morning during harvest season, when, as always, he was in the fields before dawn. Under the sun, poppy sap was too dry, too crusted, doubling or tripling his work. And the labor was hard enough as it was. That day he was on his knees, lancing the bulbs and watching the sap dribble out, then lancing them again and a third time, the sap richer with every cut. It was good work. Ever since Manan's defeat in 2001 at the battle of Tirin Kot, opium had been his provider. It paid for his sister's salwars, for his nephews' school supplies, for their daily naan. The Taliban's collapse, it turned out, had been a great boon for the village: everyone was able to get back to growing the stuff, which was hardier than wheat or corn and had two harvest seasons to boot. In fact, poppy cultivation was flourishing province-wide, and everyone from tribal elders to government functionaries to Jan Muhammad himself had a hand in it.

With the sun high he went inside, his muscles burning, his knees tender. In the early days after the invasion, Manan had listened to the hand-cranked radio on his breaks. The BBC would discuss President Karzai and the international donors helping to develop the country, and Manan felt that, despite the ignominy of his defeat, it was a great thing the Americans were doing. Nowadays, however, he wasn't so sure.

In the afternoon, when the air cooled, he returned to the field and crawled from bulb to bulb, collecting sap. In a few weeks brokers would arrive and pay good money for it, then carry it off to other countries for processing. For a kilo of sap, he could get almost double compared to potatoes or wheat.

He was scraping the bulbs when he looked up to see plumes of smoke rising from a neighbor's plot. He went over to take a look. The farmer was frantically hacking down his own poppy field, like a man possessed. Flames danced and leapt from one patch to the next.

The farmer saw Manan and shouted, "Jan Muhammad is coming!"

Manan raced back to his field. He knew that the government did not look kindly on people like him growing poppies. But they had never bothered him before.

He saw a group of vehicles nearby with American Humvees idling behind them. Four Afghans, wearing bandoliers and salwars, ran toward him with weapons raised. He threw his hands up and soon they were on him, shouting, "Get down, you dirty Talib! Get down, you dog!" In a moment he was lying facedown in the dirt, being kicked and jabbed in the ribs with the barrel of a gun. He was dragged to a jeep and tossed into the backseat. The militiamen returned to the fields and retrieved other farmers, and soon the jeep was bursting with bruised and bewildered men. The Americans stood in the distance, watching.

As the jeep pulled away, he looked back and saw the militiamen setting his field aflame.

In prison, Manan discovered that he'd been rounded up as part of an American program to eradicate poppy cultivation, conducted with the help of JMK, who was seemingly using the program to wipe out Ghilzai competition and keep prices high. For twelve days, he and the other farmers were kept in a claustrophobic cell. Freedom was reserved for those who could pay, so he passed word to his family to auction off their livestock.

When he returned home, he walked out onto the field and looked over what had become of his livelihood. The soil was ashen, covered with rotting opium paste. The bulbs had charred to nubs. Even part of the mud-walled enclosure was torn down. He wanted only one thing, to walk into the governor's mansion and shoot the man himself. Or onto an American base and gun down the whole lot of them. But what could he do? There was no one to complain to, no advocate for his village. His best hope, the Ghilzai elder Muhammad Nabi, had disappeared after repeated American arrests.

Every Friday, the ruined farmers gathered at the local mosque after prayers to discuss the situation. Among them was the charismatic Mullah Dil Agha, an ex-Taliban commander who had sworn off politics and taken to a life of quiet preaching. Now, seething with anger at what was happening to his village and to Ghilzai elders across Uruzgan, he did most of the talking. Manan was happy to listen because Dil Agha had the gift of a silver tongue. Manan had assumed that the campaign of persecution was just one in a long line of injustices, stretching back to the civil war, that people of his lot were destined to suffer forever. This was how things were and how they would always be. Dil Agha begged to differ. This abuse, he said, felt more immediate, more personal. Their community was being targeted simply because they were from the Ghilzai tribe—and it did not stop there. Their Pashtun ethnicity was similarly in the crosshairs, for it was clear that Hazaras were escaping the worst of this. And with the American raids, with the assassinations and disappearances of their elders, their very way of life as Afghans and Muslims was under threat.

Mullah Dil Agha would repeat that phrase often: "our way of life." The Americans, he explained, invaded because they hated the Afghan way of life. It was not long before Manan finally asked Dil Agha how they could sit idly by while this was going on.

"In Kandahar people have already started work," he replied. "They are brave and they are doing something about it."

It seemed to Manan that it would be an impossible task to stand up to the likes of JMK and the Americans. Dil Agha reminded him that their fathers had thought the same of the Russians. "If it's in your heart," he said, "if you love your country and your religion, that's what matters."

Then he cited a Pashtun proverb: "A dog curls his tail, but a man fights."

Later that summer, his field unsown, his relatives idle indoors, his household finances stretched to the breaking point, Mullah Manan, too, went back to work.

For a week, Akbar Gul had been mulling over the question of weapons. From his initial meeting of eleven, eight had pledged to fight under him, eight men to be fed and armed and led as well as he could. One day, a potential solution suddenly came to him. It depended on a friendship he had made with a man named Pir Mohmand a decade earlier on the front lines of the civil war. Mohmand hailed from Akbar Gul's neighborhood in Kabul and had fought with him in Hizb-i-Islami and then the Taliban. Now he worked for the US special forces as a member of a private militia operating outside government jurisdiction. His job was to transport fuel from Kabul along hundreds of highway miles to American bases near the Pakistani border. The pay for the lonely six-hour haul was modest, and Akbar Gul wondered whether he could entice Mohmand with the promise of something better.

The plan went like this: during an early-morning delivery, Mohmand would hand over a full tanker of fuel to Akbar Gul and go into hiding for a few days. He would then claim that he had been kidnapped and the fuel stolen at gunpoint. Akbar Gul would sell the fuel on the black market and the pair would split the profits. Mohmand spent some days mulling it over, then called to say he was in.

It was long before dawn when Akbar Gul set out again for the Tangi Valley. He drove through the night, the spur of the mountains ahead lying dark against the sky. Crossing the valley floor, the gravel road banked up and hugged the northern slope. He passed some mud villages and some made of stone, and he saw in the valley below him the darkened minaret of the Tangi mosque. Farther on the valley widened and the road sloped down into it, and the valley basin gave way to a broad pied-mont plain marking the beginning of Logar Province. He drove on, and there was not a house in sight.

The gravel road crossed the plain to meet with another, which had once been asphalted and now lay fractured. He looked to the direction of Kabul, an hour off, and saw only darkness. In the other direction, the road ran to the far horizon, where it was swallowed by a mountain range beyond which lay the provinces bordering Pakistan. At the intersection of the two roads stood the broken remains of a mud village wiped away by some battle or some neglect of which he did not know.

He turned off the engine and waited. Somewhere in the distance, he could hear the first strains of the morning's call to prayer. The roads were empty and still.

The sky began to pale. It was possible that Mohmand had lost his nerve or, worse, had tipped someone off. He sat in the dawn light think-ing about all the things that could go wrong or probably had gone wrong and the trouble he'd find himself in when a police truck rolled up to ask what business he had out here. It was arrogance to have assumed that he could pull this off. He would get what he deserved.

Then he spotted a pair of headlights off in the distance, bouncing toward him. It was soon followed by a second pair of headlights. *Two* tankers. Something must have gone awry. Then the lead tanker flashed its lights three times—the prearranged signal—and Akbar Gul knew that he was in business. Mohmand had recruited an accomplice.

He casually slipped his station wagon ahead of the vehicles. Turning back onto the gravel road, he led them straight into the Tangi.

– – –

By that spring, there were twelve small, nearly autonomous Taliban groups operating in Wardak Province, all under the authority of former field commanders like Akbar Gul. Each group was left to its own devices to raise funds and weapons, resulting in a weak and divided movement. Commanders were scrounging for money, some even traveling to Pakistan in search of donations and often returning empty-handed. In this atmosphere, news of a Taliban commander wheeling two fuel trucks from the hated Americans through the Tangi must have seemed like the heist of the century. Sure enough, word of the conquest spread through the valley as farmers gossiped, and the tankers multiplied in the telling.

Within days, Akbar Gul sold off all the fuel, split his share with Mohmand and the other driver, and set the trucks ablaze. News outlets reported that the two trucks had been attacked.

With this windfall of cash, Akbar Gul contacted Jabbar, an old acquaintance adept at finding whatever was needed and ready to deal with anyone for the right price. What Akbar Gul needed was weapons: Kalashnikovs, rocket-propelled grenade launchers, mines, mortars, and—his weapon of choice—the DShK, a Soviet-made heavy machine gun.

Jabbar took Akbar Gul on a three-hour drive to Behsud, a Hazara district at the far western edge of Wardak. Many Hazara warlords, enthusiastic backers of the Americans and the Karzai government, were being forced to surrender their weapons for nominal compensation as part of a UN disarmament program—weapons that would fetch a far higher price on the black market. So they were selling their stocks to Hazara arms smugglers instead, and Jabbar was in contact with one of them. Akbar Gul returned home with mortars, RPG rounds, Chinese-made AK-47s, and a gritty old PK machine gun.

The irony ran deep: the main former Taliban commanders in Wardak had sided with the Americans after 2001 and publicly surrendered their weapons only to end up in prisons, while not long after, US-backed commanders like these Hazara strongmen began secretly selling their weapons to the newly reconstructed Taliban.

Back home, Akbar Gul called his group in and showed off his haul. No one could believe that he had gotten guns so quickly. He handed one to each man.

That evening, long after the village had retired, he and his fighters stepped out onto the darkened macadam road near the bazaar. The shops were shuttered and the night was as perfectly still and black as a country night could be, save for the occasional headlights of an oncoming vehicle. Akbar Gul studied the traffic. Then he walked into the middle of the road and pointed his gun at an approaching car.

It was the very first Taliban checkpoint in Chak District.

The summer of 2005 was long and hot and angry. American fatalities countrywide began to rise, nearly doubling from the previous year, and kidnappings and assassinations of government officials came in record numbers. Newspapers started writing about the resurgence of the Taliban, and for the first time Washington contemplated sending in more troops.

For Akbar Gul, the summer officially commenced late one June night when he directed his men to dig a hole under the highway leading to the turnoff to his village. Jabbar had provided the bomb, smuggled in from Pakistan and triggered by a pressure-plate mechanism. To ensure that they took out a suitable target, Akbar Gul posted observers about a mile ahead to radio back when the right vehicle approached. Sometime after dinner, a police Ranger drove slowly up the highway. As it neared the turnoff, it exploded into flames. Everyone inside was killed.

Later, Akbar Gul complained to Mufti Latif that pressure-plate bombs were too dangerous and indiscriminate, requiring constant supervision if civilian deaths were to be avoided. Latif arranged for a visitor from Pakistan, a bespectacled, clean-shaven Arab in his twenties, to instruct the group on more advanced bomb-making techniques. This would be the first and last time Akbar Gul met anyone from al-Qaeda. The relevance of bin Laden's organization to Afghanistan had diminished since 2001. Still, the group wielded a certain tactical influence on the resurgent Taliban movement. In that 2005 summer, for example, suicide bombings first began occurring in Afghanistan in significant numbers. The Taliban's senior brass had been divided on their use, with many in the old guard, including Mullah Omar, pointing to Koranic prohibitions against suicide and harboring a general distaste for the sort of indiscriminate violence then tearing Iraq apart. But politics has a way of making a virtue of necessity, and soon suicide bombers became the outgunned Taliban's answer to B-52s and up-armored Humvees.

It would be some years before Akbar Gul saw his first suicide bomber. For now, he was content to deploy the newfangled Arab bombs, command-detonated and devastatingly effective. Soon, his unit was burying roadside bombs up and down the highway near Chak, then waiting, hours sometimes, for a target. Within a week they had taken out four police vehicles. Twice, American convoys drove right into their trap. The first time, Akbar Gul hit the lead vehicle and watched from a nearby field as it popped straight up in the air, landing armor cracked and smoking. The second time he struck a middle vehicle with a large antenna, which he hoped signaled the presence of a commander inside. The blast tore a hole clean through it and left the trailing vehicle jackknifed.

By summer's end, that stretch of road had come to be known among Americans as IED Alley, a billing that, when Akbar Gul learned of it, filled him with pride. The police, in fact, quit patrolling the road after dark altogether. Americans passed through rarely and only with their lights off. He had been in business for less than a year, and already he owned the night.

In winter, snows set upon Wardak and many roads become impassable. Orchards frost over and only a few scattered pine forests survive, and people stay indoors, feeding wood or sawdust to their *bukhari* heating stoves. Akbar Gul stored his gun and retired to his village for the season. Only when the valleys thawed in late spring did he return to work. It was now 2006, and with a successful year under his belt he set his sights on a new goal: daytime missions. He was intent on keeping his promise: to operate unafraid of the enemy, hitting them "out there." The first such assault took place in late May, when he and Ghulam Ali, another local commander, brought their men—about thirty in all—to a Tangi hilltop overlooking a police outpost. Akbar Gul could see seven poorly equipped policemen eating lunch, their guard down in the daylight. On his command, the two teams swarmed down the hillside firing RPGs. The police barely had a chance. Four were killed instantly. The three others fled into the open scrubland near the highway, where Akbar Gul's fighters picked them off like hunted game.

Inside the outpost, the fighters discovered cases of precious ammunition and four Kalashnikovs. Using his cell phone, Akbar Gul snapped a photo of himself standing triumphantly amid the weapons and sent it to Mufti Latif. This was how Taliban commanders now proved their worth; the movement that had once shunned moving images and photography could no longer operate without them. The photographs wound up in the possession of Taliban leaders in Pakistan, and Akbar Gul was soon rewarded with a few thousand dollars. With the fresh infusion of money and weapons, he was able to attract more farmers to the group. His force expanded to fifteen.

That summer, his attacks grew ever bolder. Each one left him wanting more, each a high for which the only fix was greater, grander, showier. In August he again teamed up with Ghulam Ali, attacking and briefly over-running the Chak district governor's compound, the first such conquest in Wardak. To carry out the raid, he had resorted to tricking some of his own men. "Whenever we went on big missions, the important ones," he recalled, "there were a few of my guys who'd volunteer to stay back and guard the village. They were terrified of bullets." He grinned at me. "Two of them were newly married. They liked to spend time with their wives. You know, they were addicted to it." He had convinced them that they were only going to attack a small outpost near the governor's mansion—until the very moment when he opened fire at the mansion itself, leaving his shocked fighters no choice but to join in.

The momentary capture of a government headquarters made the national news and brought Akbar Gul further acclaim from the leadership. His group now numbered thirty strong.

Another winter came and went, and 2007 brought more violence than anyone had seen since the civil war years. The UN estimated that the Taliban had reclaimed control of more than half of rural Pashtun territory countrywide. By year's end, officials had logged more than five thousand security incidents—roadside bombings, kidnappings, assassinations, ambushes. Akbar Gul and Ghulam Ali were no longer alone in Chak, as farmers and religious students of all stripes began to join the fray. By now, there were a half-dozen Taliban groups active in that district alone.

In the winter of 2007, for the first time, some Taliban groups remained active despite heavy snows, as ever more villagers flocked to the Taliban's side. And after only a few months, 2008 had already broken the previous year's record for violence. Most of this was unfolding far from the eyes of Kabul-based reporters. Through contacts with the Taliban leadership I was able to secure permission to venture into Taliban country, and that summer I hopped on a motorcycle with an Afghan friend and headed for Chak.

We zipped along the country's main arterial highway connecting Kabul to Kandahar, which slices right through Wardak Province. Paved five years prior, to the tune of millions of dollars, it now stretched out before me as a roadway devoured, pocked and cratered with culverts here and there burst open. We passed the disemboweled remains of fuel tankers, charred vendor stalls, and small police outposts where the officers holed up, refusing to step out day or night.

In Chak, we pulled into a small village. We spent the afternoon with the malek eating watermelons in the shade of almond trees, near a small stream of tea-colored water with a few sun-blanched mud homes on the opposite bank. Village children sat nearby, watching us talk. Occasionally a Taliban fighter walked past, looked at us, and continued on.

The malek told me that the village had been under Taliban control for nearly two years, and in that time crime had vanished. The Taliban court adjudicated disputes and sentenced criminals, something only a bribe would have achieved in government courts. He explained how Taliban "police" had captured a known child molester and turned him over to Islamic justice, with judges tarring his face, parading him around Chak, and forcing him to apologize publicly. If caught again, he was told, he would be executed.

The malek would not say it, but this service, as important as it may have been, was the extent of the Taliban's governing activities. For the rest, life remained frozen—no jobs, no development, no aid. Still, for the time being at least, people preferred Taliban austerity to government and foreign impunity.

These transformations were unfolding only fifty miles from Kabul, with its embassies and aid offices and government ministries. Wresting control of Wardak—which the Americans referred to as "Kabul's doorstep"—from the Taliban would become a major goal of the Obama administration's attempts to turn the war around. Shortly after assuming office, President Obama ordered a mini-surge of troops into the country, including a battalion from the Tenth Mountain Division dispatched to the strategically crucial Logar and Wardak Provinces. The Americans were coming to Chak.

The first time Akbar Gul saw a US soldier, he was amazed. "You know, I'll never forget it," he recalled. We were sitting in a guesthouse, nursing steaming cups of cardamom tea. It had taking him a while to get to the Americans in his story, perhaps because in the early days of our meetings he could never quite shake the suspicion that I was a spy. "I was in the bazaar, chatting with some shopkeepers who were my friends. I didn't have a weapon or anything with me, I was just relaxing, and all of a sudden they came by." He counted more than a dozen soldiers. "You know, they were all different colors. I was so surprised. I saw white ones and black ones." He pointed a bony finger in my direction. "Even some that looked like you. I realized on that day that I didn't know the first thing about these people."

The soldiers were swaddled in gear—helmets, vests, wires poking out of various pockets. They walked uncomfortably, as if in great pain. Akbar Gul glanced down at his own unadorned salwar and sandaled feet and couldn't decide which of the two sides was more foolish. The soldiers worked their way through the bazaar single file. When they reached his stall the man in front turned to Akbar Gul and smiled, but the others eyed him coldly. An Afghan translator, looking awkward in his uniform, followed close behind. Within seconds, the group had passed, and soon they returned to their vehicles and drove off. Akbar Gul knew that he must be on some list of theirs, but fortunately no public photographs of him existed. Still, he decided to play things safe and spend a few nights away from home with his friend Ismael.

He woke late that night to the sound of distant thunder. Straining to listen, he could hear a helicopter hovering somewhere nearby. *Americans*, he thought. He reached for his Kalashnikov. Lights flashed outside. Every few minutes, he heard a dull thud and realized these must be explosions. They were doing house searches. Blowing off gates.

Ismael appeared in the doorway. "What do you want to do?"

Akbar Gul studied the window. If he ran for it, he might make it to the fields abutting the village. But if the Americans were there already?

"We'll stay here," he decided. "They won't search every house." He knew that they were probably looking for him. He was, after all, one of the most prominent commanders in the province, and the only one in this village. He looked over at Ismael, who was a worried mess. He was a civilian, a poor farmer, who opened his guesthouse to the Taliban, tribal elders, or whoever else passed through; he had certainly not signed up for this.

"You should get out of here," Akbar Gul said. "I'll take care of it." Ismael shot him a grateful look and left.

Akbar Gul hid his weapon and for the next hours sat in the guesthouse, waiting. The Americans, he knew, would be angry. In the previous week he'd planted a bomb that destroyed one of their vehicles and probably killed one of their soldiers.

By the morning's first light the explosions had ceased and the sky had fallen silent. He decided to test the outdoors. Slipping through a warren of donkey trails between the houses, he emerged onto the escarpment leading away from the village. At the next village, he took shelter in the house of a friend and waited. The sun was high by the time he sent the friend out and learned that the Americans were again approaching. He was spirited away to a small hut, perched atop a hill from which he could observe the houses below. He scanned the roofs and the narrow lanes. And then he saw them, gathered around the compound of an elder: meaty men in sunglasses and hats. One of them sat down with the elder. On a nearby hill, four soldiers stood guard. *Four exposed soldiers*, he realized, for all the world to see. That was when he got the idea.

He stole back to his village to retrieve his walkie-talkie and radioed Ghulam Ali and three other commanders, asking them to rendezvous in a nearby fruit orchard with men ready to fight.

It was late afternoon when the four commanders gathered in a thicket of apple trees near the occupied village. They had nearly a hundred fighters under them, but only twenty had shown up. Ambushing the Americans, after all, was a far cry from hitting the hapless Afghan police. Akbar Gul divided the group into four: two teams moving under tree cover toward the hill, one in a nearby graveyard with a good line of sight to the target, and the fourth in the orchard as a rear guard.

He led one of the mobile teams through the fruit farm. About half a mile ahead, he could see the small knoll and the Americans still pacing atop it.

He came to a ten-foot-high mud enclosure, the back wall of a farmer's compound, at the foot of the hill. Climbing onto the shoulders of one of his men, he peeked over, balancing an RPG launcher with one arm.

The Americans stood talking among themselves. *This is it*, he thought. *This is how great men are made.*

"Ready for lunch," he spoke into his walkie-talkie. "Let's eat." Within seconds, gunshots erupted from the far side of the hill. As the American soldiers scrambled for cover, Akbar Gul aimed his launcher and fired. The Americans were shooting back wildly. He reloaded and fired again. There was gunfire coming in now from multiple directions. His man was beginning to wobble under him, so he climbed off and onto another fighter. Three of the Americans had taken cover behind some boulders; the fourth was nowhere to be seen.

Many minutes passed as the firing continued, and in a haze of smoke and dust Akbar Gul could no longer see what he was shooting at. He began to worry about American reinforcements. He had just radioed his concern to Ghulam Ali when the air pulsed with a sound that did not belong. Suddenly, the world exploded.

Unbearable heat. Smoke mud-thick. A ringing in his ears. He'd fallen off his compatriot's shoulders, and he could hear the plane returning. Reaching for his walkie-talkie, he spoke in the calmest tone he could muster. "It's okay! Just run! Don't worry—just run, run, run!"

That evening, the commanders regrouped in the mountains. Remarkably, there were no injuries. They spoke among themselves of how cowardly the Americans were, how without their airplanes this war would be over in months. The mood was triumphant, their narrow escape evidence that God was on their side.

Then they received news from the village. The air strike had flattened the house whose wall Akbar Gul had used for cover and ravaged the apple orchards through which they had escaped. Akbar Gul felt deeply ashamed. He wondered how he could possibly face the villagers. But was it his fault? The Americans had chosen to come to Wardak, he reasoned. He'd never asked for it. They had placed themselves in the middle of the village and he was doing the best he could, the best anyone could, under such conditions.

Much later, I asked him if he felt remorse. He gave me a surprised look and said with a touch of rancor, "You can't ask me that. Americans won't ever feel what we feel. Your problems have solutions." We both fell silent and he looked hard at the floor. Finally, he said, "Yes, it was a terrible thing. But we were scared. When death appears in front of you, no one hugs it. This is war."

Still, he felt that the mission had been a success. Days after the attack, he had trekked up the hill and found blood splattered on the rocks. That evening, he called Mufti Latif and reported that four Americans had been killed.

Later, trying to verify his account, I came across the US military log for the skirmish, released by WikiLeaks in 2010. No one, it turned out, had been killed in the incident.

Back in Chak, though, that mattered not. The death of four American soldiers at the hands of Akbar Gul's fighters became truth itself, and soon he was awarded more money by the leadership. His group now numbered nearly forty strong, and Akbar Gul's name was catching attention in Taliban ranks across Wardak Province. Fresh off his success, he set to devising even more daring assaults. As with any great ambition, however, war has a stubborn way of becoming an end in itself. Like the Americans, Akbar Gul would learn this the hard way.

12

No-Man's-Land

On the old rutted gravel road by the grassy bank the young men squeezed aboard the buses, carrying only their knapsacks and their hopes for a better year. The buses followed the road as it crossed a rolling country covered with soft yellowing grass, dotted here and there with the occasional banyan or sissoo. There were creeks bluer than any sky, their waters braided over gravel bars. There were also fruit farms, but after a hard and dry summer here in Laghman Province, the trees stood bare. For the farmers on the bus, there had been no work to be found here.

They rode on through the Hindu Kush, following the rapids of the Kabul River alongside sheer cliffs dropping almost a thousand feet, and on to the shallow hills of Kabul. Looking through the window, the men could see low-slung concrete buildings and glimmering wedding halls. But without access, there was no hope of work here either. So they switched buses and headed south, into the bare country of Wardak. With the roadside craters and unpredictable checkpoints, each trip through Wardak was a perverse lottery. The men said their prayers.

It was past dawn when they pulled into Kandahar city and switched buses again. From here it would be a good fifteen hours to the Iranian border, to the traffickers who would arrange their crossing and help them find work. The two new buses took the highway west into the deserts of Maiwand District. It was open country for miles around, not a building or shack in sight.

Then some armed men ran onto the road ahead. Thinking fast, the driver of the first bus accelerated. Before the gunmen could close ranks, he had sped past them. But the trailing bus was forced to stop. When the gunmen boarded and the passengers saw them, their hearts sank: it was the Taliban.

The captives were brought to Band-i-Timor, to the same clutch of villages that, when I'd visited earlier that year, had held only children or no one at all. For three days, the men were kept in a series of small houses as the Taliban decided their fate. Years later, I obtained an account of what happened as told by Rahim, a Taliban fighter. "When I went there," he said, "it was late evening and all the passengers were there. They were yellow with worry." As he recalled it, Mullah Adaam, the local commander, addressed the group. "When you were coming from Kabul to Kandahar, we received a credible report that you were coming to join the National Army. We have good sources."

"What did you say we came for?" a captive asked. They could not believe it. They were simply in search of jobs in Iran, of a better life.

"Sons of Gulab Mangal!" he shouted, referring to the Karzai-appointed governor of Helmand, the next province on the bus's route. "You've come here to join the National Army and start fighting against us!"

The young men pleaded with Adaam, swearing that they had never laid eyes upon Gulab Mangal and would never join the Afghan army. But he appeared unmoved.

However, Rahim noticed doubt in his commander's eyes. Sure enough, Adaam soon phoned Taliban leaders in Quetta, Pakistan, for advice, pointing out that some of the captives were clean-shaven "like Americans." He listened and then replied, "Don't worry, we'll do our thing to them and then you'll say 'well done' to us."

Adaam turned to his fighters. "Only one phone call remains. After that, we'll send these guys to hell."

In the meantime, the captives were kept in a series of huts, one of which Rahim was assigned to guard. Sometime after midnight, he heard a commotion behind the door. He opened it and saw men crying.

"What are you doing?"

"For God's sake, we are going to Iran for work. We've even paid money to traffickers. They are going to take us there."

"Keep quiet," Rahim said. If his commander heard them talking, they'd all be in trouble.

Another, heaving, cried out, "My brother! I've got a little brother and three sisters. My mother and father are old. If something happens to me, what will they do?"

Doubt began to gnaw at Rahim.

The next day, the crowd of Talibs had doubled. Rahim suggested to Adaam that the men might indeed be innocent. Adaam called a Taliban cleric in Pakistan and put the phone on speaker. High-ranking clerics typically decided matters of law and order of significant magnitude—and a busload of captives was one of the biggest abductions of the war so far.

"I'm sure the other scholars have informed you of their decision, but I wanted to hear it from you with my own ears," Adaam said.

"I was with the others when they made their decision," the voice said. "Just go on and behead them."

Adaam hung up and looked at Rahim. "This isn't my decision. It's the decision of all the scholars. Now do you agree?"

Rahim asked how scholars sitting in Pakistan could possibly decide on issues here in Maiwand, but Adaam waved him off.

The next morning the captives were brought out in groups to a canal at the edge of the village. On their motorbikes, armed Taliban had gathered across the way. At once, the prisoners realized their fate. Some began wailing, some pleading for mercy. The young man to whom Rahim had spoken earlier was sobbing, calling out his parents' and siblings' names.

Shots rang out. The cries grew louder. The Taliban kept firing. The bodies kept falling.

Rahim couldn't bring himself to squeeze the trigger. Adaam pulled up on his motorcycle. "What are you looking at? Shoot!"

Rahim fired a shot haphazardly and Adaam cried, "No, Talib! You can do it." He grabbed the gun and started firing himself, hitting one captive in the foot. The man lay moaning until Adaam walked over and aimed two bullets at his head.

After a while, there was no longer any noise, no wailing, no gunshots. Rahim crossed the canal. Lying there were the bodies of some of the captives. And, nearby, four severed heads.

Twenty-five civilians in total died in the massacre, but incredibly enough two managed to escape. One of them, Bashir, recounted his ordeal afterward to a reporter: "They tied our hands behind our backs. When they began firing at us, I ran." The four others in his group were gunned down, but he escaped with a bullet in his leg. "I ran and hid," he said. "When God Almighty wants to rescue a person, he can rescue them anywhere, under any circumstances."

News of the slaughter sparked a public outcry. The Taliban insisted they had received reliable reports that the victims were Afghan army recruits. Even when it became clear that there had not been a single enlistee among them, they held fast to this fiction. It was autumn 2008, and for the first time anti-Taliban protests erupted countrywide. In villages that had rebelled against American and government abuses, the dark realization was setting that the Taliban were, in fact, no different from all the rest.

Not far from the homes of the victims' families, on the grassy banks of the Alingar River, you can find a simple tarpaulin lash-up that serves as the home of a one-eyed man named Hazrat.

"Nothing you see here in this country belongs to us," he told me when we first met. "You see that road out there? That's not ours. Everything is borrowed and everything can be taken back." Hazrat was the malek of a village that no longer existed. Some twenty miles off to the west, Garloch had been a hamlet of poplar trees and irregular patches of wheat and barley, its few hundred straw and mud homes there since the time of Hazrat's grandfathers and his grandfathers' grandfathers.

The war had slipped into Garloch like a thief. One summer night in 2008, a Taliban commander from a nearby village showed up with his men and established a checkpoint. Before anyone realized it they had become a fixture, though the people of Garloch had no vote in this. Not long thereafter, in a valley ten miles away, insurgents ambushed a French patrol, killing ten soldiers and wounding almost two dozen—France's biggest battlefield loss in a quarter century. American intelligence came to believe that one of the commanders involved, a man named Qadir, hailed from Garloch.

Two weeks passed. Then, early one morning, Hazrat awoke to a vibrating sky. Shelving shook in its place. Lights flashed outside. A friend arrived with news that the Americans had cordoned off the village. They were going house to house, blowing off gates and searching every room. Men and boys were being thrown to the ground, their hands tied behind their backs.

The operation lasted six hours, after which the villagers watched soldiers board helicopters and fly off. Then an aircraft swooped in, dropping its payload on a house.

Afterward, the government announced that the Americans had hit the house of Commander Qadir. When I suggested this to Hazrat as an explanation for the raid, he snorted, "You want to meet Qadir? I'll bring him right now." He stepped outside and headed over to a row of tents, their blue UN-issued tarpaulins flapping in the breeze. He returned with a pole-thin old man—Hajji Qadir, a village elder. Qadir explained that he had been hosting a wedding party at his home the night of the raid. The bomb had split his house in two, killing sixteen guests, including twelve members of his family. Dozens were wounded. He walked me to his tent to show me his mementos from that day. A chalky white chunk of ceiling; a mangled sliver of metal railing; a smiling toddler, his eyes daubed with kohl, his foot missing.

The air strike had targeted the wrong Qadir, though the Taliban commander did indeed live in the village and survived unscathed. Afterward, Hazrat, the village malek, went to the governor of Laghman Province and demanded an explanation. He was told that as long as the Taliban Qadir made Garloch his home, residents would not be able to allay American suspicions. Hazrat returned to his village and confronted Commander Qadir.

"Don't be a coward and hide among civilians," he told him. "If you want to fight Americans, go down south and leave us alone."

Eventually, Commander Qadir and a fellow insurgent departed. The troubles, Malek Hazrat told his grieving neighbors, were over.

A month later, however, just after dawn, residents awoke to the same pulsating sky. Some farmers, already in their fields, watched as American helicopters alighted on the wheat farms abutting the village. The choppers fired at something unseen and, in a panic, villagers fled from their homes into the fields. What they did not know was that the US forces were locked in a battle with Taliban insurgents in a nearby valley, and the fighting had spilled over to Garloch. In the havoc, two shepherds and a woman were gunned down. Warplanes then appeared overhead and bombed the village, destroying many homes.

From then on, the whirling chop-chop of rotary blades in the middle of the night brought cold sweats and prayers. To some, the copters seemed almost magical. "They wait in the sky, up there, behind those clouds," a boy told me. "When they want to attack, they drop like this." He held his hand parallel to the ground, bringing it down in a rapid glide. "There's nothing you can do."

Two months after the assault, the Americans returned yet again, acting on a tip that there were 100 antigovernment militants in the area. Afterward, however, it was found that the only casualties were two hundred dead sheep. Laghman police chief Abdul Karim Omaryar chalked up the incident to a NATO-led drive against terrorism, and a local news outlet ran the headline: "This Time Sheep Mistaken as Enemy Combatants." The humor was lost on the inhabitants of Garloch, however, many of whom were herdsmen and saw their livelihoods vanish in a single night. They carried the eviscerated carcasses to the governor's house and deposited them in front of his gate in protest.

Malek Hazrat also protested, to the media, to lawmakers, even to the president's office, and Karzai himself called to assure him that he had spoken to the Americans and that such tragedies would not be repeated. Hazrat returned home and once again promised his villagers they would be safe.

A few weeks later, in the pre-morning dark, the Americans returned. As the soldiers approached a home, a dog growled and they shot it. A villager ran out, thinking a thief was on the premises, and they shot him too. His younger brother emerged with a gun and fired into the darkness, yelling for his neighbors. The soldiers shot him as well, and the barrage of bullets also hit his mother as she peered out a window. The soldiers then tied the three bodies together, dragged them into a room, and set off explosives. A pair of children stood watching, and they would later report the scene.

An old man stepped out of the neighboring house holding an oil lamp. He was shot. His son ran out to help, and he, too, was shot. By night's end, seventeen residents lay dead. When people came out of their houses to collect their loved ones, they found a body swinging from a tree. Some believed that the Americans were behind the hanging, while others guessed that it was a result of neighborhood retribution against whoever may have provided false intelligence, but no one could say for sure.

US officials announced that the dead were "mostly militants," but villagers showed me photos of bloodied, lifeless women and old men. This time, Hazrat and his people had had enough. They descended upon the governor's house, burning President Obama in effigy. When the governor attempted to calm the crowd, protesters hurled stones at him. In the wake of the uproar, American authorities backtracked on their earlier claims. "I would say there was some potential that some of those killed were civilians," Colonel Greg Julian, a spokesman for US forces, told a reporter, "because some of those men shooting at our troops may have been civilians." Subsequently, the United States paid $2,000 in compensation to each of the victims' families.

Sitting with me in his tent, Hazrat railed, "That's what our lives are worth to you Americans—two thousand dollars? You want to kill us and then pay to keep us quiet?" An old man nearby leaned forward and shouted, "My daughter is buried in the ground! You can give me every dollar on Earth, but I won't touch it. It won't bring her back."

Hazrat's eyes were burning. "When you go back to America, give Obama a message. You say you'll give us roads and schools? I don't give a shit about your roads and schools! I want safety for my family."

After four deadly raids in the space of five months, Garloch residents faced a choice. They could take up arms in resistance, join the Taliban, and fight as their fathers had against a foreign occupation. But in this section of Laghman, haunted by the ghosts of Taliban brutality, resistance did not seem a viable option. Neither was neutrality, not in a war that had rendered the notion obsolete. So they took the only course remaining: they left. On foot, by car, by motorcycle, across an open country of crabgrass and gravel, they left. Across long harsh miles, taking their clothes and their bedding and their animals, they left. Some did not quit until reaching Pakistan. But most, like Hazrat, stopped by the grassy riverbank near Laghman's main highway, far enough from trouble but close enough to the world they knew, and erected a new village of tarpaulin and plastic. They called this canvas hamlet "New Garloch," although it didn't feel much like home. Occasionally, someone felt the urge to return to the ghost-town Garloch. Matiullah, a young farmer, once made the trip, but upon arriving he spotted a dog with its teeth clamped around the bones of a human hand. He promptly turned back.

Life in New Garloch was hard going. Men and boys scavenged for food or cadged for UN handouts. Women were restricted to their tiny tents all day long. Every winter, a few children were buried. Quitting entirely and heading for Pakistan seemed more appealing by the season. But Malek Hazrat refused to leave. "I'll stay here until I can go home," he told me, "or until they bury me, too."

Mullah Manan and I were in a cramped hotel room in downtown Kandahar city. A queen-size bed occupied most of the room, but Manan insisted on sitting on the floor. Photographs of the Swiss Alps and Indian cricketers hung on the wall. A small white refrigerator hummed in one corner, and Manan stared at it for some time, as it was new to him. The air conditioner blasted frigid air and the television silently played scenes of a Bollywood starlet frolicking in a flower bed.

I asked him to describe his home village, and as he did I used Google Earth to pull up its overhead image on my computer.

"My God!" he said, smiling. He shook his head in amazement. "I don't know how you're able to see that." He could not read or write, nor had he ever seen a map of any kind, but he grasped the picture's value at once. "America must be glorious," he said, not taking his eyes off the screen. "Maybe one day Afghanistan will become like that."

It was summer 2010 and Manan now commanded nearly a hundred men, a stature he hadn't experienced since his defeat by Jason Amerine. Yet he sat before me in nothing more than an old pattu and frayed sandals, carrying the Afghan equivalent of a few dollars. Money, in fact, was the abiding challenge. Scrounging together funds for ammunition or weapons had become part of life's daily struggle, and as his unit grew the problem was only getting worse.

"In the beginning, we had nothing," he said. "It was hard for us to even get batteries for our walkie-talkies. No one was helping us, just occasionally some rich people from the village, who gave us donations. When we went on raids, we divided the spoils and I told my men, 'Here, these are your expenses for the month. Use it to survive.' We never called it a salary."

As the insurgency grew, funds began to trickle in to the Quetta-based Taliban leadership from private donors in the Gulf and merchants in Pakistan. Some of them were shunted to the movement's so-called district governors, who took a cut and disbursed what was left to field commanders like Manan. "They would tell us, 'This money is just for weapons, just for walkie-talkies and daily expenses. It's not for personal use,'" he recalled.

While Karzai and the Americans could peddle influence through patronage—that is, by spending large sums of money—the Taliban was left to corral support mainly through sheer force. You stood in their way at your peril. Once, Manan's unit came into the possession of a list of NGOs operating in the area and the amount of aid they were receiving for various projects. Manan noticed that, not far from his home, a businessman had obtained funds to repair a small community bridge.

"So we warned him," he recalled. "We used a trusted elder from the area. We did this so that if we acted, the elders wouldn't blame us. We told the elder to order the businessman to surrender his money to us and halt construction of the bridge." If villagers wanted a bridge, Manan said, he'd use his money to build it. He simply couldn't allow the government, or Jan Muhammad, to take credit—not after everything that had happened, everything he'd been through. It would be the Taliban's way, or none at all.

In this developing system, Manan and other commanders would issue a warning to anyone caught working for the government or handling government money, a category that included aid workers, police officers, and, most frequently of all, schoolteachers. Schools that had reopened their doors after 2001 were now again forced shut. Sometimes they were burned to the ground. Bridges, culverts, and irrigation ditches went unrepaired.

"Those who were warned and did not quit, we arrested," he said.

I asked what became of those he arrested.

"We had no option but the sword," he answered.

It occurred often enough, but it was the first time that he'd never forget. The man's name was Sidiqullah and he had taken a job running a government checkpoint on the highway. Manan issued a warning, but Sidiqullah ignored it. With jobs scarce and families to feed, such defiance was not uncommon. Manan waited a few weeks and then showed up at Sidiqullah's doorstep with dozens of men.

"Sidiqullah, son of Akram," he said in his wispy voice. "You've been told by our religious leaders to stop working for the government. Now you have no right to complain."

Sidiqullah started pleading. The men forced him into their jeep and drove out of the village. At a grassy escarpment, with the mountains looming, they ordered him out.

Manan wanted it done quickly, before elders or family members had a chance to intervene. Once they became involved, things would get difficult.

They made Sidiqullah sit by the stump of a large tree, and, when he struggled, two of the men placed their weight on his arms and body and tied his hands behind his back. He began to scream, a deep madman's scream, and the Talibs looked on and waited. One of them lowered a butcher's knife onto Sidiqullah's neck, as if measuring, and began to cut. It surprised Manan how long it took, how much work it was, to decapitate a man. Afterward, when they tossed the head aside, it looked to him like a deflated balloon.

I asked Manan if he'd ever done such a thing again.

He looked at nothing in particular and appeared to think this over, as if it were some technical question or some subject that he had not considered until then, and answered in his shy and quiet voice: "We were doing this two, maybe three times a month."

One night, Akbar Gul again awoke to a loud rumble. The sky outside was flashing white. Stepping into the street, he could smell burning rubber and smoke. He'd been staying with a friend, and the smoke appeared to be coming from the far side of the village, over by the mosque—not far from the direction of his house. He ran as fast as he could. His fears were quickly confirmed: a sizzling pit had swallowed his home's mud wall. The front yard was smoldering. His wife and daughter were inside. *Please, God*, he said to himself, *please, God*. The door had been locked from the inside. He kicked with all his might, kicked again, and finally it succumbed. He called out their names and they came running, terrified but unharmed.

After sunrise, he inspected the blast site. It betrayed all the telltale signs of explosives: an epicenter, a radial discharge of some sort, concentric circles of damage. The Americans had combed through the village only days earlier—he had been away on a mission—and he was sure that this was their doing. But how had they known which house was his?

He spent the day investigating and came up empty. The only lead he had was a list of names of those seen chatting with soldiers on their patrol, which he'd collected from his scouts. Akbar Gul couldn't prove it, but he felt in his bones that one of the people on the list, a neighbor named Raqib, was the culprit. He had never liked Raqib, who was always making excuses for not donating to the cause.

The next morning he showed up at Raqib's house with his men. "You're coming with me," he ordered.

"Why? What did I do?"

"This is over," he said, pointing to his damaged house down the street. "My wife and child were in there."

"What does this have to do with me?"

Akbar Gul said nothing and the others forced Raqib into their truck. As they drove up the mountainside, Raqib started wailing. He had a wife and children at home, he pleaded. Akbar Gul ordered him out of the truck, put his Kalashnikov to Raqib's temple, and shot him dead.

In general, informants were rare, although he'd heard stories of spies in other villages. Sometimes, when he drove his motorcycle along the rutted mountainside trails behind those villages, he came upon corpses dangling from trees. He tried not to think too much about them, instead spending his time dreaming up schemes to get himself funded. Those plans would get hashed out in his guest room, where he passed long hours with friends and fellow commanders sipping cardamom tea and hacking into a spittoon. It was a room no simpler or grander than any other, with *toshak*s on the floor for sitting and an old tea-stained rug in the center. On the wall hung a picture, cut out from a magazine, of a crystal blue wave crashing onto a beach, and another of a giant red rose. Like many Pashtun men, Akbar Gul adored roses, their reds and pinks burning in a dun-colored world.

When he wasn't working, he and his comrades would watch films of Taliban attacks on their cell phones and, when bored of those, clips of Bollywood movies. The Taliban's old injunctions against television and music had more or less fallen by the wayside. Back in the 1990s, Akbar Gul had embraced the puritanism with fervor—he'd been Mullah Cable, after all, enforcing the rules with his whip—because in a world turned upside down by civil war, where women could be dragged out of a home and dishonored in the open street, it seemed that the best medicine was to boil things down to their bare Islamic essentials. Anything that left the door open to sin was banned; television, as a possible venue for pornography, had been high on that list. Now, looking back, Akbar Gul could hardly recognize his old self or his old group. The commanders he knew in Wardak wore beards of differing lengths. Some, to avoid detection, even went clean shaven. Nearly everyone he knew listened to music and traded cell phone video clips. And activities that he would have found abhorrent before, such as suicide bombing, now seemed a logical expression of religious faith and patriotic duty.

Sometimes, when the group tired of watching movies, Syed Muhammad, the only one among them with a religious education, would start up with his impromptu sermonizing. He would remind them that the Americans were on Afghan soil to convert the population to Christianity, to eradicate their way of life. To those present in the room, this explanation made perfect sense: they had all heard stories of the proliferation of brothels in Kabul, of US soldiers flushing Korans down the toilet. Syed Muhammad was also an accomplished poet. Often, he would conjure up verses on the spot—of unrequited love, of forbidden romance, of friendship, or of fear, the kind of fear that weighs upon you the first time you leave home to fight.

Even on those slow afternoons, money was never far from Akbar Gul's thoughts. Fund-raising proved to be a challenge no matter how well they did on the battlefield, so he began to diversify his approach. About a third of his operating expenses now came from donations, another third from various forms of coercion such as the "taxation" of local construction firms, and the rest from Quetta. By 2008 he had also expanded into heroin trafficking, with policemen and government employees as his biggest customers.

Through it all, Akbar Gul built himself the village equivalent of a mini-empire. Still, something was missing—it didn't feel like enough. For one thing, there was Ghulam Ali, the other top commander in Chak, who owned the only gas station for miles around. That brought in a steady revenue with which he attracted fighters and purchased weapons. One success begat another, and soon Ali was fielding one of the most formidable forces in the province, a development the Quetta leadership was quick to notice. He was appointed as Chak's "district governor," usurping Akbar Gul, who was then awarded the sinecure of "police chief." Akbar Gul never complained, but it ate away at him. He was sure that if he could command Ali-like profits, he'd run the Americans out of Wardak in no time. If anyone should be governor, it was he.

Matters came to a head one afternoon in 2009, when he learned that Ghulam Ali was demanding that villagers stop paying taxes to the government for the operation of a community power station and instead hand the money over to the Taliban—specifically, to him. In a meeting with graybeards and elders, Akbar Gul listened as they complained bitterly about the new policy. Then he asked them, "Under what authority does Ali want to take this money?"

"He says he wants it for jihad, for the sake of God."

"God?" he responded. "If you are fighting for God, God will provide everything for you." The men nodded in agreement. "If Ali really wants the money, will he guarantee that the power station stays working? Will he pay the electricians to maintain it? Will he pay the station's staff? Will he supply fuel for the generators? Where will he get that from? His mother?"

The men laughed. "If the harvest is bad one year, will he keep the thing running like the government would?" Akbar Gul was hardly one to defend the government under normal circumstances, but the idea of Ali lording it over his district was too much to bear.

"But there's nothing we can do," an elder replied. "You know he'll beat us if we refuse. Everyone is afraid of him."

Akbar Gul flashed with anger. "No—he's a dog. Ignore him. If he gives you any trouble, you tell me. I'm the commander here."

Emboldened, the elders went to Ghulam Ali and announced that Akbar Gul had ordered them not to pay the tax. In a rage, Ali demanded a meeting, to which Akbar Gul immediately agreed.

The elders were seated in a circle the next day, with Taliban commanders from around the district in attendance, when Akbar Gul strode in with his fighters. Ali was sitting with a few of his fighters, who wore bandannas to cover their faces.

"Are we meeting thieves or the Taliban?" Akbar Gul asked as he sat down.

"What is your problem?" Ghulam Ali snarled.

"You act like you're the king of Chak. Look at these poor people," he said, pointing to the elders. "You're making problems for them."

"You're making problems for my people," Ali snapped back. "You're telling these people to oppose my orders." Since when, he asked, did a Taliban commander direct people to pay the government? "Maybe you love the Americans, maybe you want to see the Taliban fail."

This was more than Akbar Gul could bear. "No, I just want to fuck your wife," he said.

Ghulam Ali leapt up. "Who do you think you are?"

"Who do you think *you* are?" Akbar Gul shot back.

"I'm the district governor of Chak, appointed by our leaders."

"I don't care if Mullah Omar himself appointed you. If you ever set foot in my village, I'll make you my bitch."

"Now let's see what happens," Ghulam Ali shouted back, pounding a number into his phone and placing it on speaker. It was Mufti Abdul Latif, their immediate superior, speaking from his home in Peshawar, Pakistan. He was saying something, but Akbar Gul, clouded over with rage, could not stand to listen and stormed out.

Later that evening he received a phone call from Mufti Latif. He was to report to Peshawar immediately.

--- ---

The dust kicking up from Peshawar's streets seemed thicker than usual, made all the worse by the humid summer air. It reminded Akbar Gul of just how much he despised Pakistan, particularly its weather. A war was raging here now between militants—who also called themselves "Taliban," though they had little to do with his movement—and the Pakistani government. He wondered how anyone could actually fight in such wet heat.

It had taken him almost two days to reach the city, as he'd used a circuitous route in order to avoid the main highway. As soon as he arrived, he borrowed a cell phone from a pedestrian and dialed Mullah Latif, who dispatched a car to pick him up. He stood on the street watching autorickshaws and motorbikes scoot by, some of them carrying women in burqas, in headscarves, and a few even with their hair as naked as when they'd risen that morning.

A black Land Cruiser pulled up. A man leaned out the window. "Are you Akbar Gul?"

He nodded and climbed into the backseat, where two others were already seated. Another man sitting in the front turned to greet him and then held up a black hood. "I'm sorry, but rules are rules," he said.

Before Akbar Gul could react, a hood was forced onto his head and he felt the weight of two men on top of him. When he tried to cry out, his voice was muffled. He couldn't believe this was happening. He lay struggling for air, cursing himself for his bravado, bargaining with God that he'd change his ways.

No one spoke, and he could hear horns and street vendors outside. After some time, those, too, faded away. The car was moving fast now, very fast. Out on the open highway somewhere.

An hour passed. He felt the vehicle turn and halt. A horn blared. Something, maybe a gate, squeaked open. Then a handler removed his hood and he sat there, gasping for air and looking around. He was in the driveway of a large country house, surrounded by towering cement walls. Mountains were peeking over in the distance.

He was led into the compound. Standing in the hallway, arms folded, was Mufti Abdul Latif. For a moment everyone was silent. Then Latif broke into a wide grin. "You crazy troublemaker! What kind of problems are you making for us out there?" He laughed and embraced his old friend.

The two sat down to dinner, talking about their families and the latest news of the war. Afterward, Latif suggested that Akbar Gul catch some rest.

Around one in the morning, Latif woke him up. "Time to go. Everyone is waiting." A white Toyota TownAce minivan stood outside in the darkness, curtains drawn over its side windows. Latif motioned Akbar Gul to climb into the tiny space behind the back window and the rearmost seats.

No one spoke during the journey. After about thirty minutes, they arrived at a house even larger than the previous one and made their way down to a long, brightly lit hall, finally entering a room near the end. There was no furniture or even rugs, only a glaring white fluorescent light set in the ceiling.

After a few minutes another door swung open, and Taliban commanders whom Akbar Gul recognized from Wardak streamed in. Sometime later, religious clerics entered. Then Ghulam Ali himself strode in. They all sat wordlessly, sipping tea and playing with their phones. Akbar Gul realized that they were waiting for someone.

Nearly an hour had gone by when he appeared. He wore a crisp, cream-colored salwar, more perfectly tailored than any Akbar Gul had ever laid eyes on. He had large, tired, puffy eyes and was beardless, with a close-cropped mustache and a crew cut.

Akbar Gul knew immediately that he was in the presence of Pakistani intelligence. *So this is what they look like*, he thought to himself. Growing up in Afghanistan, you'd hear about the shadowy Inter-Services Intelligence, or ISI, spoken of the way people spoke of malevolent jinns, omnipresent and responsible for the ills of the world. Few had ever seen an operative in the flesh.

"We have a problem in Wardak," the man began, "and we're here to solve it." He looked around the room. "We need to appoint some new people. So which one of you is Akbar Gul?"

He raised his hand.

"Ah, I should have guessed. You look like the kind of guy that likes to argue."

Akbar Gul smiled his most disarming smile, and said, "No, I'm not like that."

"So tell me, why do you create problems for Ghulam Ali? Why don't you let him do his job, and you do yours?"

Akbar Gul resented this tone. Who was he, hundreds of miles from the battlefield, to question him?

"Let me ask you something first, if you don't mind," Akbar Gul said, as Mufti Latif pinched his leg. "Why do you help America? You take their money and work with them, then you work with us as well. What kind of business is this?"

Everyone was quiet. Finally, the ISI officer said, "Go on, I'm listening."

"Well, let me start with a joke. People talk about overpopulation on Earth, about having too many people. But I don't see the big problem." He paused. "You see, some people are actually just jackasses." He pointed at Ghulam Ali. "And we don't have to worry about including donkeys in the count."

The agent burst out laughing. A few of the others giggled.

"Look, in my area, I have support. I don't want this power plant to become useless. That's what this is all about."

The agent turned to Ghulam Ali. "Let's say the Americans are on patrol and you want to plan an ambush. What do you do?"

Ghulam Ali thought about it and then answered, "I just grab my guys, however many I need, and we attack. We're brave."

The agent turned to Akbar Gul. "And you?"

"Well, first I'll watch them, the Americans. I'll position my guys ahead of them, between them and their base. We'll watch sometimes for an hour. Sometimes we'll mine their escape route. And when I feel the time is right, and I'm sure that my guys can escape alive, I'll order them to fire."

The agent nodded and stood up. "Thanks for your time. We're done here." He turned to Akbar Gul. "I don't have answers to your questions right now, but I'll send them to you."

Mufti Latif and Akbar Gul were escorted back to their vehicle. The sun was breaking through the morning fog and they could hear the call to prayer. They were blindfolded and driven back to Peshawar.

The following day, Akbar Gul returned to Afghanistan to learn that Ghulam Ali had been ordered to abandon his power plant scheme. Mufti

Latif also passed along the message that Akbar Gul was expected to be more of a team player, to not lose sight of the mission.

He never did receive those answers, however.

Akbar Gul knew that this was how things worked in his country. Pakistan had long been the éminence grise of Afghan politics, stemming from a generations-old rivalry between the two neighbors. Tensions had reached a fevered pitch in the 1970s when Afghan dictator Daud Khan attempted to whip up nationalist fervor among millions of Pashtuns living in Pakistan for a united "Pashtunistan," a Pashtun homeland that would straddle both sides of the border and necessarily implied the breakup of Pakistan. Khan also harbored separatist insurgents looking to make the Pakistani province of Baluchistan into an independent state. Islamabad had retaliated in kind, supporting Islamist rebels—precursors to the mujahedeen—in Afghanistan.

It might have remained little more than a simmering neighborhood rivalry if not for the Soviet invasion and the US proxy war, which, through billions of dollars in aid and military equipment, helped assure the rise of the ISI as a formidable player in regional politics. In the 1990s the Pakistanis had backed the Taliban, only to abandon them after the US invasion, appearing ready to at least tolerate a new Afghan order. It was soon clear, however, that Karzai and the Northern Alliance were too closely linked to India for Pakistan's comfort. When the Taliban revived itself, the ISI threw its support behind the insurgency—even as it publicly proclaimed support for the US mission.

Pakistan could bring pressure to bear on the Taliban at any moment. In 2010, for example, it arrested a number of leading Taliban figures on suspicion that they had contacted the Afghan government to explore possible future peace talks. To Akbar Gul, it all seemed like a big, scandalous game. One group of Taliban commanders in Wardak were known ISI favorites, regularly reporting to their handlers in Pakistan. A second group maintained subterranean links with the Afghan government, an insurance policy if the going got too tough. The unfortunate ones—and he counted himself in this last category—floated between these two poles, working for whoever could keep the guns and money flowing.

Through it all, Ghulam Ali's stature continued to grow. Akbar Gul watched as, over the months, alliances shifted and three of Chak's top seven commanders fell under Ali's influence. He complained to Mufti Latif, but there was little that Latif or the ISI could do, for Ali was undeniably effective and had the ear of top figures in Quetta. So Akbar Gul requested a meeting with the leadership. Connecting with a member of the so-called Quetta Shura face-to-face was difficult, if not impossible, without access—and there were no Wardakis on the grand council. Still, Akbar Gul knew of a Quetta-based Talib named Rehmatullah who hailed from Chak and had some links to the senior leadership, so he decided to make the trip to Pakistan to see him.

He set out in a shared minivan taxi, stopping overnight at a hotel in Ghazni city, where he spent a sleepless night thinking about Hajji Mullah —a Taliban commander he knew who had upset the leadership and simply disappeared after a Quetta meeting. The following day, he arrived in the border town of Chaman and hopped into another shared taxi. He was about an hour into Pakistan when they encountered a checkpoint. A Pakistani policeman peered through the window and motioned for him to step out. They spent twenty minutes there at the roadside negotiating the bribe. It was early evening when he arrived in a Pashtun quarter of Quetta, filled with men in turbans and beards like his own, some carrying walkie-talkies and others driving brand new SUVs and still others loitering outside mosques, talking. He dialed Rehmatullah.

Late that night he was brought by rickshaw to a small house and led to an underground bunker of some sort. Opening the door, he found six or seven men seated on toshaks. He greeted Rehmatullah and then the others in turn; two of them he recognized as commanders from his province but the others he could not place, though judging by their accents they hailed from Kandahar or Chaman. Rehmatullah did most of the talking while the Kandaharis sat watching. Finally one of them, the most heavy-set, disheveled-looking of the lot, spoke up.

"Tell me, are you in this for jihad, or for your country? Do you love all Muslims, or just your people in Wardak or in Afghanistan?"

It seemed like a trick question to Akbar Gul. He was there to complain about Ghulam Ali, but somehow this had become about him.

"I love jihad and my people. It's the same."

The Kandahari continued to grill him with such logical puzzles and riddles. "Do you believe that educated people or uneducated people know best?"

"Educated, of course. I'm illiterate and you are educated. That's why I've come to you."

"And if I ordered you to do something you disagreed with, what would you do?"

Akbar Gul squirmed and gave a halfhearted answer, and the interrogation continued. He desperately wanted out. Finally, he offered a compromise:

"If you want me to work with Ghulam Ali, I'll do it. Just please don't ask me to work *under* him. We're more effective together, as one."

The men nodded and seemed pleased. Eventually, food arrived. It was the most sumptuous meal he'd had in some time, plate after plate of meatballs, and sweet rice pudding for dessert. They sat and talked long into the night, about war and friendship and poetry. They spoke of the good things in life and how those things were gone forever. They talked until dawn, and when the men rose to leave, Akbar Gul embraced each of them in turn. He told them, "I'm a loyal guy. I'll do whatever it takes. If you want me to put a bomb in a crowded market, if you say that's the right thing to do, I'll do it."

He spent the next day touring the Taliban infrastructure in Quetta with Rehmatullah, visiting mosques to speak with scholars and bazaars to speak with important benefactors of the movement. In the evening he was taken to one of Rehmatullah's madrassas, where hundreds of skullcapped boys sat in a chain of rooms reciting from the Koran and writing on the chalkboards. "These are my little warriors," Rehmatullah said proudly.

Akbar Gul could hardly believe what he was seeing, but he told Rehmatullah that it was good these boys were being taught to fight for their country and their religion. Rehmatullah smiled and replied that it was difficult to raise them this way, but necessary. Before Akbar Gul boarded a taxi back to the Afghan border, Rehmatullah promised him that he'd keep an eye on Ghulam Ali and see that he didn't grow too strong—and that he'd talk to the leadership about finding Akbar Gul more funds.

— — —

The summer of 2009 saw an increase in infighting among Wardak's Taliban, and growing tensions with their co-insurgent allies in Hekmatyar's faction. At the same time, because the Taliban leadership paid units a "bonus" for outstanding attacks, the number of fake assaults, staged for video, surged. Akbar Gul played the game as well as anyone, but as the days went on he slid into despair. He hated those men in Quetta, he hated the ISI, and, most of all, he hated Ghulam Ali and his success. But he kept it all to himself. It was a dangerous new world, and you couldn't trust anyone, even your own allies.

Countrywide, his movement was losing steam. The Taliban were now responsible for more civilian deaths than were the Americans. In some communities, roadside bombs, assassinations, and summary executions had come to take their place alongside Guantanamo and the door-kicking night raids of US troops in the pantheon of fears that kept villagers awake at night. Meanwhile, the insurgency was spreading from marginalized, cut-off communities into those that had fared better in the post-2001 years, whether it was welcome there or not.

In Chak, many of the commanders Akbar Gul knew had been killed in night raids, leaving Ghulam Ali's crew and a smattering of independents, most younger than he, with no memories of the old Taliban days. It became increasingly difficult to defend their actions—which included, in one case, beheading a schoolteacher—to the village elders. He turned inward, planning operations on his own, without other commanders, and keeping away from Pakistan. Then, one day, he received a surprising phone call. It was the government's new chief of police for Chak, an old war buddy from his Hizb-i-Islami days. They had ended up on opposite sides through chance more than anything else. The man spoke of a government program that invited fighters to switch sides in return for money and a guaranteed job. Akbar Gul listened and wondered where such a program had been years earlier, when he would have given anything for a normal life. But things were different now, more complicated. He realized that it had been a long while since the Taliban meant anything to him. But he couldn't imagine himself openly joining forces with the government either. In fact, he knew that friends who'd gone down that route were languishing in a dangerous political no-man's-land: Karzai's government had not fulfilled its promises, and for the Taliban they were now marked men.

"What are you fighting for? The Americans are going to leave anyway," the police chief said. "We are building Afghanistan." The Taliban, he added, were terrorists, enemies of the country, stooges of Pakistan.

Akbar Gul was unmoved. "There are no good men among the living, and no bad ones among the dead," he replied, reiterating one of his favorite Pashtun proverbs. This war had left no group, Afghan or foreign, with clean hands. You had to be careful to survive. Today, the government said the Taliban were terrorists—but what about tomorrow? Would the Taliban be venerated, as the mujahedeen were now venerated? Would the Americans change their allegiances, as it seemed they had done after the 1980s, and brand the Karzai government as their enemy? It was too much for Akbar Gul to grapple with just then. He knew only that to trust the categories put forth by the Americans or the government was to go down the road to ruin.

He told the police chief that he wasn't interested. He said he was satisfied with his life as it was, thanked him for his call, and hung up.

The next morning, with new presidential elections looming, with American patrols crawling here and there, with Taliban groups erecting their usual checkpoints to hunt for spies and possible kidnap targets, he hopped on his motorcycle, headed for the low hills behind the village, and began another day of work.

PART FIVE

13

Stepping Out

Home had never felt so strange. Heela's apartment was on the first floor of a house on the edge of Kandahar city, and when she stood by the compound wall in the backyard, she could sometimes hear the laughter of young men as their hashish smoke drifted over. It wasn't long before she avoided that side of the house altogether. But the front wall proved no better. There, she could hear men arguing and laughing and spitting onto the sidewalk, and they sounded like police but she had no way of knowing. It wasn't long before she started avoiding the front wall, too. She tried befriending the widow upstairs, who worked as a cook for an NGO. With the month drawing to a close and rent looming, Heela asked her about finding a job. As it happened, the cook said she knew of the perfect one—working with the director of the Kandahar government's Department of Youth Affairs.

"How much does it pay?" Heela asked.

"Oh, that doesn't matter! He'll help you, I promise," she replied.

"What do I do?"

"This isn't a regular job. Just go whenever he calls you, whenever he needs you, and he'll pay you."

"What do you mean?"

The cook blushed and laughed giddily. "You'll enjoy the work."

From that moment, Heela avoided her, too.

It was early winter 2005. Nearly three months had passed since

Musqinyar's murder, and in that period she had been moved three times without ever quite fitting in anywhere. First, there had been the American camp in Tirin Kot, where she'd been brought by helicopter from Khas Uruzgan. At the camp she was housed in a small tent and nearly starved herself because she wasn't convinced the food was halal. For days on end, it was only fruits and chocolate, delivered by friendly soldiers. She kept herself inside, with her two boys, living a waking dream, never quite sure just what had happened to her. The days were long and quiet, until one afternoon she was brought to an office in town and told to wait in the courtyard. After some time she noticed the faint, distant chug of a car. It grew louder and stronger, and soon it was right outside. The gate opened. Standing there on crutches, in bandages, was nine-year-old Jamshed, her second child. She ran out and pulled him in tight. They both wept.

He asked, "Where is Baba?"

She looked him over. "Father is injured. He's in Kandahar."

"No," answered Jamshed. "No—I know what happened. There were so many shots."

Heela said nothing.

"Just tell me the truth," he said.

She held him close and sobbed.

Some weeks later she and the boys were moved to Kandahar Airfield. The prefab container serving as their home there was the cleanest space she'd ever seen. Too clean, in fact, leaving her little to do but count the daylight hours and think back over choices made and those made for her. Finally, she was brought to Omaid. That a boy of eleven could take four bullets and still hold on to life was miraculous—though that miracle would have been inconceivable without the heroic work of US soldiers and the doctors at KAF. When he saw his mother, Omaid sat up and held her hand, and she spoke to him words of comfort.

He was soon transferred to the Kandahar city hospital, and it was there that Heela had her first stroke of luck. A doctor took pity on the family and gave her about fifty dollars' worth of Afghan currency, which she used to find herself a small apartment in the city.

It was as far removed from the countryside as you could get. There were no courtyards or stand-alone guest rooms or gardens out back, just tightly packed mud and cement houses, clotheslines and electrical wires webbed between them. She could hear a television playing from the apartment of a family upstairs and she was eager to see it herself, but she did not go up to meet them.

The first days had been the hardest. The morning light, the first notes of the muezzin's call, the growing clamor of the street—to Heela, these were rude interruptions of the few hours that still belonged entirely to her, the few hours when her life seemed whole again. She no longer had Musqinyar in the flesh, but he still dutifully visited in dreams, where everything was as it had always been. He spoke to her and walked with her and they went to all the places they were meant to go until the night was over, and they started again the next night. It took great effort to manage the tyranny of daylight, and some days she failed. In time, she began to see that each visit of his was a message, a map, charting her life ahead.

The immediate challenge was finding work. Without stepping out-doors, this was no easy task. Even though there was no one to restrict her movements, she felt it simply wasn't proper to move about without a mahrem. She swore to herself that she wouldn't become one of those widows one occasionally heard about, the sort who cavorted with unre-lated men and went wherever they pleased. So she relied instead on an acquaintance of Musqinyar's, who came every so often to check on her and bring naan for the family. Once, an aid worker showed up with blan-kets, two spoons, a bowl, and a mattress. Heela would cut bread into strips and portion them out during the day, and if they grew stale she would soak them in the bowl with green tea. When Walid woke up crying with hunger, she would rub his belly and rock him back to sleep.

By the end of her first month, she was out of options. Some days they survived only on green tea. Some nights she would think back to her Kabul days and remember the burqa-shrouded widows sitting cross-legged on the sidewalks, children by their side, begging for change. Alone in the world, forgotten. Unaccounted for.

It was a Friday, the day of mosque-going and shopping. One more day and the landlord would show up. She stood watching the children. Omaid had her eyes but he had his father's smile. It was impossible to ignore that something within him and the others had altered, maybe forever. She urged Omaid to go out and explore, but he would have none of it. Instead, he spent whole afternoons in a corner, staring off into space. He would not say a word to anyone.

The muezzin called for the Friday prayers, and she caught herself counting the hours till sundown. The landlord had said that he would come by first thing in the morning.

Heela decided that this could not continue. She retrieved her burqa and held it aloft, studying it. She stood thinking a long while about Musqinyar and Khas Uruzgan. Then she fit herself into the burqa, opened the gate, and stepped out into the open city. For the first time in ten years she was in the streets without a mahrem. She wasn't sure what had gotten into her, but she wasn't going to turn back. She headed down the lane onto a broad dirt road. It led her to a crowded neighborhood, and she could hear scooters and autorickshaws and vendors shouting prices. There were men in pattus and swirled turbans standing around pushcarts heaped with vegetables. There was a man in a police uniform, and another on a bicycle, and another selling music CDs. Then she saw the women. There were women begging and women speaking to shopkeepers. They wore powder blue and pistachio green burqas, walking here and there with children and men—or, in some cases, by themselves. *On their own*, she realized. Heela felt as if she had walked into a different country.

She returned home, opened up her diary, and began thumbing through the pages in search of names and numbers of Musqinyar's friends. In Khas Uruzgan it would have been downright scandalous for her to call one of these men, for her to allow them to hear her voice. But she wasn't going to hold herself back, not when there were women out on the streets of Kandahar, surviving. It no longer mattered what anyone might think. She found a friend of Musqinyar's in Kandahar city and dialed him. They had a long conversation. A few days later he showed up at the house and erected a signboard on the outer wall advertising the services of a midwife. Through this work, she was able to afford another month's rent.

Not long after, however, Musqinyar's friend left town and she was alone again. Without his help and cover she could not operate her midwifery business. But her trip outdoors had awakened something within her, and she scrabbled for more contacts. She knew that she would need to rely on Musqinyar's old circle to survive. One or two kindhearted souls was all she needed. But none of his friends were in Kandahar. It dawned on her that only one hope remained, only one place in the country where she could go to find them. It was the option she had been avoiding all these months, the option she hadn't even allowed herself to consider: Jan Muhammad Khan's Uruzgan.

The bright noon sun baked the windows. Having finished a prodigious meal, JMK leaned back. A gold-rimmed portrait of Hamid Karzai hung above him. To his left, a photograph of a clock; to his right, of puppies. He spoke to me of his days as Uruzgan's governor in 2005 and 2006. "Those were good times," he recalled. "We opened up orphanages, built roads, built schools." Of humble origins himself, he was widely known and appreciated within the Popalzai tribe for his generosity. He financed weddings and built irrigation ditches, loaned farmers money for seeds and refurbished the bazaar. One of his passions was female education, so he bankrolled the construction of girls' schools in Tirin Kot. "Wherever women are educated," he told me, "the country is strong."

JMK wasn't the type to sit in an office. He was one of the few provincial governors to accompany American troops on their missions, showing up with his heaving belly and gnarled sandals, walkie-talkie in hand, alongside militiamen who functioned as his praetorian guard and private army—with Washington footing the bill.

"We went everywhere, the Americans and me," he recalled. "They were the only ones who truly cared about fighting the terrorists. Sometimes we even went into the neighboring provinces. Once I headed into Zabul, to the Dai Chopan area, and we went through their villages. The place was full of Taliban." He laughed. "We started hanging them from trees. Everyone could see them hanging. After that, there were no more security problems in Dai Chopan."

Once, during a joint Afghan-American mission to a Ghilzai region— home to Mullah Manan—they descended on a house where they uncovered weapons, a common enough occurrence in a country awash with arms. In a sequence captured by a documentary filmmaker, a villager was brought out to JMK for interrogation, with US troops and his militiamen seated around him. JMK then began rummaging through photos of young boys and men taken from the captive's house.

"Where did you find these boys? Oh God, what good looks!" he exclaimed, as his militiamen chuckled. The prisoner sat nearby uncomfortably. "Aren't they heavenly creatures? What beautiful boys they are. I wish I was young again. They're more beautiful than ten women."

After conferring with the militiamen over the evidence, Jan Muhammad told the prisoner, "Come on, man. You say this is the photo of a lion? It looks like a donkey." He glared. "I'll fuck your mother. I'll make you suck my dick." Then, through a translator, he sent a message about the captive's fate to an American officer sitting nearby. "Tell the colonel we'll take him along with us and for a few nights he will keep us entertained. He will do his thing and then we'll see."

By 2006, JMK's malign influence had become apparent to everyone— everyone, that is, except the Americans. UN officials and European diplomats came to view him as a key destabilizing influence in the province, even as US commanders stood by his side because the very traits that made him so divisive also made him an ideal ally in the war on terror. Still, with the Taliban's resurgence, Washington desperately wanted greater troop contributions in the region from its NATO allies. The Dutch government finally agreed to deploy a contingent to Uruzgan— but only if JMK was removed from office. After much wrangling, President Karzai was forced to comply. He appointed his old friend as special adviser to the president, a sinecure that brought him to Kabul.

When I asked JMK about the transfer, he leaned close and said, "The Dutch actually support the Taliban. I've got all the evidence. It's a well-known fact among certain people. You see, they want to destroy our country so they can fund the Taliban. They and the ISI work together. This is our country's tragedy, the tragedy we suffer through every day. The Dutch are weak, not like the Americans. They don't understand right and wrong. That's why they opposed me. They knew what I'd do to them. Anyone who supports the Taliban is not welcome in my province. That's been my rule from the beginning." He again praised the Americans as the only foreign nation that truly understood the stakes. The rest, he said, "want to bend us over and fuck us."

— — —

On a spring day in 2005, Heela and the boys pulled up in a taxi to a small house in central Tirin Kot. Hajji Akhund, an old friend of Musqinyar's, had arranged for her to stay on property he owned, promising to cover for her if locals discovered that a single woman was living in their presence. It was still JMK's province then, and while he would likely learn of a single female newcomer to town, he did not know about Heela's connection to Musqinyar and the politics of Khas Uruzgan. She planned to keep it that way.

Hajji Akhund showed Heela to her new lodgings, a squat house with faded butterscotch walls and a single set of windows out front. Mold clung to the eaves and the outer enclosure was crumbling to ruin. Still, Heela was grateful for what she had. Her compound adjoined Hajji Akhund's and was only a few streets from the main bazaar. Everything within a three-mile radius was government-controlled. Beyond that lay a region that had fallen in part or whole to the Taliban. Khas Uruzgan, seventy miles away, was now insurgent central.

As one of Tirin Kot's few educated women, she soon landed a job through Hajji Akhund with Afghan Health and Development Services, a local NGO that offered medical aid to women and children. They paid about $180 a month, more than she'd ever seen at one time. She would get up early to get the boys ready for school and then she'd be driven to the office in a car with tinted windows. By lunchtime she'd be back home, ready to receive the boys. Occasionally the routine was broken and she was brought to the American base, where she treated Afghan women who were casualties of the war.

Heela made sure to go about her work as quietly as possible. The car pulled in only when the coast was clear, and then she scurried out to it in her burqa. She spent the workday in a back room, away from the men, and when she returned home she did so with equal caution. It took a full year before the neighborhood discovered her presence. She had just returned from work one summer's day, and was opening the main gate when she stopped short. "I saw madness," she recalled.

Beans and sugar were scattered everywhere. Shelves were overturned, clothes spilling out. Her samovar lay smashed. Her sewing machine was missing. Shaking, Heela phoned a translator she knew at the American base, but she could not get through.

That evening she borrowed a Kalashnikov from Hajji Akhund and kept it by the bedside. By sunrise the break-in had already become the talk of the neighborhood, and the secret was out: a woman was living alone—and working—right in their midst. For some weeks she stayed away from the office and kept the children home, too. Then one night, as she was drifting off to sleep, she opened her eyes to a noise. She sat up and listened. Something like steps on gravel, or something being dragged across the outside wall. She peered through the window and saw the luminescence of a flashlight from that wall, and a man's sandals and his baggy-trousered legs and his torso blending into the darkness. She screamed. The children, jolted awake, began shouting. In the clamor, the man stumbled off the wall; she heard him slam into the roof, and the pots and pans in her kitchen came crashing down. By the time the first neighbors came running, he was long gone.

In the following days, Hajji Akhund and other well-wishers advised her to quit working until the dust settled. With money saved up Heela could afford to lie low for a while, so months went by before she ventured out into the street again. Her first foray outdoors was to the American base to gather donations to distribute to other widows. Later, she started making occasional trips to the NGO office to see friends.

Even with this restricted schedule, though, trouble found her. On an autumn evening in 2007, as she was settling into bed with the boys beside her, she heard a knock on the front gate. She put on her burqa and stepped into the dark night. When she opened the gate her eyes washed across the street and saw nothing but emptiness. Only as she turned to walk back in did she spot the letter that had been forced under the gate. Neatly written, it said:

Dear Sister,
It has come to our attention that you have been working with the occupy-
ing and crusading forces who have come to destroy our country and Islam.
Please be advised to cease this activity. If you do not, you have no right to
complain.

It bore the official seal of the Islamic Emirate of Afghanistan—the Taliban.

Some weeks later Heela received a phone call.

"Why are you meeting with foreigners?" the voice asked. It sounded like a mere boy.

"Who are you? What is this?" Heela asked.

"I'm telling you, sister. If you keep this up you'll have to accept the consequences."

Sister. The way he said it unnerved Heela. A boy that young would normally call her *auntie.*

"I'm only getting medicines," she replied. "I'm giving them out to poor widows. I'm not helping them in any way. I'm just helping our people."

"Then why don't you help us? We need medicine too."

Heela did not know what to say, so she hung up. The calls continued over the coming days, and she began to have violent dreams in which she found herself running from unknown men in the mountains. The dreams ended with her capture and execution, and she would wake up in tears. Hajji Akhund, who was well versed in matters of the dreamworld, explained that it was rare to die in your dreams. "It's a good thing," he said. "It means you'll live a long life. This is what people say."

She remembered these words the next time the boy called. "Stop calling me," she snapped. "Just tell me what you want." There was silence on the other end and then he politely said that he'd contact her at the appropriate time. That afternoon, he called back and told her to step outside. She threw on a burqa and opened the front gate. In the blinding white noonday sun it took her a moment to notice the tall, dark-skinned boy, a pattu wrapped around his face revealing just his eyes. He stared at Heela and then threw a package in her direction and ran.

She opened it to find a new SIM card for her phone and some women's clothing. The boy called again.

"You're a sister to us," he said. "We know what happened to you. Any time you want to call us, use that SIM card."

"There are clothes in here," she said.

"Our gift to you. In return, please send us medicines. We're desperate."

Later that week she gathered medicines and first-aid materials donated by the foreign agencies and the Americans and left the bundle atop her front gate. She awoke the next morning to find that it had been taken. Over the next weeks, she settled into a routine of collecting aid when she could and leaving it for her new friends. For Heela, the war was not a matter of policy, not a neat delineation of allies and adversaries—it was life itself. Living a war was different from fighting one; it meant keeping yourself somewhere in the gray area of survival. So long as the Taliban left her and her family alone, so long as they dealt with her respectfully, she had nothing against them. These were boys not much older than Omaid, and given Jan Muhammad and Commander Zahir and the others on the government's side, why wouldn't they fight? The only troubling part was rumors from the countryside that she didn't want to believe but knew were probably true, like the stories of Taliban stringing alleged spies up on trees and stuffing dollar bills into their mouths. She told herself that her Taliban unit couldn't have been involved.

Once, a Taliban friend requested that she venture into the field to treat women injured in an American attack. Eager to travel, to see, Heela thought about it long and hard, but in the end she decided not to risk it. And it would be a lasting regret because one day the calls stopped, just as mysteriously as they'd begun. She waited for weeks, then months, but nothing. Much later she heard that the Americans had paid an informer to carry a tracking device to the home of the unit leader and then dispatched an aircraft to finish them all. But it was only a rumor.

The moments after the muezzin's call and just before the boys awoke were Heela's most precious. She would write in her diary about the day ahead, about days past, about Musqinyar. She would take apart the night's dreams and Musqinyar's messages to her, as if a proper divination could bring the coming daylight under control. When the boys woke they would sit down to naan and green tea and talk about school. Shortly after they went off for the day, a car would arrive to take her to the NGO compound. She had started working again part-time, and the neighborhood was, for the moment at least, leaving her alone.

At the office, she would sort medical donations into boxes. Occasionally a foreign aid worker would show up, and Heela would receive medicines for cold and fever and menstrual cramps. She would arrange for deliveries to be made to distant parts of the province. Some days she herself would travel to villages around Tirin Kot to distribute chickens and offer women some advice on their care.

Everyone would take their nap after lunch. Heela would return home before the boys, and when they arrived she would send them out to the bazaar to collect groceries for dinner. By the time the family was in bed, the car horns and the vendors' shouts would be replaced by the distant whistle of falling rockets and the faint rapping of machine-gun fire. They were the only nighttime sounds Heela knew, and she slept soundly through them.

Since JMK's departure the province had settled a bit. The constant scrapping for territory had ceased, the Taliban holding their ground and the government theirs. The countryside remained a world removed from the streets of Tirin Kot, but for the first time in years people began to feel that things were not deteriorating—even if they were not getting better, either. Heela wished that Musqinyar could see her now, making a life for herself in ways no one in Khas Uruzgan would have dared imagine. She found herself focusing increasingly on the future, especially on the possibility that one day Omaid might study at university in Kabul, just like his father.

She might have continued this way, losing herself in the promise of new beginnings, in the hints of a world slowly righting itself, if not for the events of a spring day in 2008. It began in the morning when she was at the office and the boys were off from school. Omaid was sitting indoors reading; he had not improved much since the Kandahar days. Due to numerous surgeries one of his legs was now shorter than the other, and his eyesight was somewhat impaired. A bigger problem was the all-consuming fear he had developed of open spaces, loud noises, unfamiliar streets, and, most intensely of all, men with guns—no easy phobia to live with in Uruzgan. By rights he should have assumed his place as head of the household. Instead, he appeared perpetually sullen.

Jamshed had fared better. He harbored no lingering injuries, although he rarely spoke of what had happened that night. He, too, was at home that afternoon, resting indoors.

It was Nawid, Heela's third child, age eight, who was proving to be the strongest of the lot. He'd tell anyone who would listen that someday he would avenge his father. He was also, in Heela's eyes, the best-looking, with butterfly lashes and dimpled cheeks. On that day he was out by the front gate, playing with the youngest brother, Walid.

At some point that afternoon, a car rolled up in front of the house with two men inside. They spoke to Nawid as Walid stood watching. Nawid giggled and the men laughed, and then they opened their door and scooped him up and sat him down beside them. The door closed and the car drove off. Walid played by himself for some time, then returned to the house to relay the events to his brothers.

Omaid immediately called his mother. The news hit Heela hard. Walid had recognized the driver as Uncle Ruhollah, a cousin of JMK's who sometimes came by the house—a man notorious for his predilection for young boys.

She ran to the company driver and begged to be taken home. From there, she called Hajji Akhund, but he wasn't answering. She phoned her American contacts, but she couldn't get through. She pleaded with the driver to take her out to JMK's home village, Touri, on the outskirts of Tirin Kot, and finally he agreed. As the adobe houses and mud-and-straw shops sped by, Heela closed her eyes. She thought of Musqinyar and then thought of Jan Muhammad, and she felt sick.

14

The Leader

As the car drove slowly through Touri, men and boys came out to watch. The driver rolled down the window and asked after Ruhollah, but no one knew his whereabouts. They peered at the sobbing woman in the back and asked what the matter was and when the driver told them they shook their heads in pity.

Heading back to town, Heela hated herself. These things did not happen to good women, to good Muslims. It was her fault. There could be no other explanation for how two tragedies had befallen a single family. She should never have left the children under Omaid's care—he wasn't like other teenagers. She watched the cornfields and the poppies pass. Night was drawing in from the east and soon darkness would fall, leaving Nawid in some back room or garden house unknown to the world. Just him and that man.

They went by her house and picked up Omaid and then the car went down street after street, Heela looking at every passing child. They drove to Jan Muhammad's old compound, with its towering stucco mud walls and armed guards. The master was in Kabul, she was told. No, they didn't know when he would return, and no, they didn't have his number.

She tried the Americans again. No luck. Same with Hajji Akhund. Finally, the driver declared the search useless and dropped them off at the house and left.

Heela sat in the living room surrounded by the boys, the Koran on her lap. No one spoke. Outside, she could hear the arrhythmic clinking of goat bells and the faraway beeping of motorbikes.

And then she heard tires on gravel. Quickly donning her burqa, she went outside. A pair of green Toyota pickups were approaching in a storm of dust and pebbles, and Nawid was in the back of one of them, smiling.

He jumped down and Heela praised God and hugged him and looked him over. A pair of Kalashnikov-toting men stepped off the truck. They told her not to worry, the boy was unharmed.

Heela asked what had happened.

The *meshr*, they replied. The leader. The leader had saved him.

"The meshr?" Heela asked.

He had heard about the abduction, they said, and immediately sent them to retrieve her son and take Ruhollah into custody.

Heela didn't understand.

They pointed to a color computer printout pasted to the side of one of the pickups. It showed a thirtysomething man with a long face and an enormous wedge of a nose, a man strikingly handsome by Afghan tastes. His image was superimposed on a dreamlike background of fluffy clouds and snowcapped peaks.

Matiullah Khan. Heela had heard of him. She'd seen his men around town. He was a nephew of Jan Muhammad Khan.

The two men told her that after capturing Ruhollah and his accomplice, they'd brought them to Matiullah's compound. Upon seeing the meshr, the captives had fallen to their knees and begged for absolution. Ruhollah pleaded that Nawid was "like a brother" to him and that he'd only wanted to take the boy to "see the sights." The meshr was unmoved. He told his men to make Ruhollah "dance," and they began firing at his feet. Ruhollah was then stripped naked and locked up.

Some days later, the militiamen returned and gave Heela Matiullah Khan's phone number. "The meshr says hello," one told her, "and wants you to know that you can call him anytime if anyone bothers you." It was the first time anyone had openly backed her in Tirin Kot. Heela couldn't understand why. As she asked around, she learned that everyone held Matiullah in a mixture of awe and terror. There were stories bouncing around the bazaar: how he once tied a man down and drove over him.

How he once broke a man's legs in a fit of rage. How he once severed all of a man's fingers.

It was not long after this that Heela caught Dr. Ishan leering at her. He lived two houses down, and one night as she was preparing for bed she spotted him watching her from atop her house's outer wall. She called Omaid to chase him away, but he returned a few nights later, and again after that. Neighbors took note. In the mouths of street vendors and housewives the story morphed, as stories do, until it was said that Heela and Dr. Ishan were involved. The children were teased about it at school, and the gossip even spread to Heela's office.

Only then did her thoughts turn back to the meshr. She would have to call him. It didn't matter what people said about him. They were saying things about her, too, and they'd keep at it. She shuffled through her diary and found the number.

Matiullah's secretary picked up. Her heart pounding, Heela described the problem. The secretary listened and promised to relay the message to his boss. The next day, the meshr's gunmen showed up at the house and assured her that they had taken care of the issue. They'd locked up Dr. Ishan in a tiny cage and threatened to shoot him in the head. When they brought him to Matiullah, he had burst into tears and fallen at the meshr's feet. Matiullah had looked him over and then released him, warning him that next time he would hang.

From that day on, Dr. Ishan never bothered Heela again.

In rural Afghanistan, people discuss roads the way we discuss the weather—before they head out for work or at the mosque or in the market. On any given day, highways are prone to sudden tempests of violence between the warring sides. They can be rendered impassable by roadside bombs, or impromptu insurgent checkpoints, or trigger-happy American convoys. ("We've shot an amazing number of people," US war commander General Stanley McChrystal commented in 2010, "and, to my knowledge, none has proven to have been a real threat.") Next week's travel can be as unpredictable as next week's skies.

If the roads attracted so much violence, it was because without them there could be no resupplying of American bases, and therefore no

American mission. And with no American mission, there would have been no Matiullah Khan, no meshr. But what exactly was he the leader of? By 2009, he had become the most powerful person in Uruzgan Province and one of Washington's closest allies—all without holding a government position.

In the summer of 2011, I rented a car in Kandahar city and set out for Uruzgan to learn who exactly Matiullah was. I started on the city's outskirts, in a mud-sodden field filled with eighteen-wheelers, sixteen-wheelers, cabs with two trailers, Indian-made trucks festooned with ruby-colored mirrors and dangling metallic tassels—all of them bearing fuel or other crucial cargo for US troops, and all waiting to travel the eighty treacherous miles north to Tirin Kot. Just a few years earlier, the truckers told me, such a trip would have been a probable death sentence. The route was then under Taliban control, so trucks often ended up as charred heaps, dotting the roadside like signposts in some ravaged alien land. Drivers were losing their heads and the American base in Tirin Kot was being starved of supplies. "If you ask me what I worry about at night," said American general Duncan J. McNabb, "it is the fact that our supply chain is always under attack." As the insurgency grew stronger in 2006–7, and the Americans sent in more troops, requiring more supplies, the problem only multiplied. The Kandahar–Tirin Kot road became one of the most dangerous highways in the world. But everything changed in 2008, when an illiterate militiaman began organizing his cousins and friends to protect the trucks. His name was Matiullah.

He was a man of humble origins who, unlike Jan Muhammad and other Soviet-era mujahedeen warlords, made himself entirely in the shadow of twenty-first-century American power. In the 1990s, he was operating a taxi on the Kandahar–Tirin Kot highway, occasionally moonlighting as a driver for Taliban commanders. He may have been poor, unschooled, and seemingly without political ambition, but as a member of the Popalzai tribe and a nephew of JMK, a world of opportunities opened up for him in the wake of the US invasion. He joined Karzai's 2001 campaign to capture Uruzgan, and by the following year he had worked his way into his uncle's militia, commanding an elite Taliban-hunting unit. With no actual Taliban around, however, this effectively meant life as a hit man knocking off JMK's rivals. Soon he was providing security for the perimeter of the main US base in Tirin Kot and accompanying American special forces missions. In 2007, he was appointed to head a short-lived highway police force, and when it was disbanded a few months later, he appropriated its guns and trucks and continued to patrol the Kandahar–Tirin Kot highway on a fee-for-service basis. In no time, he was supplying heavily armed men—most of them relatives or fellow tribesmen—to protect trucks hauling American supplies into Tirin Kot. The Taliban proved no match.

It was noon at the truck depot when we spotted the seemingly unending stream of desert beige Ford pickups heading toward us, Afghan flags whipping in the wind. Some had Matiullah's image pasted decal-style to their cab windows, but most were unmarked. The supply trucks fell into place behind them, and we were off. The convoy drove along a canal as wide as the highway itself, its waters shimmering a brilliant cerulean blue against the dull brown scrubland rolling away into the distance. An hour into the trip, we passed through the shadow of a massive concrete dam. It was here that Jason Amerine's unit had called in the wrong coordinates almost ten years earlier, bombing themselves and nearly killing Karzai.

Farther north, the mud houses and rutted dirt paths by the roadside disappeared and we were in open country, with barren slopes and a naked, treeless horizon. Perched here and there on the slopes were small teams of Matiullah's gunmen, part of a private army thousands strong financed through his contracting business. For every truck escorted, he charged the Americans $1,000 to $2,000. With hundreds of trucks heading for the US base in Tirin Kot weekly, he was pulling in millions of dollars a month—in a country where the average income is a few hundred dollars a year. You could not move a truck into Uruzgan without his permission. "No one leaves without paying," said Rashid Popal, another trucking contractor. "Matiullah will kill anyone on this highway, Taliban or not." When another private security company, the Australian firm Compass, once attempted to escort US supplies up the highway, they were met by a hundred or so of Matiullah's heavily armed men, who demanded $2,000 to $3,000 per truck for "passing rights." The exchange grew so heated that the US military was called in. Eventually a settlement was negotiated and the trucks were allowed to pass, but the message was clear enough: Matiullah Khan owned the highway.

Our convoy passed through a defile that opened onto the earthen bowl where Mullah Manan's forces had battled Jason Amerine's Green Berets for control of Uruzgan. We arrived in Tirin Kot as dusk fell, without a shot fired en route, without encountering a single roadside bomb or illegal checkpoint. American officials believe that Matiullah's success hinges in part on a protection racket, in which he pays off certain Taliban commanders not to disturb his convoys—meaning that the United States, by hiring Matiullah, is indirectly paying its enemies.

Under Matiullah Khan, Tirin Kot was a changed town. Using his windfall funds he gobbled up real estate, elbowing aside his exiled uncle as the major landowner in the area. He leased bases to the Americans and financed bazaar shops. Soon, just about every business transaction of note in the city required his imprimatur. "Nothing happens in Tirin Kot without him," Hajji Shirin Dil, a wholesaler from Kabul, told me. "You can't make a single dollar without his permission, without giving him a cut."

With Jan Muhammad in Kabul, Matiullah quickly monopolized the political scene as well. Yet he was eager to distance himself from his uncle's ruinous regime. JMK's excesses had eventually turned the Dutch and other NATO allies against him, and Matiullah was keen to keep in the foreigners' good graces. He built schools, established radio stations, erected mosques, sent poor children to university in Kabul, settled land disputes, and protected widows like Heela. Through his militias and construction companies, he also provided jobs for thousands.

As with his uncle, however, governance was a sideline to Matiullah's principal occupation: fighting "terror," with no holds barred. When a roadside bomb once went off near his convoy, killing one of his men, Matiullah leapt out of his vehicle in a rage and grabbed a bystander—a shopkeeper in the wrong place at the wrong time. Matiullah tied him to the rear bumper of his pickup truck and drove around town. When the body was returned to the family, it was barely recognizable. In another village, Matiullah captured a suspected Talib (who, locals claim, was actually just a poor farmer) and took an already radical measure of emasculation—chopping off his beard—a step farther: he smashed the man's chin. And in yet another incident, Matiullah's men attacked a madrassa suspected of being a center of Taliban influence. Dozens were taken hostage and executed, most of them young boys.

In the town that had become Matiullah's, new offices opened almost monthly. The summer of 2008 saw an aid organization with foreign ties set up shop down the road from Heela's house. Not long after, a Western woman from the agency showed up at Heela's office and asked if she would help deliver medicines to the countryside. It had been years since Heela had set foot in a district outside of Tirin Kot, but she felt ready for the challenge. Through Hajji Akhund, she recruited one of Musqinyar's old friends, a doctor working for the government hospital. He, in turn, contacted a friend in an outlying village—and so it began. In no time, medicines were beginning to reach needy women outside of the capital in a regular fashion, and soon Heela was devoting much of her energy to this new project. But as quickly as the opportunity materialized, it vanished. The foreign-linked NGO closed down, and weeks later so did the Afghan organization that was her main employer.

Heela did not remain out of work for long. One of her colleagues from the Afghan NGO had moved on to work at the local hajj department, which coordinated travel for pilgrims to the Muslim holy city of Mecca in Saudi Arabia. His office had no means of processing the handful of requests that came in from female pilgrims, though, so he brought Heela aboard to help. Unlike her previous workplace, this office was all-male, so she wore her burqa eight hours a day. At first she was placed in a back room, helping to fill out paperwork for female applicants. But there were, in fact, so few of them that she spent her days largely idle at her desk, her restless mind spinning. Before long, she was helping illiterate farmers complete their applications, and not once did she request a bribe. It was only a matter of time before she became the most popular bureaucrat there, more so than any male counterpart.

Heela wished that Musqinyar could see her now, climbing from nothing to make a life in this town. In fact, she sensed that he *could* see, that he *was* watching. In some of her dreams she worked with him in a clean white office, with dozens of employees under them. It was a reminder of her days teaching in Kabul, university degree in hand. A reminder that she had been destined for so much more. The men around her at the hajj office, good souls all, had never been anywhere near a place of higher learning. Most of them had not finished high school. Even her supervisor could read only haltingly. She felt that, as a woman, she wasn't fit to run an office full of men, but still she wondered if she could do more. One afternoon, impulsively, she decided to sit for the certification exam for hajj instructors. She would teach pilgrims the basics of the travel process.

The exam was given a month before the start of the pilgrimage season, and Heela studied day and night to pass. A few weeks later, having received her certificate, she found herself in front of a roomful of farmers and tribal elders, chalk in hand. All those men, all those eyes watching her. Not since her wedding had she stood in front of so many people. Her words came out weak and soft, but the men said nothing and listened attentively. She continued to speak and no one laughed or scolded her, they just sat listening. It was hard for her to believe. After the class was over, they thanked her and called her "daughter" or "sister." One elder told her that while this type of work wasn't good for "our women, in the villages," it was fitting for "educated women like you."

She was working late at the office one day when she received an unexpected visitor: Musqinyar's uncle, who had come to apply for hajj. She hadn't seen him since leaving Khas Uruzgan, and there was so much she wanted to know. What had happened to her house, her property? What was Shaysta up to? They talked for hours. Commander Zahir, she learned, had fallen out of favor with JMK some years before, supposedly over opium profits. In the end, JMK had reported Zahir to the Americans as a Taliban agent, and, in a twist of fate, the police chief was now sitting in Bagram. In the meantime, nearly the entire district had fallen to the Taliban, with government-controlled territory whittled down to a mile or so around the governor's house.

They continued talking into the evening, and then the uncle looked at her and asked: "Would you like to come with me? To do hajj?"

The thought had never occurred to her. The very idea seemed wild, impossible—to go all the way to Saudi Arabia, when she could hardly walk to the bazaar?

"If you take me, you will do a great thing," she replied.

Heela sat in a window seat and fiddled with the emergency card in the pocket in front of her. It was her first flight since being ferried to Kandahar to see Omaid. Through her burqa netting she could see the Tirin Kot mountains, far off the runway's edge. She was the only woman on the plane. Her uncle sat beside her. She glued her face to the window and watched the honeycomb of mud-walled houses recede from sight.

During the layover in Kabul she explored the airport, which had barely existed during her last visit to her home city. She changed from her burqa to a headscarf, and hours later they were in Mecca. She'd never seen a place so organized, so clean, so metallic. The roads were pitch-black, wide and unblemished, not a crater in sight. Buildings towered over her, blotting out the sky like so many human-made mountains. A model of efficiency, the Saudis had already erected a tent city for the pilgrims, each tent containing the machines for blowing cold air that she had first seen on US military bases.

On her return home, she was addressed as *hajjanay*. Men spoke to her with the deference accorded to the elderly. But her success inspired jealousy among neighborhood women, who spoke among themselves of how she was too familiar, too comfortable, with the men in her office. More than once, rocks rained down on her windows. She decided that it was time for a change, and with the money she'd saved up over the years she moved to a larger house, not far from Matiullah's compound. Now, with the hajj season drawing to a close, she turned her attention to finding a new job.

Afghanistan's second presidential election was scheduled for the late summer of 2009. For Heela, it was impossible not to relive that autumn week five years earlier. Sometimes she spoke to Hajji Akhund about it, but mostly she kept her thoughts to herself.

That summer, Hajji Akhund found temporary work for her at an aid agency whose focus was raising election awareness among women. It felt like Khas Uruzgan all over again. She and the team would travel to outlying villages where a sympathetic malek might allow her to visit house to house. Most women took her pamphlets, but she knew that few would actually vote.

A month into the job, she was flown to Kabul for an elections workshop. She spent two days cloistered in an office with no chance to explore the city of her birth, just as if the Taliban were still running affairs. On returning to the airport, she took leave of her mahrem and slipped into the bathroom to exchange her hijab for an Uruzgani burqa. As she walked out, she noticed that she'd forgotten to change her heels for flats, but she was running late so she told herself she'd do it later.

The waiting room was packed with farmers and businessmen who looked like farmers, with crying children and clutches of burqa-clad women. The place smelled like a stable. Heela closed her eyes and waited for the flight announcement. Suddenly a group of men burst in, shouting, and people seated on the ground scattered away. The men kicked boys who did not move fast enough and put their hands on women to clear space. They pushed whole rows of plastic chairs to one side.

"What's happening?" Heela asked her mahrem.

He walked over to take a look and returned. "The meshr is coming."

"Here? He's coming *here*?"

"He's flying back to Uruzgan today. He was visiting Kabul."

The door swung open again and more men streamed in. They wore rich gray and silver turbans, and some had walkie-talkies. Then they parted to reveal Matiullah Khan. Some people ran up and clasped his hand. Others simply stared. Suddenly, to Heela's horror, he walked right toward the chairs where she was seated.

He exchanged greetings with the men nearby and then peered into Heela's burqa-shrouded face. "Who's this?"

"That's hajjanay," one of them said. There were only a few females in all of Uruzgan who had made the pilgrimage to Mecca, and only one likely to be in Kabul. Matiullah laughed and pointed to her shoes. "Great to meet you. I didn't know you were such a fashionable woman!"

Heela couldn't make a sound. In a life vulnerable to the whims of strongmen, every word had to be chosen with the utmost care.

"You do speak, don't you?"

"Yes," she said quietly. He was taller than she expected, and simpler, too. He wasn't carrying a weapon. His clothes were old and dirty. He slouched, his arms close to his sides. This was the king of Uruzgan? She began to feel a little better, more sure of herself. The two started talking. Heela explained the work she had done in the previous elections, pinning Musqinyar's murder on the Taliban just to be safe.

It was then that he asked, "Do you want to work for me?"

"Doing what?"

"We're setting up a campaign office for President Karzai in Uruzgan. I want you to run the women's section."

Heela wondered if this was why Matiullah had taken an interest in her over the months, why he had been so quick to come to her rescue. She wasn't sure how to respond.

He smiled and said, "You have to be a brave woman doing the work you do in Uruzgan. That's why I want you."

The campaign office was situated on the ground floor of a large house in central Tirin Kot. Photographs of Karzai with various tribal elders adorned the walls, and an American flag hung in one corner. Heela's days became a blur of appointments with election workers and Karzai boosters and government officials checking on the work. The goal was to ensure that women cast ballots, or, even better, that their husbands did so on their behalf. The men in the office performed the valuable work of liaising with the village elders and maleks, for whom a vote was not an exercise of democracy but a down payment on access, an effort to ensure that the right people were in power when the time came to call in a favor. So votes typically came in blocks, and it wasn't unusual for a village to report 90 percent support for a single candidate.

The real problem, as Heela and her colleagues quickly realized, was that with so little of the countryside under government control, only a few villages would vote on election day. A Taliban campaign to intimidate potential voters was already in full swing, which meant the campaign staff would need to get creative to avoid the embarrassment of a minuscule turnout. Arrangements were made with maleks province-wide to return full ballot boxes by whatever means they saw fit. Heela knew that there was no other option, and so as long as she got to travel, she was content. An adviser from Kabul had provided her with thousands of new pamphlets

for housewives, which she took on escorted trips to the few villages outside Tirin Kot where it was still safe to visit. She would speak to housewives
about President Karzai. Usually they would listen politely until she finished and then ask her about life in Kabul. They found her stories of
streets and markets open to women hard to fathom and while some of
them admired such a lifestyle, most condemned it.

When she wasn't traveling, work was slow, and Heela found herself
drifting from meeting to meeting. Things picked up only when a new
team arrived from Kabul that included Hanifi, an old friend of Musqinyar's. He had been serving on the provincial council, an elected body of a
dozen members that was supposed to advise the governor. Each province
designated two of its councilors to serve as senators in the upper house of
parliament in Kabul. When one of Uruzgan's members bowed out before
his term was up, Hanifi, a well-regarded tribal elder, had been chosen as
his temporary replacement. Now, returning to Uruzgan for the campaign season, he served as Heela's guardian as they visited neighborhoods across Tirin Kot.

For Heela, Hanifi's arrival was both a breath of fresh air and a painful
pull at the heart. No one at the office understood her ordeal; most of her
coworkers, in fact, didn't even know her story. But Hanifi was a Khas
Uruzgan native, and Heela felt that she could confide in him. At the same
time, he was fresh from Kabul, and it was impossible not to wonder what
life might have been like had she never left her home city. Where would
they be now? Musqinyar would be working for the health ministry. She
would be teaching schoolchildren, maybe girls. Omaid would be at university. Almost nightly she dreamed that she was wandering through
Kabul's streets, searching for Musqinyar and the children. She would
hear their voices around every corner, but when she looked it would be
empty. The Kabul of her dreams was not the place of her childhood, but
the modern version that Hanifi told her about, a chaotic metropolis of
luxury hotels and blast walls and unbearable traffic. It was not any city
she could identify, yet even so she felt that Kabul was hers.

In fact, Heela was known in the neighborhood as "the Kabul woman,"
and Hanifi could see why. She spoke with a certain city-bred confidence
that set her apart from the few other women he'd met in Uruzgan. Her
mind worked like that of a Kabuli. She even walked like one. So one day,

in the midst of a long conversation about work, he asked her, "Do you really want to go to Kabul?"

She told him she did.

"Then you should run for the provincial council."

By law, two of the twelve council seats were reserved for women. And council members did often travel to Kabul for training and meetings with officials. Heela laughed and jokingly said she'd do it. But she saw that Hanifi was dead serious. He looked at her thoughtfully, and then the conversation turned elsewhere. Back at home, Heela sent out the boys to buy cooking oil and vegetables and naan. As she set about making dinner, she found her thoughts wandering back to their discussion. Could a housewife really run for the council? What would people say?

Weeks passed and Hanifi never mentioned it again, and Heela began to feel foolish for having even considered it.

What she did not know, however, was that Hanifi had already broached the subject with Matiullah Khan. The meshr, of course, had had his eye on Heela for quite some time. She was a rare and potentially useful commodity, for only educated women could work in government. Various forces were trying to block Matiullah's ascent to absolute power—the Dutch, for instance, who (unlike the Americans) worried about his human rights record, and local officials such as the Uruzgan chief of police, who bristled at his informal authority. Matiullah needed to stack the local government with allies. Now it appeared that his stars—and Heela's—were about to align.

Hanifi arrived at the office one morning and handed Heela a few hundred dollars. "For registration," he said.

They found a boy to act as her guardian during the registration process. By that afternoon, Heela was officially running for a seat on the provincial council.

Matiullah Khan provided her with a car and a staff, and that summer she went almost daily from house to house around Tirin Kot and a few select villages nearby. She sat across from maleks in her burqa, her guardian by her side, and discussed village needs, a careful political dance that involved making promises and offering favors in the guise of polite generalities. It was the subtle give-and-take that Musqinyar had been so adept at, the sort of honor-conscious repartee where the quick-witted and gracious thrived—and she turned out to be a natural. She distributed fertilizer and seeds to farmers, chickens to poor widows, and notebooks to schoolchildren. She played up her credentials as a potential access broker, touting her ability to arrange visits from Kabul officials and reminding people of her own time in that city.

Around town, Matiullah's men put up campaign posters—with her face exposed, following regulations—and printed ten thousand leaflets with her image. It wasn't long before Heela became a household name in Tirin Kot. It was true that the population of Tirin Kot represented a tiny percentage of the electorate, but this would matter little. Rather, her presence around town was a clear signal to elders and power brokers that the forces that mattered stood behind her.

For the international community, however, numbers were everything. Their claims of legitimacy hinged on Afghanistan being an unfolding democracy, and a low turnout would be disastrous. So Western officials pushed ahead, insisting that the vote would go off without a hitch, even though holding polls in an embattled country with a nearly nonexistent state was like building a dam where there was no water, a project only for show. The UN and other agencies covered up growing evidence of fraud, and the charade continued up to election day, despite overwhelming evidence of ballot-stuffing on Karzai's behalf. In most of Uruzgan, there had hardly been anything resembling an election at all.

Still, "votes" were tallied and winners declared. Heela sat at the campaign headquarters with the rest of the team as merchants and wealthy farmers periodically stopped by to check on the results. Outside, she could hear occasional gunfire and the deep thuds of rocket explosions.

Late in the afternoon, Hanifi burst into the room, beaming. "Hello *wakil*," he said.

It took a moment for the word to register. Lawmaker.

With the quota system, Heela effectively had run only against other female candidates, all of them Hazaras. Without a ballot-stuffing operation of her own, she had received just seven hundred votes—2 percent of the total—but it was enough for victory. She immediately dialed one of Matiullah's wives, with whom she had become friendly, to share the news.

For the rest of the afternoon, government officials, tribal elders, maleks, and even local farmers came to congratulate her. Matiullah sent a car for her, and when she went looking for her mahrem, the driver told her: "You're a wakil now, you don't need anyone." Not quite a man, but no longer just a woman, in victory she had become a category unto herself.

At Matiullah's compound she met yet more dignitaries. It occurred to her that she had no idea what to do next, how to actually *be* a provincial council member. But she wasn't bothered, not when she was standing there talking and laughing with the governor and the police chief and other men she'd only heard about until this day. It was not long before the meshr himself arrived to congratulate the victors, then promptly left. His aide announced that he would be returning that evening.

The group sat down to discuss the coming senate selections: each provincial council was to pick two of its members for the senate in Kabul. Everyone knew that whoever was anointed would function as a de facto representative of Matiullah, whether they wanted to or not, since you could not get selected without his approval. And the meshr, under pressure from the interior minister to rein in his militia, needed allies in the capital at least as much as he needed them in local government.

The discussion lasted an hour. Abdul Ali insisted that he deserved to go because his Hazaras had made up the bulk of the actual turnout. After much wrangling, Uruzgan governor Asadullah Hamdam threw his support behind Ali and the mood began to tilt in his favor.

That was when Heela spoke up. "I think I should go." Everyone turned and stared at her. She regretted the words as soon as they came out of her mouth.

"What?" said Hamdam. "A woman senator?"

Whatever thoughts Heela had of dropping the matter instantly dissolved. "There are other women senators," she said calmly. "I have a lot of support from the people. And besides, I'm from Kabul. I know the culture well."

"This is Uruzgan," Hamdam reminded her. "We don't send women." The others concurred.

After the meeting, she worked up the courage to call Matiullah directly. He sounded annoyed by her open campaigning and curtly informed her that she would have to "allow the system to do its work."

Heela went back to the provincial council office feeling slightly ridiculous. She had overreached, letting the first taste of power go to her head. Governor Hamdam and the others knew better than she—they'd been doing this for years.

After dinner, a call came from the Independent Election Commission in Kabul. The first senatorial seat for Uruzgan was going to Hajji Azmi, a newly elected councilor and tribal elder.

The second seat was awarded to Heela.

In Heela's dream, a deep purple covered the nighttime sky, so deep that she couldn't see the stars. She was standing on the roof, colder than she had felt in years. All around her mountains rose from the earth, blue and dark and jagged, stretching as far as the eye could see. There were houses built right into the mountainside—hundreds of them, lit up like candles, like some votive offering from the earth itself. All around her, thousands of women, in all manner of clothing, were standing and watching, waiting for her. "I was giving a speech," she recalled. "Everyone was listening to every word." And there were those mountains, unlike any in Uruzgan, yet so strangely familiar—the mountains of her childhood.

When she awoke, she dressed quickly and stepped out into the crowded streets of Microrayon, her old Kabul neighborhood. Hailing a taxi, she watched the passing scenes as if she had stumbled onto a lost world. A new city had sprung up during her fifteen-year absence, leaving hardly a trace of the civil war that had devoured its predecessor. She saw steel glass buildings and foreign banks and supermarkets. She saw women in headscarves and girls in school uniforms, men in suits and boys in jeans.

Within city limits the ongoing insurgency had been largely kept at bay, but traffic conquered all. The car worked its way slowly to the western edge of town, turning through a roundabout onto a broad, busy road. It was here that, during the civil war, militiamen had ordered a pregnant woman out of her taxi to give birth in full view of everyone. In that spot now stood a traffic policeman's stand. Farther on she passed the street corner where, during her Taliban-sanctioned nurse training trip, she had witnessed a whip-wielding religious officer chasing boys through the rubble. In place of that rubble there now stood a gaudy glass structure, its enormous sign announcing the Kabul Dubai Wedding Hall. Blinking neon lights and large plastic flowers adorned the front entrance.

Farther on down the road, the traffic ground to a complete halt, so Heela paid the driver and walked. She turned down a side street leading into a maze of blast walls. Armed men stood near a driveway checking credentials. Journalists loitered nearby, some setting up cameras. It was the inaugural day for the new parliament. Other members of the senate were pulling up in tinted SUVs. Heela approached the gate on foot. Seeing that she was a woman, the guards waved her on. She entered a wide parking lot and made her way toward a registration table. A man was slouching behind it.

"What do you need?" he said.

"I'm a new senator from Uruzgan," she replied.

He sat up. "I'm sorry, Senator *sahiba*." He ruffled through his papers. "Welcome. We'll take care of everything." He pulled out some documents and proceeded to take down her information. Another man in a three-piece suit appeared and escorted Heela to a waiting room, where she was photographed and processed.

"So you are Heela," he said. "Senator Heela. But what's your full name? Your father or your husband?"

Heela didn't know what to say. She thought for a moment about Musqinyar, about her long-gone life in Khas Uruzgan. Was she Heela Musqinyar? That was the tradition, to take your husband's name, even as a widow. What would Musqinyar have wanted?

No, she decided. She had done this on her own. She was there to represent the people of Uruzgan, and her tribe, the Achekzais. It was a new beginning, and whatever hope had drained from her country, she still believed in a future that could be reclaimed.

"I'm Heela Achekzai," she said. The man noted it, completed the questionnaire, and led her to a plush antechamber where secretaries and assistants were waiting.

Senator Heela Achekzai of Uruzgan Province had arrived.

Epilogue

On an autumn afternoon in 2010, I met Akbar Gul for our regularly scheduled interview session. Although violence countrywide was at record highs, the United States had announced that it would start withdrawing troops in less than a year. I wondered if it was not too early to begin asking the question: Who won the war? But Akbar Gul, consumed by his troubles in the field, was in no mood to answer. "You can't trust anyone anymore," he said. "Those days are gone. We're just doomed to have a life of problems." We were at my house in Kabul, seated around a spread of meatballs and Uzbek-style mixed rice. He picked at his food. The many sides of the war had finally blended together into something unmanageable, for him at least, and he could see no way out. "I now understand why people become suicide bombers. What else do you have in this life?"

I had never seen him in such despair. I wanted to ask him what turn of events had precipitated this bout of self-loathing, but I knew by then to tread carefully when he was emotional. It had taken me more than a year to fully win his trust. He was unfamiliar with Western journalistic standards, so when I first attempted to corroborate his stories by independently contacting those involved, he felt wounded. Later, when he realized that my interest in his story was not an indication that I agreed with his view of the world, he felt betrayed. It was only after he came to see our interview sessions as a form of catharsis, not simply a service to a foreign journalist or even to posterity, that he began to view me in a different light.

During our meal he received a phone call that appeared to distress him further, but he did not tell me why. After finishing, we walked into the courtyard and I was about to say good-bye when he stopped me. "In our country, you never know when it's the last time you will ever see someone, so you have to make your good-byes count." With a warm smile, he held out his hand and gripped mine firmly. I opened the gate and let him out, watching as he headed toward the bazaar, skullcap atop his head, checkered *dismaal* scarf over his shoulder. I watched as he worked his way through the Friday crowds, past the butcher shop, past the vegetable stands, past the shouting vendors, until he was gone. I would never see him again.

It was almost a week before I realized that something was amiss. He failed to show up for our next interview session, and, when I tried to call him, all three of his phones were off. One week turned into the next without a sign of him. I contacted fighters under his command and elders in his home village, but they, too, were at a loss. His deputy said that he had gone to meet someone in the Tangi and had never returned. Zubair Babakarkhel, an Afghan journalist and friend who helped me research this book, reached out through intermediaries to Akbar Gul's wife. She, too, was in the dark, and in great distress.

There were only two possibilities. Either Akbar Gul had fallen victim to internal Taliban rivalries, or he had wound up in the hands of US soldiers. If the former, I knew that all hope was lost. Cases of Taliban commanders killed by their own comrades, or summoned to Pakistan and never seen again, were popping up with increasing frequency. If he was with the Americans, on the other hand, it was at least possible, in theory, to find him. The Red Cross is able to track down Afghans who have been "disappeared" by the Americans and connect them with their loved ones. I contacted them, and a few days later they returned with the answer: Akbar Gul was in custody in the American prison at Bagram Air Base.

The reason for his arrest was unclear, but by now I knew that it was also irrelevant. I also knew that, some months before, Akbar Gul had begun working secretly with the Americans, sharing intelligence against those Taliban units he deemed damaging to his country. He was being paid with US taxpayer dollars and armed through the Afghan government. Yet it had soon dawned on him that his Taliban enemies were not necessarily the ones the Americans were interested in, and he was no longer sure what or whom he was fighting for. The lack of purpose ate away at him, and he desperately wanted to extricate himself from the Americans, the Taliban, and the Afghan government—but there seemed to be no way out.

If Akbar Gul was losing that war, the same could be said for the Taliban as a whole. With a new generation of commanders at the helm, the movement was riven by infighting and behaving more brutally toward civilians than ever. They lacked the military prowess or the popular support to take cities or the largely non-Pashtun north. While they were strong in the deep southern countryside, the prospect of marching through the streets of Kabul and reestablishing a 1990s-style regime seemed remote. Some old-guard Taliban commanders had already grasped this new reality. After one scrape with death too many, Mullah Manan decided that the war was pointless and switched sides, joining an Afghan government reconciliation program. But the promised job and pension never came, so he returned to his village to farm. The village, however, was now under the control of a younger generation of Talibs, who regarded him as a traitor. Manan fled to Pakistan, but the Pakistani intelligence agencies also did not take kindly to Talibs who left the movement, so he was forced to flee again. He now lives in a shantytown in Kandahar, picking up day work from time to time as a bricklayer.

Not long after my final meeting with Akbar Gul, I moved back home to the United States after being away for three years. As I followed the news of the impending troop withdrawal, it was clear to me that the Americans would not be victors either. The Taliban had not surrendered or been defeated, the Afghan army was weak and unreliable, and the Afghan government was hopelessly corrupt. I began to wonder if the true winners were the commanders whom the US had transformed into the post-2001 power elite, men like Gul Agha Sherzai and Jan Muhammad Khan. Yet starting in 2011, a series of mysterious assassinations around the country knocked off one strongman after another. The victims included Ahmed Wali Karzai, the president's powerful brother; Burhanuddin Rabbani, a key Northern Alliance figure; General Daud, an influential northern commander; and many others. It was playing out like a mafia film—except that there seemed to be no Don Corleone standing at the end.

A few days after Ahmed Wali's death, I called Jan Muhammad to express my condolences and get his thoughts. "Nowadays Taliban-style thinking is everywhere, even in our government," he said. "It's like a disease. People who should be working together are instead killing each other. I don't even know what to say." JMK had been in exile from Uruzgan for nearly five years and felt that the time was ripe for his return. He had been lobbying President Karzai to reinstate him as governor because "the current administration are lovers of the Dutch and the Taliban." His return to Uruzgan would pose awkward challenges, however, as he had long since been eclipsed by his powerful nephew Matiullah. In the past, whenever I had asked about Matiullah, JMK was uncharacteristically circumspect in his phrasing. But on this day he held nothing back. "He has gone mad with power. This is not a democracy, not when one man rules everything." If he could only return to Uruzgan, he told me, he would save the province from dictatorship.

JMK asked me when I would visit Afghanistan again and promised that he would treat me to a sumptuous meal upon my return, and I thanked him and said good-bye. Three evenings later, he was at home meeting an Uruzgani parliamentarian. He had sent all but one guard home for the night. At around eight, two men armed with Kalashnikovs and grenades walked up to the compound. JMK was sitting on a couch in his living room when he heard the shots. Moments later, the two men barged into the room, aimed, and shot Jan Muhammad dead.

Not long after, I returned to Afghanistan. President Obama's plan to withdraw US troops was well under way, with bases closing and equipment being destroyed. Could the war's true winners be found in what we were leaving behind? I traveled through Uruzgan, and on the Kandahar–Tirin Kot highway I could see Matiullah's men everywhere, as they had been during my last visit. But the road north of Tirin Kot, heading into Ghilzai country, was now dotted here and there with new militia outposts not adorned with Matiullah's photo or the Afghan flag. I stopped at one, a small wooden trellis with a canopy of leaves as cover, and met the fighters. They were under the control of a local strongman, who was being paid by a private company to protect a road construction project. Every mile or so I came upon another such militia, each run by a different strongman.

Later, I arrived at the home of Daud Khan, a leader of the local Barakzai tribe and one of the key militia commanders in the province, perhaps second only to Matiullah himself. He was heavily invested in protecting road construction crews against Taliban attacks, and the impending US withdrawal was hurting his business prospects. "We need money," he told me. "We need money because life is hard out here. We've got a lot of expenses—I need weapons, RPGs, trucks, we want body armor. I keep asking the Americans for body armor but they won't give it to me. They expect us to fight with nothing."

I asked him if he had gotten into firefights with the Taliban recently. He clasped his hands together and laughed. "The Taliban? My mother can fight the Taliban. They just put bombs in the ground. They won't be a problem after the Americans leave."

Then why the need for all the weapons?

"Matiullah," he said. "He's worse than the Taliban. After the Americans leave, we'll need to protect ourselves." Tirin Kot was now caught in a cold war between Daud Khan's and Matiullah's forces. By my count there were more than thirty pro-American armed groups operating in central Uruzgan alone, some aligned with Matiullah, some against.

Later that afternoon I visited Daud's uncle, a militia commander named Shah Muhammad. We sat in a field overlooking his poppy plantation, surrounded by nearly a dozen fighters. "There's something I want to tell you," he said, looking at me keenly. "There's only one force that can save Afghanistan. The Americans. And I want you to know how much I despise the Taliban. Even if my father was a Talib, I'd kill him." He shifted to sit next to me, nearly whispering in my ear. "I'm in trouble. You're an American. I need your help. I want to fight the Taliban, I just need contracts. If the Americans give me some contracts, I can bring security. I can turn this war around. I just need money." He begged me to pass on the message to politicians in Washington.

Such jockeying for patronage was nothing new. From its earliest days, the Karzai government was tethered to American aid, incapable of surviving on its own. It was reminiscent of the Communist regime of the 1980s, which lived and died by Moscow's patronage—except that now there was a twist. Of the $557 billion that Washington spent in Afghanistan between 2001 and 2011, only 5.4 percent went to development or governance. The rest was mostly military expenditure, a significant chunk of which ended up in the coffers of regional strongmen like Jan Muhammad. In other words, while the United States paid nominal amounts to build the Afghan state, it fostered a stronger and more influential network of power *outside* the state.

These were no conditions for nation building. Instead, as journalist Matthieu Aikins has pointed out, a weak Karzai administration found itself competing with strongmen of the countryside for funds. With warlords like JMK developing their own business and patronage relationships with the United States, the tottering government in Kabul had no choice but to enter the game itself. As a result, the state became criminalized, one of the most corrupt in the world, as thoroughly depraved as the warlords it sought to outflank.

So corrupt, in fact, that nearly every metric that US or Afghan officials pressed into service to show progress unravels upon inspection. "Under Taliban rule, only 1.2 million students were enrolled in schools, with less than 50,000 of them girls," a US forces press release stated in 2011. "Today, under the government of Afghanistan, there are 8.2 million students, of which nearly 40 percent—or 3.2 million—are girls." But these were largely phantom figures. In the central province of Ghor, for instance, independent investigators discovered that of the 740 schools listed by the education ministry, 80 percent were "not operating at all." Nonetheless, over four thousand teachers were on the government payroll. The vast majority of them, investigators found, simply collected paychecks and stayed at home, giving a cut to local officials, who in turn funneled a portion to warlords as a way to purchase influence. The story was similar around the country. Traveling through Wardak Province, I came upon one long-abandoned school after another that was still included on the much-touted government tally.

Likewise, US officials often stated that in the post-Taliban era, 85 percent of Afghans had access to health care—which would have made Afghanistan the health care capital of the region. Yet that figure turned out to refer only to the fact that 85 percent of *districts* had at least one health center, which many Afghans could not access due to distance or insecurity. "Essentially," journalist Aunohita Mojumdar wrote, "that would be akin to saying that just because every state in the US had a hospital, 100 percent of Americans had access to healthcare." What's more, many of these district health facilities existed only on paper. As with schools, government officials often purloined health care funds, using them to buy influence with local power brokers.

Throughout the south, the US military supported showpiece projects—a new well or a refurbished school, in some cases even whole model villages. But if the south was dotted with Potemkin villages, Afghanistan itself had become a Potemkin country, built almost entirely for show. As the situation devolved, President Karzai and top officials began pointing fingers bitterly at the United States. Meanwhile, Washington began to view the corrupt central government as the key roadblock to its mission—even though American patronage was ultimately responsible for the mess. In frustration, US officials redoubled their efforts to circumvent Kabul and deal with local power brokers, unwittingly cultivating a new generation of strongmen.

So in Matiullah Khan and those like him across the country, the American war regenerated itself. The new class of warlords was more sophisticated than their predecessors. Weaned on the Washington way of doing business, their militias were rebranded and formalized as "private security companies," chartered through contracts with Western firms or the US military itself. Unsurprisingly, this only unleashed further corruption on a scale that dwarfed that of even the most unscrupulous Afghan government agency.

To grasp the enormity of the problem, you need only picture the most elementary aspect of the US presence. At the war's height there were more than four hundred American bases scattered around the country, nestled in craggy valleys and perched on barren hilltops, days apart and reachable only over crumbling, perilous roads like the Uruzgan–Kandahar highway. The United States and other NATO countries contracted out the arduous task of delivering supplies to an array of Western and Afghan companies. The largest of these deals was a $2.16 billion Department of Defense contract called Host Nation Trucking, split among eight multinational firms. Some of these companies fielded their own fleets of trucks, but others did not even have vehicles and subcontracted out the job to Afghan companies. Either way, the trucking companies then hired local warlords to protect their routes. They, in turn, provided militiamen—"private security guards" in the new parlance—for Matiullah-type fees. The warlords had outlays of their own, including bribes to Afghan army and police commanders along the route and protection money to the Taliban, all of which guaranteed unfettered passage for the trucks. Upon learning that US tax dollars were going to support warlordism, racketeering, and the insurgency, Congress launched an inquiry and Pentagon officials promised to reexamine the whole system. But reform was impossible because the new contracting economy was inexorably bound up in the project of counterterrorism. As long as US troops remained on Afghan soil, there was no other option—short of bringing in hundreds of thousands of additional soldiers to take the place of the Western subcontractors, possibly sending the American body count skyrocketing.

The Soviets, too, had outsourced their war. After their 1989 withdrawal, Moscow funded militias to protect the Kabul government against mujahedeen groups in the pay of the CIA, and for the most part the status quo held even without Russian boots on the ground. The Soviet-backed government clung to the cities, while the insurgents claimed the countryside. But when the two nations cut off funding in 1992, the commanders on both sides—who had men to feed and arm—were forced to "privatize" their activities by robbing homes or setting up checkpoints to shake down travelers. The ensuing turf battles quickly spiraled into all-out civil war.

The American war has renewed this cycle. In 2013, there were, by some estimates, 60,000 to 80,000 armed private security employees in the country, almost all of them working for Afghan strongmen. Add to this 135,000 Afghan army soldiers, 110,000 police, and tens of thousands of private militiamen working directly for the Afghan government, the US special forces, or the CIA, and you have more than 300,000 armed Afghan men all depending on US patronage. You can't help but wonder: What happens when the troops leave, the bases close, and the money dries up?

During my most recent visit to Afghanistan I met Senator Heela in the garden of a friend's home, and for many hours we drank tea and ate raisins and talked about the people we'd known in Uruzgan. If she had learned anything, she said, it was that triumph and fear come together, that all positions and titles were fleeting. She expressed dismay at the impending US withdrawal. We both knew that her life in Kabul depended on the war staying in the countryside, and after 2014 all bets were off. It was a subject better left unspoken, and I steered the conversation away from the conflict. Soon she was telling me of her attempts to fix Omaid's limp and of her dream to see America.

The darkness was coming on, and the mountains around the capital were already burning bright. Heela said it was time for her to go, and as she left, I knew I didn't need to ask her the final question I'd had in mind. The answer was right in front of me. Winning a war such as this was not about planting flags or defending territory or building fancy villas. It was not about titles or promotions or offices. It was not about democracy or jihad, freedom or honor. It was about resisting the categories chosen for you; about stubbornness in the face of grand designs and schemas. About doing what you had to do, whether they called you a terrorist or an infidel. To win a war like this was to master the ephemeral, to plan a future while knowing that it could all be over in an instant. To comfort your children when the air outside throbs in the middle of the night, to squeeze your spouse's hand tight when your taxi hits a pothole on an open highway, to go to school or the fields or a wedding and return to tell about it. To survive.

A NOTE ON SOURCES

In southern Afghanistan, there's an old joke that goes like this: a group of inmates at an asylum are gathered around a hole in the ground. They've been staring at it intently for hours. A doctor comes by, peers into the hole, and looks at the inmates with bemusement. "I don't see anything," he says. "What are you looking at?"

Comes the reply: "How can you expect to see anything? You just got here. We've been staring at it for hours, and we still haven't seen anything."

In Afghanistan, truth is an evasive thing. Part of the reason is that human memories are notoriously unreliable—especially when those memories are ones that people would rather forget. It is also because Afghan storytellers are often less concerned with literal truth than they are with the deeper moral truth of a story.

This doesn't mean that a truthful rendition of events is impossible, only that it takes effort. The stories in this book are the result of countless hours of interviews over the course of three years. The names of some individuals, such as Akbar Gul, have been changed for their protection. Where relevant, I've interviewed multiple witnesses for the events in question. I have traveled to nearly every province, district, and village detailed in this book, and in many cases I was able to retrace my subjects' steps. There are newspaper accounts and official documents detailing aspects of many of the events I've described, and I've made use of them to verify and augment my reporting. You can find the sourcing below. In the end, though, there are still elements of any story that are by their nature unverifiable—someone's thought process, for instance— and in those cases I've relied on my feel for the person in question, on his or her track record for accuracy and demonstrated understanding of my project.

NOTES

1 · THE LAST DAYS OF VICE AND VIRTUE

8   *Mullah Cable. The very name spoke of:* There were at least three people known as "Mullah Cable" on the front lines. It is unclear if the other two are still alive.

11   *President George W. Bush's warning:* Kathleen T. Rhem, "Bush: No Distinction Between Attackers and Those Who Harbor Them," U.S. Department of Defense, American Forces Press Service, September 11, 2001.

12   *The Taliban, for their part, doubted the objectivity:* Abdul Salaam Zaeef, *My Life with the Taliban* (New York: Columbia University Press, 2010), 136–39.

13   *"Osama is like a chicken bone":* Alex Strick van Linschoten and Felix Kuehn, *An Enemy We Created: The Myth of the Taliban/Al-Qaeda Merger in Afghanistan, 1970–2010* (London: C. Hurst, 2011), 166.

13   *President Bush increased the pressure:* "Bush Gives Taliban Ultimatum," *Telegraph*, September 21, 2001.

13   *"You just care about your posts":* Van Linschoten and Kuehn, *An Enemy We Created*, 225.

13   *Twice he sent his top deputy to meet covertly:* George Tenet, *At the Center of the Storm: My Years at the CIA* (New York: HarperCollins, 2007).

13   *a gas mask by his side:* Scott C. Johnson and Evan Thomas, "Mulla Omar Off the Record," *Newsweek*, January 20, 2002.

13   *Contravening dictator Pervez Musharraf's stated policy:* Ahmed Rashid, "Intelligence Team Defied Musharraf to Help Taliban," *Telegraph*, October 10, 2001.

14   *On October 6, he received word from Pakistani agents:* Interview, Kandahar, 2010.

14   *"My family, my power, my privileges"*: Claudio Franco, "The Tehrik-e Taliban Pakistan," in *Decoding the New Taliban: Insights from the Afghan Field*, ed. Antonio Giustozzi (New York: Columbia University Press, 2009), 272.

14   *The next evening, a few minutes before nine p.m.*: This scene is drawn from interviews with Mullah Omar's driver and from news accounts (2010).

14   *"He had very bad abdominal injuries"*: Charlie Bain, "Omar Came into the Hospital and Said: This Is My Son. Please Help Him," *Mirror*, October 22, 2001.

14   *"Go! Go to Sangesar!"*: Interview with Mullah Omar's driver. See also "Taliban Leader 'Survived Direct Hits,'" Reuters, January 21, 2002.

24   *Late on November 12, 2001, Mullah Cable entered Kabul*: This description of Kabul is based on my interview with Mullah Cable and interviews with others who were in the city at the time.

27   *A* New York Times *reporter traveling with them*: David Rohde, "Executions of P.O.W.'s Cast Doubts on Alliance," *New York Times*, November 13, 2001.

2 · THE BATTLE FOR TIRIN KOT

31   *Karzai vowed to do whatever it took*: Material on Karzai in this chapter is based on interviews with aides, relatives, and publicly available sources.

33   *A Taliban guard pointed to the large sack*: Bette Dam, *Expedite Uruzgan: De weg van Hamid Karzai naar het paleis* (Amsterdam: Arbeiderspers, 2008).

33   *The elders listened politely, but it soon became apparent*: Ibid.

34   *"Have the Americans bomb the Taliban command"*: Eric Blehm, *The Only Thing Worth Dying For: How Eleven Green Berets Fought for a New Afghanistan* (New York: HarperPerennial, 2011), 73.

38   *Mullah Manan rose nervously to greet me*: "Manan" is a pseudonym that I have given him.

41   *"Hey, what the fuck is going on?"*: Blehm, *The Only Thing Worth Dying For*, 130.

41   *every available air asset across the theater*: Ibid., 131.

46   *When he looked up, he saw smoke and blood*: Description of US bombing from interviews in Shah Wali Kot, 2010. Description of Karzai from Nick B. Mills, *Karzai: The Failing American Intervention and the Struggle for Afghanistan* (Hoboken, NJ: John Wiley & Sons, 2007). Details of US casualties and Amerine from Thom Shanker, "Applying Early Lessons to Build Afghan Security," *New York Times*, May 20, 2013.

46   *"What's your reaction to being named as prime minister?"*: Author interview with Lyse Doucet, August 2013.

46   *"believe only in Islam and my Afghan bravery"*: Franco, "The Tehrik-e Taliban Pakistan," 272.

46   *bouts of boundless terror that brought him close to tears*: Interviews; and van Linschoten and Kuehn, *An Enemy We Created*.

48   *Mullah Omar and other senior Taliban leaders were huddled together:* This
        and subsequent info on Mullah Omar's actions from interviews with Tali-
        ban official, Kandahar, 2010.

3 · THE WAR FROM YEAR ZERO

56   *financed textbooks for schoolchildren in refugee camps:* Matthew Hansen,
        "Soviet-Era Textbooks Still Controversial," *Associated Press,* September
        23, 2007.

57   *"Aleph [is for] Allah":* Craig Davies, "A Is for Allah, J Is for Jihad," *World
        Policy Journal* 19, no. 1 (Spring 2002): 90.

57   *The US-backed mujahedeen branded those:* See, for example, "Afghani-
        stan," *Bulletin of Atomic Scientists* 39, no. 6 (June/July 1983): 16–23.

59   *permissible to rape any unmarried girl over the age of twelve:* US Depart-
        ment of State, Bureau of Democracy, Human Rights, and Labor, "US
        Department of State Country Report on Human Rights Practices
        1994—Afghanistan," February 1995.

59   *outlawing love songs and "dancing music":* John Baily, "Music and Censor-
        ship in Afghanistan, 1973–2003," in *Music and the Play of Power in the
        Middle East, North Africa and Central Asia,* ed. Laudan Nooshin (Burling-
        ton, VT: Ashgate, 2009), 143–64.

59   *"schools are whorehouses and centers of adultery":* Helena Malikyar,
        "Development of Family Law in Afghanistan: The Roles of the Hanafi
        Madhhab, Customary Practices and Power Politics," *Central Asian Survey*
        16, no. 3 (1997): 396.

59   *"Women are not to leave their homes at all":* Hafizullah Emadi, *Repression,
        Resistance, and Women in Afghanistan* (Westport, CT: Praeger Publishers,
        2002), 124.

65   *Sher Muhammad climbed to the roof of his house:* John Pomfret, "Rocket
        Attack Terrorizes Musicians' Neighborhood," *Associated Press,* May 5,
        1992.

65   *Muhammad Haroun was arrested by an ethnic Hazara militia:* Afghani-
        stan Justice Project, *Casting Shadows: War Crimes and Crimes Against
        Humanity: 1978–2001* (Afghanistan Justice Project, 2005).

65   *Hazara militiamen stormed the house of Rafiullah:* Interview, Kabul, 2009.
        ("Rafiullah" is a pseudonym.)

65   *fighters broke into apartment number 38:* "From Fundamentalism-Blighted
        Afghanistan" (excerpts from *Payam-e-Zan* reporters in 1992–96), Revolu-
        tionary Association of the Women of Afghanistan, accessed October 9,
        2013, http://www.rawa.org/reports.html.

65   *A month later another group came to the housing complex:* Ibid.

66   *lobbing mortars blindly into the densely populated neighborhood:* Human
        Rights Watch, *Blood-Stained Hands: Past Atrocities in Kabul and Afghani-
        stan's Legacy of Impunity* (New York: Human Rights Watch, 2005).

66   *"They held him and asked where his father was"*: Afghanistan Justice Project, *Casting Shadows*, 87. Here, I have given her the pseudonym "Mina."

66   *Some Hazaras, like resident Abdul Qader:* Human Rights Watch, *Blood-Stained Hands*. Here, I have given him the pseudonym "Abdul Qader."

66   *An unknown number of people—probably at least one thousand:* Afghanistan Justice Project, *Casting Shadows*, 20.

66   *Fazil Ahmed was decapitated:* Human Rights Watch, *Blood-Stained Hands*, 87.

67   *Human rights investigators subsequently found:* Ibid.

67   *Still, when Zbigniew Brzezinski:* Zbigniew Brzezinski interview, "The CIA's Intervention in Afghanistan," trans. Bill Blum, *Le Nouvel Observateur*, Paris, January 15–21, 1998.

4 · THE SEWING CENTER OF KHAS URUZGAN

73   *Only 12 percent of Afghan soil is arable:* World Bank, *World Development Indicators, 2013* (Washington, DC: World Bank, 2013).

74   *typifying what some sociologists call a culture of honor:* See, for example, Dov Cohen and Richard E. Nisbett, "Self-Protection and the Culture of Honor: Explaining Southern Violence," *Personality and Social Psychology Bulletin* 20 (October 1994): 551–67.

75   *mountain clans even tattooed their animals and their women:* Emadi, *Repression, Resistance, and Women in Afghanistan*, 32.

75   *may have helped spark violent riots in Kandahar:* Some scholarship suggests that the riots had more to do with taxation than with women.

80   *British documents from as early as 1901:* A. H. McMahon and A. D. G. Ramsay, *Report on the Tribes of Dir, Swat and Bajaur Together with the Utman-Khel and Sam Ranizai*, reprint of 1901 edition (Peshawar, Pakistan: Saeed Book Bank, 1981). See also Magic ud-Din, "1901 Taliban," *Language, Politics, Pakistan* (blog), http://languagepoliticspakistan.blogspot.com/2011/10/1901-taliban.html.

81   *"The religion of God is being stepped on"*: Husayn ibn Mahmud, *The Giant Man* (At-tibyan publications, http://ebooks.worldofislam.info/ebooks/Jihad/The_Giant_Man.pdf, accessed November 4, 2013), 16.

5 · NO ONE IS SAFE FROM THIS

103   *The sky clotted gray:* This scene is from interviews in Maiwand (2010) and the 2010 TLO report "Maiwand" (unpublished).

104   *fifteen truckloads of weapons:* Interviews, Kandahar, 2010; Bill Powell, "Warlord or Druglord?," *Time*, February 8, 2007.

104   *via clandestine meetings with US officials:* James Risen, "An Afghan's Path from U.S. Ally to Drug Suspect," *New York Times*, February 2, 2007.

104   *in January 2002, he showed up at an American base*: Gregg Zoraya, "Taliban Money Man Reportedly Freed," *USA Today*, January 25, 2002.

104   *"the Taliban system is no more"*: "Taliban Official Asks Pakistani Islamists Not to Collect Donations in the Name of Militia," Associated Press, December 16, 2001.

104   *"If a stable Islamic government is established"*: Hilary Mackenzie and Michael Petrou, "Mujahedeen Routs al-Qaeda, But bin Laden Remains at Large," *Edmonton Journal*, December 17, 2001.

105   *"Ministers of the Taliban and senior Taliban are coming"*: Brian Knowlton, "U.S. Seems Sure to Oppose Amnesty Proposed by Afghan Captors: 3 Taliban Leaders Said to Surrender," *New York Times*, January 9, 2002.

105   *the Taliban ministers of defense, justice, interior*: Anand Gopal, "The Battle for Kandahar," in *Talibanistan: Negotiating the Borders Between Terror, Politics, and Religion*, ed. Peter Bergen and Katherine Tiedemann (Oxford, UK: Oxford University Press, 2012).

105   *"We are giving advice to Hamid Karzai"*: Amir Zia, "Taliban Leaders Defect Orthodox Islamic Militia," Associated Press, December 9, 2001.

105   *At Kandahar's soccer stadium*: Ellen Knickmeyer, "Afghans Rally for Peace on Former Taliban Execution Ground," Associated Press, January 24, 2002.

105   *fields were lavender bright*: Author interviews in Kandahar, 2010.

106   *Abdullah, the family driver, would usually be dispatched*: "Abdullah" is a pseudonym.

106   *ran into the courtyard with other guests*: Jon Stephenson, "Eyes Wide Shut: The Government's Guilty Secrets in Afghanistan," *Metro* (New Zealand), May 2011.

107   *"The war in Iraq drained resources from Afghanistan"*: Seth Jones, *In the Graveyard of Empires: America's War in Afghanistan* (New York: W. W. Norton, 2010), 127.

108   *one of Sherzai's lieutenants met Master Sergeant Perry Toomer*: Michael Phillips, "Battlefield Business Deals Are Cut in Afghanistan as Marines Find Willing Contractors Among Locals," *Wall Street Journal*, December 19, 2001.

108   *an $8-a-load job*: Sarah Chayes, *The Punishment of Virtue: Inside Afghanistan After the Taliban* (New York: Penguin Books, 2006).

109   *"Get Wealth and Power Beyond Your Dreams"*: Herbert A. Friedman, "Psychological Operations in Afghanistan," Psywarrior website, http://www.psywarrior.com/Herbafghan02.html, accessed November 4, 2013.

110   *constantly scratch and massage his back*: Christopher Torchia, "Short of Money, Staff and Equipment, Kandahar's Intelligence Chief Directs Search for Taliban Leader," Associated Press, December 18, 2001.

110   *"could get into places and exact payback"*: Anonymous, *Hunting al Qaeda: A Take-No-Prisoners Account of Terror, Adventure, and Disillusionment* (St. Paul, MN: Zenith Press, 2009).

111   *a poisoned tablet for $100,000:* Stephenson, "Eyes Wide Shut."

111   *"an elderly father died while in custody":* David Pugliese, *Shadow Wars: Special Forces in the New Battle Against Terrorism* (Ottawa: Esprit de Corps Books, 2003).

111   *"we hope we got some senior Taliban":* Vernon Loeb and Thomas E. Ricks, "1 Killed, 59 Held in Raid on Suspected Taliban Camp," *Washington Post*, May 25, 2002.

111   *"If we did any crime, they must punish us":* Patrick Quinn, "All but Five Villagers Detained in U.S. Raid on Suspected al-Qaida Leadership Released," Associated Press, May 30, 2002.

111   *"If they touch our women again":* Michael Ware, "We Were Better Off Under the Russians," *Time*, June 10, 2002.

112   *"She was the laughter of the house":* Ibid.

112   *As Major A. C. Roper explained:* Nahlah Ayed, "Majority of Suspects Captured by Canadians and U.S. Special Forces Released," Canadian Press Newswire, May 30, 2002.

112   *announced that the captives were "al Qaeda-Taliban":* "Afghan Military Arrests 95 After Receiving Reports of Links to al-Qaida, Taliban," Associated Press, August 29, 2002.

112   *"The government paid for their salaries":* Tini Tran, "Afghans Cry Foul over Police Roundup," Associated Press, August 31, 2002.

113   *the captured policemen in US custody were beaten:* Author interviews in Kandahar, 2010.

113   *admitting that officials "never had hard evidence":* Tini Tran, "U.S.-Afghan Raid Speaks Volumes," Associated Press, September 1, 2002.

113   *If the government could do this "to their own people":* Tran, "Afghans Cry Foul."

113   *this time detaining Hajji Nasro, a local leader:* Matthew Rosenberg, "U.S. Special Forces Take Seven People into Custody; Find Large Weapons Cache," Associated Press, September 19, 2002.

113   *"to make the situation in Afghanistan stable":* Powell, "Warlord or Druglord?"

113   *"Why don't we have any Afghan drug lords":* Ibid.

114   *the home of Akhtar Muhammad Mansur:* Gopal, "The Battle for Kandahar."

6 · TO MAKE THE BAD THINGS GOOD AGAIN

118   *Abdul Ali approached the main schoolhouse:* "Abdul Ali" is a pseudonym.

119   *"US Pat. No. 5651376":* Interviews, Uruzgan, 2010; and Michael Ware, "How the U.S. Killed the Wrong Afghans," *Time*, February 6, 2002.

121   *a sound unlike any of them had heard before:* Ware, "How the U.S. Killed the Wrong Afghans."

121   *Shah Muhammad, one of Qudus's bodyguards:* Carlotta Gall and Craig S. Smith, "Afghan Witnesses Say G.I.'s Were Duped in Raid on Allies," *New York Times*, February 27, 2002.

122   *As Pryor later recounted it:* Gregg Zoraya, "Inches Divide Life, Death in the Afghan Darkness," *USA Today*, October 19, 2003.

123   *"they are our friends":* Gall and Smith, "Afghan Witnesses Say G.I.'s Were Duped."

123   *"We're friends! Friends, friends, friends!":* Molly Moore, "Villagers Released by American Troops Say They Were Beaten, Kept in 'Cage,'" *Washington Post*, February 11, 2002.

123   *"Have a nice day. From Damage, Inc.":* Craig S. Smith, "A Nation Challenged: U.S. Raid; After a Commando Operation, Questions About Why and How 21 Afghans Died," *New York Times*, January 28, 2002.

123   *twenty-one pro-American leaders and their employees dead:* Figures from Khas Uruzgan government officials, interview, Uruzgan, 2010.

124   *"We're Karzai's people!":* Interviews, Uruzgan, 2010; and Moore, "Villagers Released."

124   *"walking on our backs like we were stones":* Moore, "Villagers Released."

124   *"I did not expect to remain alive":* Carlotta Gall, "Released Afghans Tell of Beatings," *New York Times*, February 11, 2002.

124   *"Whoever is responsible should be executed":* Ibid.

124   *both pieces of intelligence from the rival camps:* Charles H. Briscoe, Richard L. Kiper, and James A. Schroder, *Weapon of Choice: U.S. Army Special Operations Forces in Afghanistan* (Fort Leavenworth, KS: Combat Studies Institute Press, Military Bookshop, 2003).

124   *a mission designated as AQ-048:* Ibid.

125   *"there are no friendlies at the site":* Ibid.

127   *Aziz Mansour was staying indoors:* "Aziz Mansour" is a pseudonym.

130   *"We never even spoke to Ghilzais in those days":* Interview with Dan Green, Washington DC, 2010.

130   *"Two of the four aircraft commandeered by terrorists":* Alex Belida, "US Troops Uncover al-Qaida Weapons, Model of 757 Airplane," State Department, September 23, 2002.

131   *I asked Eckart Schiewek:* Interview, 2009.

131   *Coburn found a similar dynamic in his study of Istaliff:* Noah Coburn, *Bazaar Politics: Power and Pottery in an Afghan Market Town* (Redwood City, CA: Stanford University Press, 2011), 146.

7 · BLACK HOLES

132   *Noor Agha could feel the shackles:* Noor Agha's story is based on interviews, Paktia, 2011; Anand Gopal, "America's Secret Afghan Prisons," *Nation*, January 28, 2010.

133   *to end his "armed defiance of the interim administration":* "Eastern Afghan Militants Wanted Peaceful Resolution: Commander," Agence France-Presse, March 6, 2002.

135   *anyone caught opposing Kabul would have his house burned down:* Kathy

Gannon, "Guantanamo Prisoner Returns, and Is Arrested Again," Associated Press, February 7, 2009.

135   *a probe into a reported theft of $3,000:* Interviews, Paktia, 2011; and WikiLeaks Guantanamo Files—ISN 1001.

135   *"operational and logistical support for al Qaeda operations":* WikiLeaks Guantanamo Files—ISN 1001.

136   *"They stripped me naked, out in the open":* Nancy A. Youssef, "Did 'Returning' Terrorists Become Extremists in Guantanamo?," McClatchy Newspapers, May 26, 2009.

136   *"We were without hope":* "Prisoners: Guantanamo: Muhammad Naim Farooq (Released)," Cage Prisoners website, http://old.cageprisoners.com/prisoners.php?id=465, accessed November 4, 2013.

137   *Parre was forced to kneel on stones:* Craig Pyes, "A Torture Killing by U.S. Forces in Afghanistan," Crimes of War Education Project, http://www.faculty.umb.edu/gary_zabel/Courses/Morals%20and%20Law/M+L/news-tortureafghan.html, September 20, 2004; Craig Pyes and Kevin Sack, "Deaths Were a Clue That 'Something's Wrong,'" *Los Angeles Times*, September 25, 2006.

137   *if he sided with those "opposing the Coalition":* Pyes, "A Torture Killing."

137   *"They didn't allow us to sleep":* Gopal, "America's Secret Afghan Prisons."

138   *"This is Guantanamo! You are in Guantanamo!":* Ibid.

141   *accused of supporting the followers of Hekmatyar:* WikiLeaks Guantanamo Files—ISN 798.

141   *"If somebody is a leader of a tribe":* Guantanamo Administrative Review Board Round 2 Transcripts.

142   *"why are you here?":* Guantanamo Administrative Review Board Round 1 Transcripts, http://projects.nytimes.com/guantanamo/detainees/798-haji-sahib-rohullah-wakil/documents/2, accessed November 4, 2013.

142   *"All I can tell you is that I fought":* Guantanamo Combatant Status Review Tribunal Transcripts.

142   *"one of the wealthiest men in eastern Afghanistan":* U.S. Embassy Cable 06KABUL5008.

143   *"For six years, I was ready to go to court":* Nancy Youssef, "Where's Pentagon 'Terrorism Suspect'? Talking to Karzai," McClatchy Newspapers, July 7, 2009.

143   *"key affiliate of the al Qaeda network" had been killed:* Heidi Vogt and Rahim Faiez, "Saber Lal Melma, Ex-Gitmo Detainee, Killed in Afghanistan," Associated Press, September 3, 2011.

143   *caught up in this universe of rivalry and intrigue:* Gopal, "America's Secret Afghan Prisons."

144   *supporting the political organization of Ahmed Shah Massoud:* WikiLeaks Guantanamo File US9AF-000949DP.

144   *alleged to have been a member of Herakat-i-Inqilabi:* WikiLeaks Guantanamo File US9AF-000007DP.

144 *"defected to the Taliban in 1998"*: WikiLeaks Guantanamo File US9AF-OOO453D.

145 *Abdullah Khan found himself in Guantanamo*: WikiLeaks Guantanamo File US9AF-00095ODP; Wikileaks Guantanamo File US9AF-000952DP; Andy Worthington, *The Guantanamo Files: The Stories of 774 Detainees in America's Illegal Prison* (Ann Arbor, MI: Pluto Press, 2007).

145 *Swat Khan's internment stemmed from an accusation*: WikiLeaks Guantanamo File US9AF-000933DP.

145 *Hajji Bismillah, the director of transportation*: WikiLeaks Guantanamo File US9AF-000968D.

145 *Abdul Rahim al-Janko, a Syrian*: Details on al-Janko are drawn from *Al Ginco v. Obama*, 626 F. Supp. 2d 123 (D.D.C 2009) Official Traverse; Spencer S. Hsu, "Freed Guantanamo Detainee Sues U.S. Military over Alleged Torture," *Washington Post*, October 6, 2010; Andy Worthington, "Judge Orders Release from Guantanamo of Al-Qaeda Torture Victim," *Huffington Post*, June 24, 2009, http://www.huffingtonpost.com/andy-worthington/judge-orders-release-from_b_219959.html, accessed November 4, 2013; Tim Golden, "Expecting U.S. Help, Sent to Guantanamo," *New York Times*, October 15, 2006.

146 *Perhaps the unluckiest of this lot is Hamidullah*: WikiLeaks Guantanamo Files US9AF-001119DP.

147 *Mohebullah, a bus driver detained in Uruzgan Province*: WikiLeaks Guantanamo Files US9AF-000974D.

147 *"I am very happy to be in the Tribunal"*: Combatant Status Review Tribunal Transcripts.

10 · BACK TO WORK

190 *all sixty-five members of the police force*: Robert Kluijver, "Study of Subnational Administrative Structures in Afghanistan, Wardak Political Context and Security Structures," wardak.de, accessed February 2012.

192 *Muhammad Haqqani, a former Taliban deputy minister*: Sami Yousafzai, "The Taliban in Their Own Words," *Newsweek*, September 25, 2009.

192 *in return for amnesty, he would pledge loyalty*: See, for example, Malcolm Garcia, "Seven Senior Taliban Officials Freed After Questioning by U.S.," *Kansas City Star*, January 10, 2002.

193 *"there was insufficient evidence to connect detainee"*: WikiLeaks Guantanamo File USAF-001043DP.

194 *the case of Mullah Ahmed Shah*: Gopal, "The Battle for Kandahar."

195 *the simple mud house of Feda Muhammad*: Ibid.

196 *"I still get flashbacks"*: James Fergusson, *Taliban: The Unknown Enemy* (Cambridge, MA: Da Capo Press, 2011), 319. For an alternative (and confused) account, see Jason Meszaros, *Interrogation of Morals: The Truth About Courage and Integrity* (St. Michael, MN: J. P. Hewitt Press, 2008).

11 · THE TANGI

201   *There was Yunis, his closest friend:* The names in this paragraph are all pseudonyms.

204   *a friendship he had made with a man named Pir Mohmand:* "Pir Mohmand" is a pseudonym.

209   *officials had logged more than five thousand security incidents:* Data courtesy of Sami Kovanen, Indicium Consulting.

211   *a few nights away from home with his friend Ismael:* "Ismael" is a pseudonym.

12 · NO-MAN'S-LAND

216   *as told by Rahim, a Taliban fighter:* All descriptions and quotes from Rahim's story are taken from an account of his interview with Ghulam Sarwar. His account also appears in "One Talib: I'm Fed Up of Jihad," Larawbar.com, October 23, 2008. "Rahim" is a pseudonym.

218   *"They tied our hands behind our backs":* "Purported Survivor Recounts Horror of Afghan Bus Ambush," Radio Free Europe Radio Liberty, October 22, 2008.

218   *"Nothing you see here in this country belongs to us":* This section is adapted from Anand Gopal, "Uprooting an Afghan Village," *Progressive* 73, no. 6 (June 2009): 24–27.

218   *a man named Qadir, hailed from Garloch:* See Abdul Moeed Hashimi and Najib Rahman Enqilabi, "Laghman, Sarobi Bordering Areas Bombed," *Pajhwok Afghan News*, October 19, 2008; author interviews, Laghman, 2009.

220   *"This Time Sheep Mistaken as Enemy Combatants":* Najibullah Inqilabi, "This Time Sheep Mistaken as Enemy Combatants," *Pajhwok Afghan News*, December 3, 2008.

221   *"That's what our lives are worth to you Americans":* Author interview, Laghman, 2009; see also Kim Barker, "Embittered Afghans Blame U.S. for Civilian Deaths," *Chicago Tribune*, February 17, 2009.

13 · STEPPING OUT

243   *In a sequence captured by a documentary filmmaker:* Taliban Country, directed by Carmela Baranowska (Eight Mile Plains, Queensland: Marcom Projects, 2007), digital video.

14 · THE LEADER

253   *Heela caught Dr. Ishan leering at her:* "Dr. Ishan" is a pseudonym.

253   *"We've shot an amazing number of people":* Richard A. Oppel Jr., "Tighter

Rules Fail to Stem Deaths of Innocent Afghans at Checkpoints," *New York Times*, March 26, 2010.

254   *"If you ask me what I worry about at night"*: Majority Staff of the House Subcommittee on National Security and Foreign Affairs, *Warlord, Inc.: Extortion and Corruption Along the U.S. Supply Chain in Afghanistan* (Washington, DC: Government Printing Office, June 2010).

255   *"No one leaves without paying"*: Ibid., 29.

255   *the Australian firm Compass*: WikiLeaks War Log, Kandahar Province Incident Report, "Illegal Checkpoint," November 22, 2009.

257   *Dozens were taken hostage and executed*: Author interviews, Kabul, Kandahar, and Uruzgan, 2010.

EPILOGUE

271   *Jan Muhammad was sitting on a couch*: Interviews; also, Julius Cavendish, "Killing of Karzai's Advisor Takes Another Hit at the President's Circle," *Time*, July 18, 2011.

273   *Of the $557 billion that Washington spent*: Amy Belasco, *The Cost of Iraq, Afghanistan, and Other Global War on Terror Operations Since 9/11*, CRS Report RL33110 (Washington, DC: Congressional Research Service, March 29, 2011), table 3.

273   *As a result, the state became criminalized*: This line of argument was first developed in Matthieu Aikins, *Contracting the Commanders: Transition and the Political Economy of Afghanistan's Private Security Industry* (New York: Center on International Cooperation, New York University, 2012).

273   *"Under Taliban rule, only 1.2 million students were enrolled"*: Allied Command Services, "ISAF Spokesman Discusses Progress in Afghanistan," news release, July 26, 2011, http://www.aco.nato.int/page424205131.aspx.

273   *740 schools listed by the education ministry*: Mohammad Hasan Hakimi, "Afghanistan: The Ghost Teachers of Ghor," Institute for War and Peace Reporting, March 29, 2012.

274   *"just because every state in the US had a hospital"*: Aunohita Mojumdar, "An Inflated Claim of Health Success in Afghanistan Exposed," *Christian Science Monitor*, December 5, 2010.

275   *contract called Host Nation Trucking*: Majority Staff of the House Subcommittee on National Security and Foreign Affairs, *Warlord, Inc.*

276   *60,000 to 80,000 armed private security employees*: Belasco, *The Cost of Iraq, Afghanistan, and Other Global War on Terror Operations*.

ACKNOWLEDGMENTS

I owe my deepest gratitude to the countless Afghans I have met over the years who provided me, a complete stranger, a glimpse into their anguishes and their desires. In particular, I am profoundly lucky to have found Heela, Akbar Gul, and Jan Muhammad, gifted storytellers in their own right, who spent hundreds of hours with me retracing their steps, poring over maps, and finding old friends for me to interview.

In many ways, this book was a partnership between me and Zubair Babakarkhel, a talented Afghan journalist. I met Zubair when he was reporting for *Pajhwok Afghan News*, and was immediately won over by his unique combination of reporting chops, intelligence, and generosity. In our year of collaboration, Zubair dug deep, traveled far and wide, and taught me much about Afghanistan. He regularly made connections that I'd missed, and knew just how to guide interview subjects through delicate topics.

While living in Afghanistan, I was fortunate to have made Afghan friends who took me into their homes and guided me through their country. Hamid Asir traveled with me across the countryside on motorcycle, giving me a glimpse of an Afghanistan foreigners rarely get to see. Habib Zahori was a colleague who quickly became one of my dearest friends in Kabul. M.S.S. embodies the best of the country's vaunted hospitality. I am also indebted to Frotan Ghausuddin, Gul Kaka, Dr. Nasir Malikzai, Haroun Mir, Edris Nawin, Waliullah Rahmani, Habib Khan Totakhel,

Dr. Roshanak Wardak, Shahir and Melek Zahine, and many others who, for security reasons or otherwise, I cannot name here.

In the expatriate community, I am grateful to those who assisted me over the years, particularly when I first landed in Kabul without contacts or reporting experience. They include: Daniel Cohen, Adam B. Ellick, Konrad Fiedler, Raymond Francis, Ricardo Grassi, Nic Lee, Aunohita Mojumdar, Mario Ragazzi, Christoph Reuter, Sujeet Sarkar, Michael Semple, and Reto Stocker. In particular, I would like to thank Sami Kovanen, whose meticulous data collection and research helped me make sense of the war, and Eckart Schiewek, whose wisdom on the country was invaluable.

I wish to thank the many editors and colleagues who aided me over the years, including Ben Arnoldy, Roane Carey, Carol Huang, Dahr Jamail, and Ann Ninan.

This book could not have been written without the generous support of the New America Foundation, where I benefited from a thriving intellectual community of fellow writers and researchers. I am deeply grateful to Peter Bergen, who encouraged me to apply for a fellowship and who commissioned the study on which the central thesis of this book is based. I would also like to thank Steve Coll and Andres Martinez for their support and encouragement.

At Henry Holt, I am indebted to Sara Bershtel for taking a chance on a new author, and Grigory Tovbis, my editor, for his meticulous attention to my manuscript. In his hands, this book was vastly improved. I wish to thank John Wright, my agent, for offering many helpful suggestions during my writing process.

I am grateful to those who aided in the manuscript's completion, including: Azin Emami, whose expert research provided me with background information on northeastern Afghanistan; Becky Shafer and Kirsten Berg at New America, whose careful and rigorous fact-checking helped me spot numerous errors; Matthew Rubin, whose assistance in fact-checking material on Guantanamo was invaluable; David Pugliese, who generously provided material on the raid on Hajji Burget Khan's compound; Peter Ter Velde, who helped me understand key battles in Uruzgan province; Martine van Bijlert, for educating me on Khas Uruzgan district; Tom Peter, for giving me a home in Kabul when I visited; and Michael Hastings, a friend and colleague who is sorely missed. I wish to thank Bette Dam, one of the most talented researchers I know, for providing me with much information over the years that aided my work. In particular, she shared transcripts of her meetings with Jan Muhammad, and tracked down a detailed history of Khas Uruzgan district. Her book *A Man and a Motorcycle: How Hamid Karzai Became Afghanistan's President*, and Eric Blehm's *The Only Thing Worth Dying For*, were valuable sources for Chapter 2, "The Battle of Tirin Kot."

I have benefited from a small community of writers and thinkers on Afghanistan, whom I am fortunate to also call friends. Graeme Smith's consistently stellar journalism always gave me something to aspire to. Alex Strick van Linschoten and Felix Kuehn's work, and my correspondence with them, have taught me much about the Taliban and southern Afghanistan. In particular, I am grateful to Alex for providing me with the source of narration of the Maiwand bus massacre described in chapter 12. Matthieu Aikins is not only one of my most respected peers, he was a pillar of friendship in the long years it took to write this book.

I would like to thank my family, and in particular my parents, who put up with my long absences in far-flung places and never wavered in their encouragement of my work.

Finally, there are two people I wish to thank for their profound influence on this project. The first is Tom Engelhardt, who first suggested that I should write a book and went beyond the call of duty time and again to make the manuscript the best it could be. Any young writer would be lucky to have such an editor and mentor. The second is Anita Sreedhar, one of the best writers I know, who taught me so much about storytelling. Every single page in this book bears her mark.

INDEX

ABOUT THE AUTHOR

ANAND GOPAL is a journalist covering Afghanistan, Egypt, Syria, and other international hot spots. He has served as an Afghanistan correspondent for the *Wall Street Journal* and the *Christian Science Monitor*, and has reported for *Harper's*, the *Nation*, the *New Republic*, and *Foreign Policy*, among other publications. Gopal is a fellow at the New America Foundation.